BASIC Programming on the QL

Also by Neil Cryer and Pat Cryer
and published by Prentice-Hall International

BASIC PROGRAMMING ON THE BBC MICROCOMPUTER

GRAPHICS ON THE BBC MICROCOMPUTER (with Andrew Cryer)

BASIC PROGRAMMING ON THE ACORN ELECTRON

NOTE TO AUTHORS

Do you have a manuscript or a software program related to personal computers? Do you have an idea for developing such a project? If so, we would like to hear from you. Prentice-Hall produces a complete range of books and applications software for the personal computer market. We invite you to write to Giles Wright, Senior Editor, Prentice-Hall International, 66 Wood Lane End, Hemel Hempstead, Herts HP2 4RG, England.

BASIC Programming on the QL

Neil Cryer
Royal Holloway College, University of London

Pat Cryer
University of Surrey

Prentice/Hall International

Englewood Cliffs, NJ London New Delhi Rio de Janeiro
Singapore Sydney Tokyo Toronto Wellington

Library of Congress Cataloguing in Publication Data

Cryer, Neil
  Basic programming on the QL.

  Includes index
  1. Sinclair QL (Computer)——Programming 2. Basic
  (Computer program language) I. Cryer, Pat   II. Title.
  QA76.8.S6216C79   1985   001.64′2   84/18179

ISBN 0-13-066143-0 (pbk)

British Library Cataloguing in Publication Data

Cryer, Neil
  BASIC programming on the QL.——(Prentice Hall
  International personal computer book)
  1. Sinclair QL (Computer)
  I. Title   II. Cryer, Pat
  001.642   QA76.8.S625

ISBN 0-13-066143-0

© 1985 by Neil Cryer and Patricia Cryer

All rights reserved. No part of this publication may be reproduced, stored in a retrieval system, or transmitted, in any form or by any means, electronic, mechanical, photocopying, recording or otherwise, without the prior permission of the authors.

ISBN 0-13-066143 0

PRENTICE-HALL INTERNATIONAL INC., London
PRENTICE-HALL OF AUSTRALIA PTY., LTD., Sydney
PRENTICE-HALL CANADA, INC., Toronto
PRENTICE-HALL OF INDIA PRIVATE LIMITED, New Delhi
PRENTICE-HALL OF JAPAN, INC., Tokyo
PRENTICE-HALL OF SOUTHEAST ASIA PTE., LTD., Singapore
PRENTICE-HALL INC., Englewood Cliffs, New Jersey
PRENTICE-HALL DO BRASIL LTDA., Rio de Janeiro
WHITEHALL BOOKS LIMITED, Wellington, New Zealand

Printed in Great Britain by A. Wheaton & Co. Ltd., Exeter

10 9 8 7 6 5 4 3 2 1

(TM) Sinclair, QL, QDOS, QLUB and ZX Microdrive are trademarks of Sinclair Research Ltd.
Quill, Abacus, Archive and Easel are trademarks of Psion Ltd.

To our parents:

Florence Clarke
Leonard Clarke
Alan Cryer
Freda Cryer

Contents

	PREFACE	xv
0.	**INTRODUCTION**	**1**
0.0	About this book	2
0.1	Why use a QL?	2
0.2	Why program in BASIC?	4
0.3	What's special about the QL's SuperBASIC?	4
0.4	Turning on the QL	5
0.5	Getting to know the QL	7
0.6	Activities	8
0.7	Points to ponder	9
0.8	Discussion on the points to ponder	9
0.9	Discussion of activities	10
1.	**STARTING PROGRAMMING**	**13**
1.0	Introduction	14
1.1	Immediate actions	14
1.2	Activities	15
1.3	Turtle graphics as immediate actions	17
1.4	Activities	18
1.5	The idea of a program	18
1.6	A simple program	20
1.7	Activities	22
1.8	Editing programs	23
1.9	Activities	25
1.10	First steps in writing a program	25
1.11	Some sample procedures	28

1.12	Activities	30
1.13	Some points to ponder	31
1.14	Discussion on the points to ponder	31
1.15	Discussion of activities	32

2. SAVING, RETRIEVING AND JOINING PROGRAMS   35

2.0	Introduction	36
2.1	Preparing a cartridge for saving a program	36
2.2	Saving programs	37
2.3	Getting a directory of a cartridge	38
2.4	Loading programs	39
2.5	Activities	40
2.6	Loading and running with one instruction	43
2.7	Activities	43
2.8	Merging two or more programs	43
2.9	Points to watch with merging programs	45
2.10	Activities	47
2.11	More sample procedures	48
2.12	Activities	49
2.13	A menu-selection program 'boot'	49
2.14	Activities	50
2.15	Discussion of activities	51

3. QL SuperBASIC   53

3.0	Introduction	54
3.1	Keywords	54
3.2	Letters, characters and symbols	54
3.3	Strings	54
3.4	Activities	57
3.5	Variables and variable names	59
3.6	Activities	60
3.7	Integer variables	60
3.8	String variables	61
3.9	Activities	62
3.10	Some points to ponder	63
3.11	Discussion on the points to ponder	64
3.12	Discussion of activities	65

4. PUTTING DATA INTO PROGRAMS 67

4.0	Introduction	68
4.1	Putting data into variables	68
4.2	Entering data while a program is running	68
4.3	Activities	70
4.4	Giving values to more than one variable	70
4.5	Inputting a lot of data	72
4.6	Activities	74
4.7	Some points to ponder	75
4.8	Discussion on the points to ponder	75

5. REPETITION 77

5.0	Introduction	78
5.1	Repetition in steps of one	78
5.2	Repetition in other steps	79
5.3	Examples of the use of the FOR loop	81
5.4	Activities	82
5.5	REPEAT loops	83
5.6	Activities	85
5.7	Loops within loops	88
5.8	Which loop to use	89
5.9	Activities	90
5.10	Points to ponder	90
5.11	Discussion on the points to ponder	91
5.12	Discussion of activities	91

6. MAKING DECISIONS 95

6.0	Introduction	96
6.1	Comparisons	96
6.2	Conditional statements	97
6.3	Activities	101
6.4	Extending conditional statements	102
6.5	Activities	105
6.6	Some points to ponder	106
6.7	Discussion on the points to ponder	106
6.8	Discussion of activities	106

7. ADDING SOUND — 107

- 7.0 Introduction — 108
- 7.1 Describing sound — 108
- 7.2 The BEEP statement — 109
- 7.3 Activities — 111
- 7.4 Musical intervals — 111
- 7.5 Musical scales — 114
- 7.6 Activities — 117
- 7.7 Extensions to the BEEP statement — 118
- 7.8 Activities — 119

8. WINDOWS AND CHANNELS — 121

- 8.0 Introduction — 122
- 8.1 Windows — 122
- 8.2 Channels — 124
- 8.3 Activities — 126
- 8.4 Default channels — 126
- 8.5 Opening channels — 127
- 8.6 Controlling windows — 128
- 8.7 Closing channels — 130
- 8.8 Activities — 130
- 8.9 Resetting windows to their default values — 131
- 8.10 Activities — 131
- 8.11 Discussion of activities — 131

9. BEGINNING GRAPHICS — 133

- 9.0 Introduction — 134
- 9.1 Pixels — 134
- 9.2 Scaling windows for graphics — 135
- 9.3 Drawing points — 138
- 9.4 Drawing lines — 138
- 9.5 Activities — 140
- 9.6 Drawing simple curves — 140
- 9.7 Activities — 142
- 9.8 Drawing circles and ellipses — 143
- 9.9 Drawing arcs — 143
- 9.10 Positioning writing precisely — 144
- 9.11 Activities — 145
- 9.12 Points to ponder — 145
- 9.13 Discussion on the points to ponder — 145
- 9.14 Discussion of activities — 146

10. INTRODUCING COLOUR 147

10.0	Introduction	148
10.1	Available colours	148
10.2	Setting foreground and background colours	148
10.3	Activities	150
10.4	Filling with colour	151
10.5	Activities	153
10.6	Bordering a window in colour	154
10.7	Activities	154
10.8	Mixing colours	155
10.9	Activities	156
10.10	An example of colour graphics: a pie chart program	158
10.11	Activities	162

11. HANDLING TABLES 163

11.0	Introduction	164
11.1	Array variables	164
11.2	Arrays of one dimension	165
11.3	Introducing an array variable into a program	166
11.4	Putting data into an array	167
11.5	Manipulations using arrays	168
11.6	Activities	170
11.7	Arrays of two dimensions	172
11.8	Activities	173
11.9	Points to ponder	176
11.10	Discussion on the points to ponder	177
11.11	Discussion of activities	177

12. FUNCTIONS 187

12.0	Introduction	188
12.1	Built-in functions	188
12.2	Activities	191
12.3	User-defined functions	193
12.4	Recursion	194
12.5	Activities	195
12.6	Points to ponder	196
12.7	Discussion on the points to ponder	196
12.8	Discussion of activities	197

13. HANDLING STRINGS   199

13.0	Introduction	200
13.1	Inputting a complex string	200
13.2	Inputting a single character	200
13.3	Manipulating portions of strings	201
13.4	Searching within a string	202
13.5	Activities	205
13.6	Repetition within strings	206
13.7	Activities	206
13.8	Conversion between a character and its code	207
13.9	Activities	207
13.10	Discussion of activities	208

14. HANDLING FILES   209

14.0	Introduction	210
14.1	Microdrive cartridge as storage media for files	210
14.2	Creating and writing to a new file	211
14.3	Reading from a file	212
14.4	Activities	214
14.5	Writing to an existing file	214
14.6	Copying a file	215
14.7	Activities	216
14.8	Points to ponder	216
14.9	Discussion on the points to ponder	216
14.10	Discussion of activities	217

15. STRUCTURED PROGRAMMING   219

15.0	Introduction	220
15.1	Subroutines and procedures	220
15.2	Jumping versus branching	221
15.3	Designing structured programs	223
15.4	Flowcharting	223
15.5	Preparing flowcharts	226
15.6	Activities	229
15.7	Discussion of activities	229

16. A GAMES PROGRAM FOR THE QL 233

16.0	Introduction	234
16.1	The game	234
16.2	Programming the display	234
16.3	The core of the program	237
16.4	The strategy of the program	237
16.5	Checking for moves that are valid	238

Appendix   Glossary of BASIC terms   248

Index   260

Preface

In 1982, we wrote BASIC Programming on the BBC Microcomputer [a bestseller! - Editor], and in 1983 we wrote BASIC Programming on the Acorn Electron. We were pleased to write on these micros because we felt that they had so much to offer. One special feature was their structured BASIC, which was generally regarded as a considerable improvement over other BASICs. Now, Sinclair Computers have brought out the QL with its own highly structured BASIC. This, together with other appealing features of the machine, prompted us to write a book on BASIC programming for the QL.

Our experience with our earlier books has been invaluable. Time and use have brought their strong and their weak points to light. The former we have built on; the latter we have tried our best to improve. In designing the contents, we have borne in mind that the QL comes with a User Guide and with various software packages: QUILL (a wordprocessor), EASEL (a graphics package) and ARCHIVE (a data base). We have tried to complement these packages, not to duplicate them.

We believe that this book will be very useful indeed to anyone who wants to learn to program in BASIC on the QL. It has a number of special features. One is our structured approach to programming, which capitalizes on the special provisions of QL BASIC. Another is that we really do start at the beginning. Newcomers to programming should have no difficulty in picking BASIC up quickly, because we explain the groundwork thoroughly, in detail and with a substantial number of illustrations. Later chapters progress more quickly and should also be useful for the programmer who already has experience on other micros. Yet another feature is that after every few pages there are activities to try out on the QL. This is because we have had no reason to change our belief that the best method of learning is by doing. However, although it is preferable to try out the activities on a QL, it is not essential, because we provide illustrations and annotations to indicate how the QL would behave in various circumstances. As a result, a lot can be learnt by merely skimming through the book.

We would like to thank those people whose names do not appear on the front cover but who contributed to the production of this book. In particular Dr Tony Brain of Chelsea College made exceptionally valuable comments on early drafts of the manuscript and provided several programs. Giles Wright and Ron Decent of Prentice Hall International have both been a constant source of support and efficiency throughout the entire writing and production process. We are also grateful to Andrew Cryer for his continuous critical support and for various programs - in particular the games program in Chapter 16. The self-study aspects of the book have benefited much from the association of one of us (Pat Cryer) with the education branch of a multi-national computing concern and with the Institute of Educational Development, at the University of Surrey. Finally we should not forget the readers and reviewers of BASIC Programming on the BBC Microcomputer. Their comments have done much to mould this book into its present form.

Neil Cryer   Pat Cryer

London
October 1984

0

Introduction

0.0 About this book
0.1 Why use a QL?
0.2 Why program in BASIC?
0.3 What's special about the QL's SuperBASIC?
0.4 Turning on the QL
0.5 Getting to know the QL
0.6 Activities
0.7 Points to ponder
0.8 Discussion on the points to ponder
0.9 Discussion of activities

0.0 About this book

This book is about the interesting and exciting things you can do with Sinclair's new QL microcomputer, using the computing language BASIC. We believe that the best way of learning is by doing. So we recommend that you have a QL within easy reach as you read. Then you can try out the activities which are at regular intervals throughout the book.

The book is divided into chapters. In this chapter, we introduce you to the QL and to our way of working. Then come four chapters on the fundamentals of programming in BASIC on the QL. These are about how to start programming; how to save, retrieve and join programs; how to work with BASIC as a programming language; and how to put data into programs. Then come two chapters on techniques which are essential for any really useful programming: how to deal with repetition and how to get the QL to make decisions. Then comes a chapter on sound, followed by three chapters which are devoted to the QL's particularly special graphics features: graphics windows; fundamentals of programming; and colour. Next come four chapters which introduce techniques for rather more sophisticated programming: arrays; functions; string handling; and file handling. The penultimate chapter is concerned with good programming practice, and the final chapter gives a games program. The appendix gives a glossary of BASIC terms.

At the end of most chapters we give some points for you to think about, to help you consolidate, and we follow with a discussion of how you might have set about them. In most chapters we also include a section of hints and discussion on the activities, particularly where they involve writing programs.

We now continue this chapter with a few short and simple sample sections to illustrate our way of working. First are some sections in which we give information to you. These are about things it would be useful for you to know before you start your programming; how to turn on the QL and how to begin familiarizing yourself with it. Next we give a short section of activities where it is your turn to do something yourself. Then we give a very short section posing some simple points for you to think about, followed by an indication of how we see the answers. Finally, comes a section in which we discuss the activities.

0.1 Why use a QL?

Computers are making an enormous impact on society: in banks, in offices, in shops and the home, for booking theatre tickets, air-line tickets, ordering goods and sending messages. The list must be virtually endless.

With the coming of microcomputer technology, computers have become sufficiently small and cheap for ordinary people to own them. These are the microcomputers - or micros - and many different types are available. So why should you choose a QL? One reason is that it is made by

0 Introduction

Sinclair, who has a longstanding reputation in the computing world.

It was in 1980 that Sinclair set the computing world alight with his ZX80, which was the first of a new breed of micros. It had many of the features of much larger computers and yet it was sufficiently cheap for ordinary people to afford. The ZX80 was followed by the ZX81 which was even more advanced. It sold all over the world – including to Japan, the then leader in calculator production. In 1982, yet another advance was heralded from Sinclair, with the Spectrum which boasted excellent graphics as well as colour. By the end of 1983 over one million had been produced. Each new Sinclair micro was a considerable advance over the previous one and, at the same time, was significantly ahead of micros from other manufacturers, particularly in terms of price.

In January 1984 Sinclair surprised the computer world yet again by entering the market of more professional micros. Because he regarded his new micro as a 'quantum leap' forward in micros, he called it the QL. It is radically different from his previous micros. Not only does it have more advanced chips and a very large internal memory, it is also neat and professional-looking in appearance, with a full-sized, professional keyboard with fully depressable 'typewriter-style' keys. They are laid out in what is called the 'QWERTY' pattern, which is so called after the five letters on the left of the top row (see Figure 0.1). This is the standard layout for all professional computers, word processors and typewriters. Like these, and unlike the earlier Sinclair micros, there is no single-key entry; each BASIC word has to be typed in full. The extension on the right contains the 'microdrives' which are for storage. We shall be having more to say about these in Chapter 2.

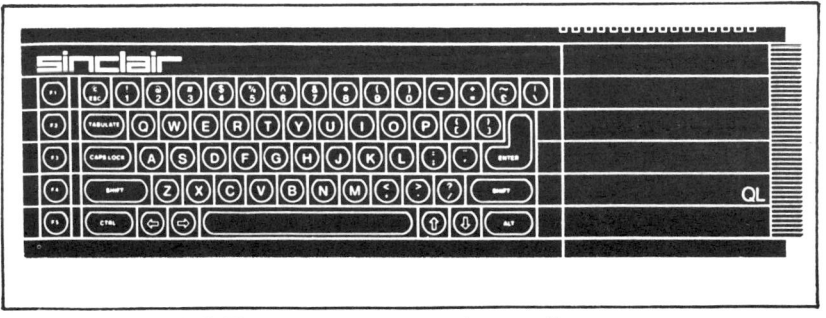

Figure 0.1. The QWERTY keyboard, so named after the five letters on the left of the top row.

The QL also has some particularly new and exciting programming features: sophisticated graphics with a wide range of colour-options and a rather special enhanced version of the computer language BASIC. The result is a professional machine, capable of performing a wide range of tasks.

The QL comes with packages for wordprocessing and for analysing trends in numbers, an archival database program and a graphics package for displaying business or other data. You can also buy packages to run on the QL. Examples include languages other than BASIC; business packages (for such things as accounts); training aids (e.g. for typing); games, etc.

There can be no doubt of the value of running specialized packages on the QL. Nevertheless, there is a unique excitement and satisfaction which comes from programming it yourself, to do exactly what you want, when you want - and that is what this book is all about. Then you can make the QL do almost anything that happens to appeal to you. Your imagination is the biggest limitation - but you will almost certainly find no shortage of ideas once you start!

0.2 Why program in BASIC?

Humans understand words - but computers understand what are called 'binary codes'. So there are very real and major differences between the way that humans would like to give their instructions to a computer and what the computer can understand. In response to this problem, various 'computer languages' have been created to convert certain words into codes that a computer can understand. When you come to learn any one of these computer languages, you don't need to know how it works. This is taken care of inside the computer - but you do have to learn the words that make up the limited vocabulary that the computer can accept - and when, where and how to use them.

This book is concerned with a language which, without doubt, is the most popular for home computers. It is called BASIC. It was developed in 1965; and stands for Beginners All-purpose Symbolic Instruction Code.

Although we shall be concerned with BASIC, we would not want to give you the impression that there are no other languages. This is by no means the case. Whereas BASIC is an 'all-purpose' language, other languages have been created for specific purposes. For example, ALGOL (Algorithmic Language) is particularly suitable for scientific problems; and COBOL (Common Business Oriented Language) is suitable for business use. Other languages in common use are FORTRAN (Formula Translator); RPG (Report Generator), APL (A Programming Language); PL/1 (Programming Language 1); Pascal (named after a French philosopher).

BASIC was created specifically for beginners. It is powerful enough for most purposes and yet it is easy to pick up because it uses words which sound like everyday English. Like most micros the QL is ready to accept instructions in BASIC as soon as it is turned on.

0.3 What's special about the QL's SuperBASIC?

Just as improvements are made to computers, so are improvements made to computer languages. Consequently various 'dialects' evolve. Until the QL came out, the best dialect of BASIC was generally considered to be BBC BASIC, which was developed for the BBC Microcomputer. This was largely because it is was particularly suitable for 'structuring' programs - and we shall have more to say about this later in the book.

The BASIC of the QL is a major departure from the BASICs of Sinclair's other computers. He calls it SuperBASIC. It has many of the features of BBC BASIC. The similarities are quite clear, yet there are some useful and imaginative differences. These improvements and extensions make SuperBASIC particularly suitable for clear and well-structured programming.

0.4 Turning on the QL

We would now like to give you a little practical information before asking you to do something for yourself in the activities of Section 0.6. Firstly something about turning the QL on. Before you can do so, it has to be connected to a television or a monitor, as described in the User Guide. We shall assume that you will be using a television.

You will than have to supply the QL with electricity by plugging the QL's power supply into the mains and then plugging its other end into the QL. There are no switches. So this is all you need do. The QL acknowledges by showing the light on its lower left-hand corner.

Finally tune the television until it gives the display shown in Figure 0.2.

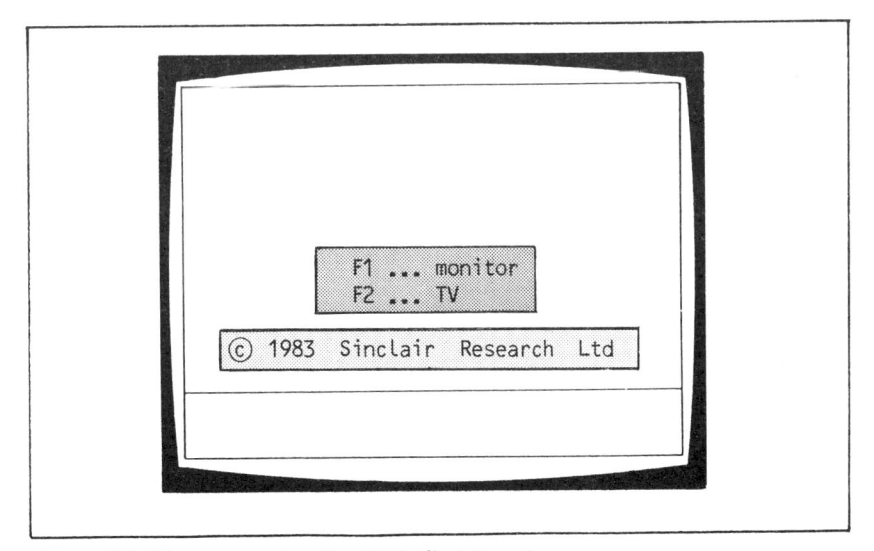

```
F1 ... monitor
F2 ... TV

© 1983 Sinclair Research Ltd
```

Figure 0.2. The screen when the QL is first turned on.

Once you see this display, you have to inform the QL that you are using a television rather than a monitor by pressing the key marked F2 on the left of the keyboard. The main area of the television screen will then clear to red (or near black with a black and white television).

Just underneath the lower left-hand corner of the main red area, there will be a small, magenta, flashing square. It is called the 'cursor'. Its presence shows that the QL is ready to receive instructions. If it is not showing, the QL will not accept further instructions – which we will be asking you to demonstrate for yourself when you reach the activities of Section 0.6. One reason may be that you need to wait a few moments while the QL finishes working out lengthy instructions. Another reason may be due to rather strange codes having been sent to the QL – perhaps because you accidentally leant on the keyboard, or perhaps by your program. When a computer is disabled in this manner, it is said to 'crash' or to 'lock up' – which should not be confused with getting an error message. These are helpful and harmless; and the cursor invariably appears afterwards, showing that the QL is ready for further instruction.

If the QL ever fails to respond when you expect it to, you can force it to stop whatever it is doing and be available for receiving instructions by keeping a finger pressed on the CTRL key while typing once on the SPACE bar – as shown in Figure 0.3. If the QL then gives the message 'not complete', just ignore it.

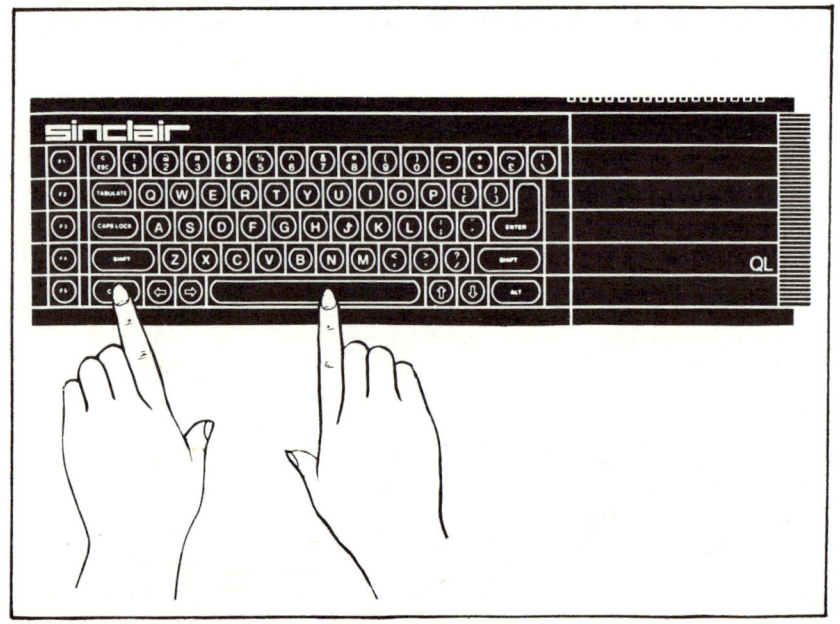

Figure 0.3. Pressing the CTRL and SPACE keys together forces the QL to stop whatever it is doing and wait for an instruction.

0 Introduction

0.5 Getting to know the QL

When you press a key, which we shall call typing, the character on the key appears at the position of the cursor, and the cursor moves along as typing progresses.

The ENTER key, which is on the right of the keyboard, is very important. The act of pressing it, as shown in Figure 0.4, is called 'entering' and this signals to the QL that you are satisfied with what you have typed and that it should now act upon it. Right up until the time you press this key, you can alter the instruction as much as you like, so giving you the opportunity to change your mind and correct any typing mistakes.

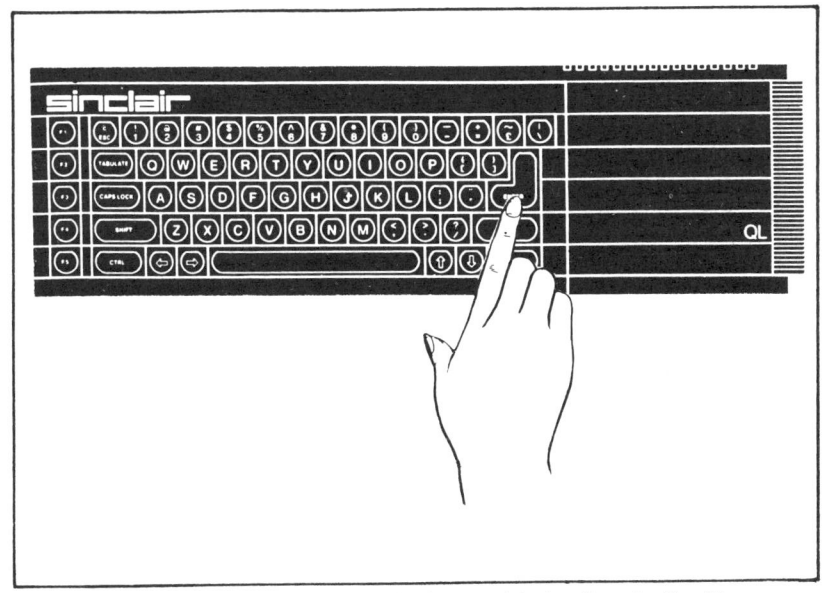

Figure 0.4. Pressing the ENTER key sends the typed instructions to the QL.

Making changes to what you have typed is called 'editing'. The simplest way to edit is to delete a single character. You do this by pressing on the CTRL with one finger, while also pressing on the left-arrow key, as shown in Figure 0.5. This deletes one character at a time, to the left of the cursor, ready for retyping. The arrow keys are called 'cursor keys'.

You can move the position of the cursor using the left and right cursor keys. This is useful for editing a mistake which is not at the current position of the cursor and for inserting characters into a line.

Now try the activities of the next section. We discuss them in Section 0.9.

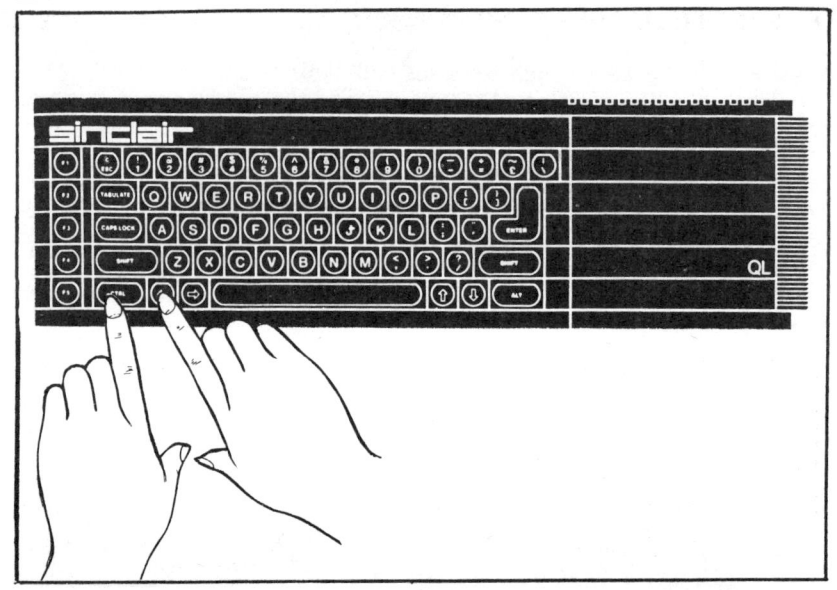

Figure 0.5. Deleting a character with the CTRL key and a cursor key.

0.6 Activities

i. Connect the QL as described in the User Guide. Turn it on and suitably tune the television. (A monitor will not require tuning.) If the light on the left-hand corner of the QL doesn't come on, or if you don't see the display shown in Figure 0.2, see Section 0.9.

ii. Type anything you like and enter it by pressing the ENTER key. Do you get an error message? Is the cursor on the next line, like this?

    asdfg12345
    Bad name
    ■

If so, the QL is ready to accept further instructions. If not, Section 0.9 gives some advice.

iii. Press any key or series of keys, including the SPACE bar at the front of the keyboard. Practise editing by using the left and right cursor keys together to bring the cursor to a suitable position and then the CTRL and left or right cursor key to delete a character. Then retype.

0 Introduction 9

iv. Type something. Now either press ENTER to enter what you have typed or try holding down the CTRL key while pressing the SPACE key to see that you get the cursor back onto the next line. What is the difference between these two methods? We comment in Section 0.9.

v. Try the effect of holding down one of the SHIFT keys at either side of the keyboard, and then doing some typing - numbers and letters. Do you get something like this when you press ENTER?

    ASDFG!@#$%
    bad line
    ASDFG!@#$%.

To get the cursor back on the next line in readiness for new instruction, hold down the CTRL key while pressing the SPACE key. We comment in Section 0.9.

vi. Now press the CAPS LOCK key once and try typing. Do you get something like this?

    ASDFG12345
    bad name
    ■

What is the difference between typing with one finger held on the SHIFT key compared to typing after the CAPS LOCK key has been pressed? Press the CAPS LOCK key again. Do you find the effect of this key is to alternate between giving lower- and then upper-case for letters? Does the CAPS LOCK key affect the number keys? (See Section 0.9)

vii. Try typing and entering all sorts of combinations of symbols, with CAPS LOCK active, then inactive and with SHIFT depressed and not depressed. How many different error messages can you get? We comment in Section 0.9.

0.7 Points to ponder

a. How do you prepare the QL to accept instructions in BASIC?
b. What damage can you cause by pressing the wrong key?

0.8 Discussion on the points to ponder

a. The QL is ready to receive BASIC instructions as soon as it is turned on. If it doesn't show the cursor at any stage, press the SPACE key while

holding down the CTRL key, as this abandons your typing.
b. It is impossible to damage the QL by pressing the wrong key, although it can sometimes produce rather strange effects. You can normally recover by pressing the SPACE key while holding down the CTRL key.

0.9 Discussion of activities

Activity 0.6i: If you don't get the light and the characteristic display, it is unlikely that your QL is faulty. You have probably not connected it up properly. If the light to the left of the keyboard does not come on then it is almost certainly a lack of any power going to the QL. If the light is on then it is more likely to be the connections to the TV or its tuning which is at fault. Reread the first few pages of the User Guide.

Activity 0.6ii: Unless you have experience with programming, you are bound to get an error message because what you have entered will not be in the BASIC language. So the most likely error message is:

bad name

It is very unlikely that your error will have made the computer crash. So probably the cursor appears on the line after the error message, showing that the QL is ready to accept further instructions. If not, hold down the CTRL key and then press the SPACE key to reset the QL and force it to wait for your instruction. Doing this will normally produce the message 'not complete' which you may ignore. If this does not regain control then as a last resort remove any cartridges from the microdrives and press the RESET button which you will find on the right-hand side of the QL. This button is purposely hidden from view, round the side of the microdrives (see Figure 0.6), because of its drastic action. It destroys everything that you have put into memory and restarts from scratch!

Activity 0.6iv: You can get the cursor back either by pressing ENTER or by pressing the SPACE key while holding down the CTRL key. The former enters your typing, and probably gives you the error message 'bad name', whereas the latter abandons the line. In either case the QL awaits your next instruction by flashing the cursor.

It is just possible that you will get the message 'bad line'. If so this will be followed by the reappearance of the line with the cursor at the end of it. The QL now waits for you to edit the mistake in the usual way. Alternatively, you can abandon the line by holding down the CTRL key and pressing the SPACE bar. This will produce the message 'not complete' which you can ignore.

Activity 0.6v: The SHIFT key changes the case of all the characters, i.e. letters come out as lower-case and the number/symbol keys give symbols.

0 Introduction 11

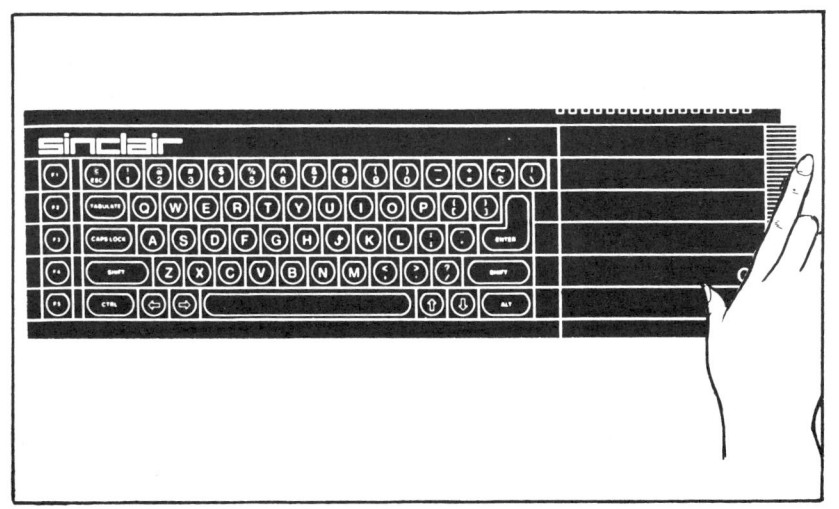

Figure 0.6. Pressing RESET sets the QL to its turning-on conditions. It destroys everything that you have put into memory.

You will find the SHIFT key essential for getting these symbols when you come to program.

Activity 0.6vi: With CAPS LOCK inactive, you get lower-case letters and numbers. This is useful for typing in messages that you want the QL to display to other users. With CAPS LOCK inactive and with SHIFT depressed, you get capital letters and symbols. We recommend that you normally keep the CAPS LOCK inactive, for lower-case writing.

Activity 0.6vii: There are many different and reasonably helpful error messages, and we will be introducing you to some of the more common ones as you progress through this book. In this activity, we managed to get the following error messages:

> **bad line**
>
> **bad name**
>
> **not complete**

You may have managed more.

1

Starting programming

1.0 Introduction
1.1 Immediate actions
1.2 Activities
1.3 Turtle graphics as immediate actions
1.4 Activities
1.5 The idea of a program
1.6 A simple program
1.7 Activities
1.8 Editing programs
1.9 Activities
1.10 First steps in writing a program
1.11 Some sample procedures
1.12 Activities
1.13 Some points to ponder
1.14 Discussion on the points to ponder
1.15 Discussion of activities

1.0 Introduction

This chapter introduces the idea of programming. We explain what a program is and give some hints to help you with your own programming.

1.1 Immediate actions

Suppose you type and enter:

> print "hello"

The word 'print' is part of the BASIC language. So the QL understands it and causes the message 'hello' to appear on the screen, as shown in Figure 1.1. 'hello' is said to be 'printed on the screen' or just 'printed'.

This is where your typing appears

hello

This is where the processed result appears

print "hello"

The main screen area changes colour when you press ENTER

Figure 1.1. An immediate action.

There are various instructions that the QL responds to immediately, like this. Such a mode of use is described as an 'immediate action'. Here is another example of an immediate action:

> print 3+4

It causes 7 (the sum of 3 and 4) to be printed to the screen.
Immediate actions can consist of more than one line. For example, if

1 Starting Programming

each of the following lines is typed and entered in order, 7, the sum of x and y, appears on the screen, as shown in Figure 1.2.

```
x=3
y=4
print x+y
```

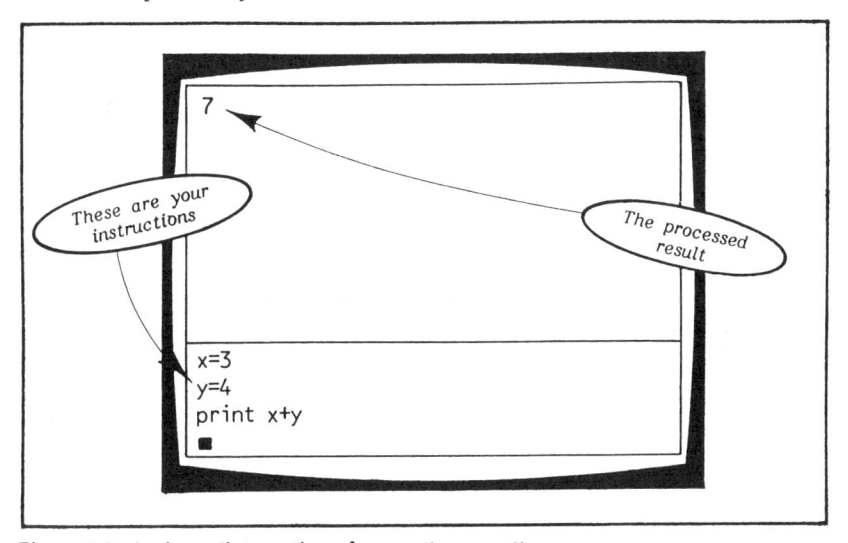

Figure 1.2. An immediate action of more than one line.

The following activities illustrate immediate actions, and you may like to try them before reading any further.

1.2 Activities

i. Enter each of the following separately into the QL. Remember to press ENTER at the end of the line to signal that you are satisfied with what you have typed and that the QL should respond.

```
         print 5+9
and
         print "5+9"
```

Is the display as shown overleaf in Figure 1.3? What does it tell you about the use of quotation marks in the 'print' instruction? (We comment in Section 1.15.)

```
5+9
```

This is printed exactly as it is

```
print "5+9"
```

```
14
```

This is evaluated

```
print 5+9
```

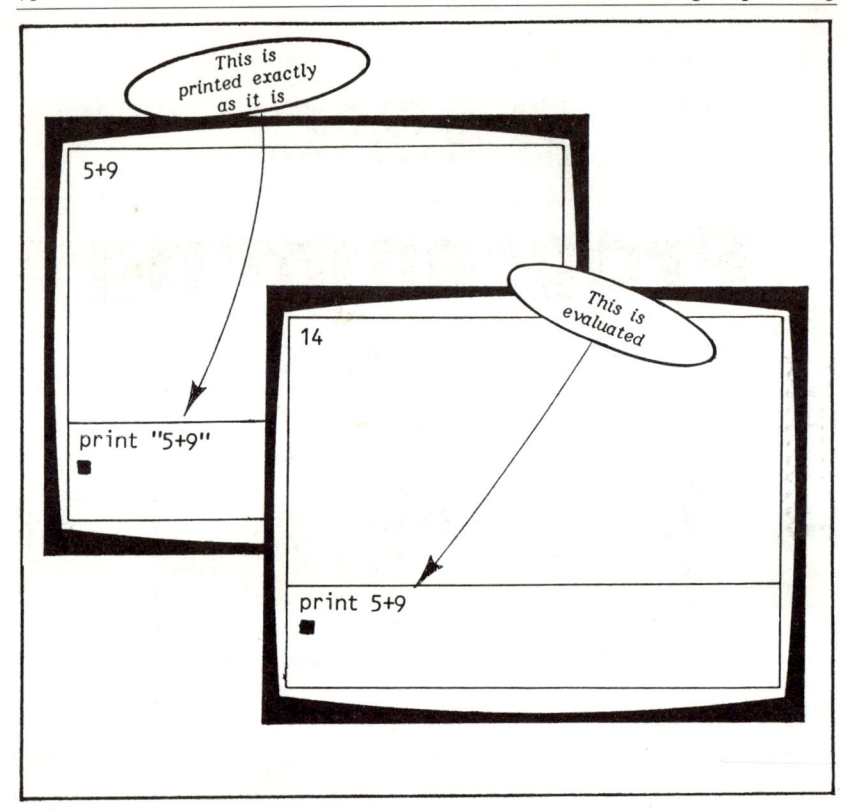

Figure 1.3. The effects of quotes with a 'print' instruction.

---

ii. Repeat the previous activity, but this time press CAPS LOCK first so that your entries are in upper case, like this:

        PRINT 5+9

and

        PRINT "5+9"

Is there any difference? (We discuss this further in Section 1.6.)

iii. Enter each of the following:

        print "hello"

and

        print hello

1 Starting Programming 17

Can you explain why the second instruction gives an error? What form does it take? (We comment in Section 1.15.)

iv. Experiment to see when spaces are optional and when they are essential. For example, try entering each of the following:

```
print 5+7

print5+7

print "hello"

print"hello"

x = 4
y = 3
print x+y
```

Can you come to any conclusions about where spaces are optional and where they are essential? (We comment in Section 1.15.)

1.3 Turtle graphics as immediate actions

You may be interested in drawing pictures with immediate actions. The method uses something called 'turtle graphics' which is not really BASIC at all, although it is available from within BASIC.

Turtle graphics were invented to go with small robot 'turtles' which crawl around, tracing out shapes, under the control of a computer. They carry a pen which can be raised or lowered to give a record of the turtle's path. The QL provides simple turtle graphics to move an imaginary turtle around the screen.

The instructions for lowering and raising the 'pen' are:

        pendown

and

        penup

The instruction for moving is 'move' followed by a number indicating how far the turtle is to move. At this stage, it is probably best if you experiment with these numbers, rather than try to understand their significance.

There are two instructions for changing direction. One is for turning left relative to the current heading of the turtle, and is 'turn' followed by an angle in degrees. The other specifies a heading relative to the horizontal and is 'turnto', followed by an angle in degrees.

1.4 Activities

i. Experiment with turtle graphics by entering the following as immediate actions:

```
pendown
move 50
turn 90
move 90
turn -135
move 60
```

ii. Experiment with some turtle graphics instructions of your own. If the turtle goes off the screen, press RESET and start again.

1.5 The idea of a program

We shall now introduce the idea of a computer program. We shall do so by asking you to consider the following single instruction:

    print "hello"   *(The space is optional)*

As you know from the previous sections, it is an immediate action. Once the QL has acted on it, it is forgotten. You could, however, turn the same instruction into a program by giving it a line number, as follows:

    1 print "hello"   *(The space is optional)*

This time, when you enter, the line you have just typed appears at the top with BASIC words changed to upper-case, as shown in Figure 1.4. A number of things happen in this simple process: The QL assumes that it should not act on any line which starts with a number – and so stores it instead. The QL also checks the line to see if it is written in an acceptable form, and while doing so, it changes BASIC words into upper-case. This is the standard way of listing programs from all computers.

If the QL decides that something is wrong as it checks the line, it will display the message 'bad line' and will redisplay the line at the bottom of the screen, exactly as you typed it. It will then wait for you to edit it by deleting or inserting characters in the usual way. When you are

1 Starting Programming 19

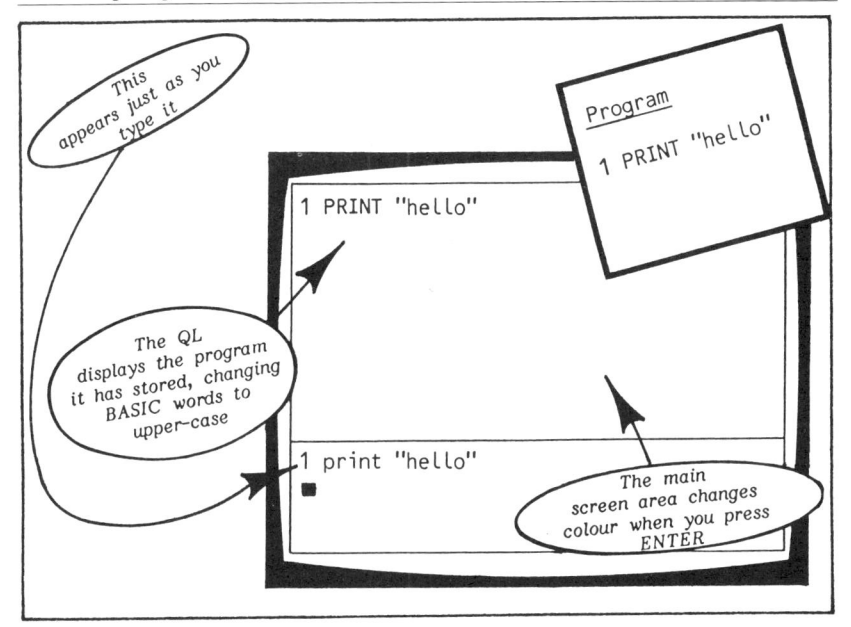

Figure 1.4. The QL displaying a program.

[Figure shows a screen displaying "1 print "hello"" with annotations:
- "This appears just as you type it"
- "The QL displays the program it has stored, changing BASIC words to upper-case"
- "The main screen area changes colour when you press ENTER"
- A separate note showing: Program / 1 PRINT "hello"
- On screen: 1 PRINT "hello"]

satisfied with the edited line, you press the ENTER key to re-enter it.

To get the QL to respond to the stored instruction – which is a program – you must enter:

    run

You may, if you like, enter it again and again. Each time you do so, the program runs and the message 'hello' appears on the screen.

In a simple case like printing 'hello', there is little point in using a program rather than an immediate action. The value of a program comes when you want the QL to carry out a number of instructions in sequence – because a program is a set of instructions which a computer stores and carries out as soon as you instruct it to, by entering 'run'. The computer then 'executes' or 'runs' the whole program.

Each line of a program begins with a line number which indicates the sequence in which the computer should carry out the instruction. By convention line numbers go up in increments of ten, giving program lines of, for example: 10, 20, 30, etc. or of: 100, 110, 120 etc. This allows you to insert up to nine additional lines between the existing lines, if you feel like modifying the program. Such editing leaves rather untidy-looking line numbers, but you can renumber to multiples of ten by entering:

renum

This both renumbers and gives a copy of the renumbered program on the screen, so that you can check it.
You can also get a copy of your program on the screen by entering:

list

1.6 A simple program

We shall now see how a program can contain various instructions. We begin by reconsidering the one-line program of the previous section - this time letting it have 100 as its line number, and showing it with upper-case instructions, as it would appear on the blue area of the screen and on a printed listing:

100 PRINT "hello"

When you run such a program, you will see that the screen looks untidily cluttered because the 'hello' appears on top of the listing of the program, partially obscuring it. A way round this is to extend the program by including a CLS instruction to clear the screen first. You could incorporate it into the program as follows:

90 CLS
100 PRINT "hello"

Then when you enter 'run', the screen clears before the 'hello' is printed. Figure 1.5 shows the sequence of events.

You might think that the appearance would be better if the 'hello' were in the centre of the screen. You could accomplish this by using an AT instruction in the program. This sets the position at which any future printing will occur. The instruction might be as follows:

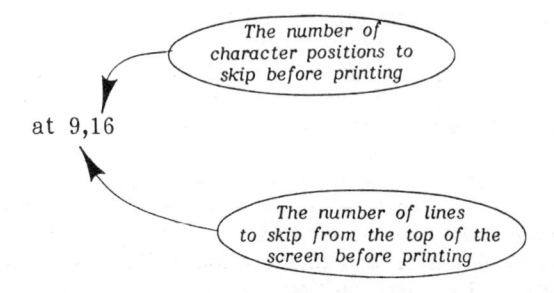

at 9,16

(The number of character positions to skip before printing)

(The number of lines to skip from the top of the screen before printing)

1 Starting Programming 21

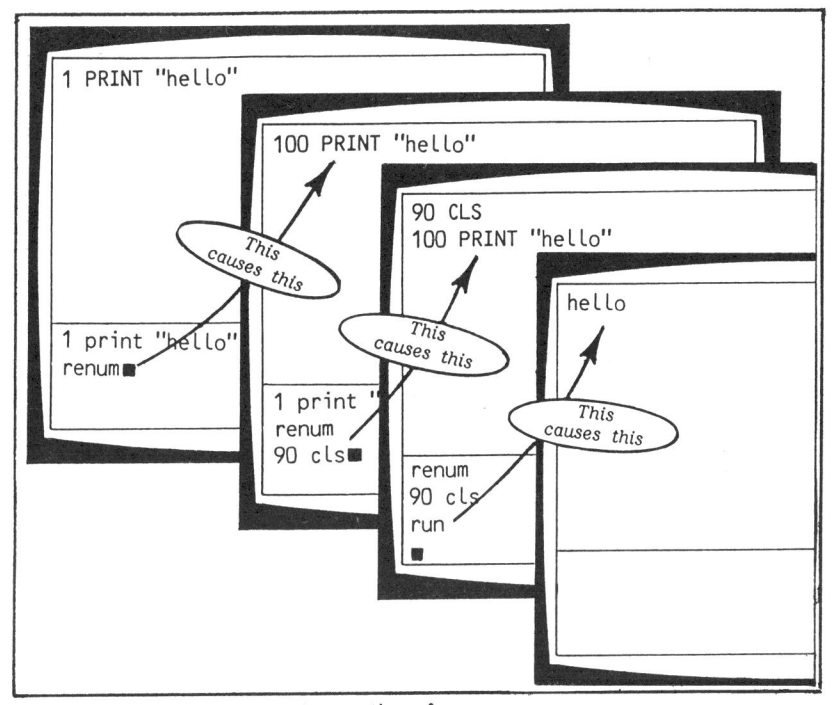

Figure 1.5. Stages in entry and execution of a program.

You could incorporate it into the program like this:

    100 CLS
    110 AT 9,16
    120 PRINT "hello"

It is worth repeating that this listing is in the form in which the QL displays it once you have pressed the ENTER key, which is also the form in which programs are given in books and magazines - and we will give all our listings this way. However, there is no need for you to enter BASIC instructions in capitals. Merely type them in lower-case, and the QL will do the conversion. Figure 1.6 (overleaf) shows how you should enter the above program.

Incidentally the QL does accept instructions in upper-case, which you can easily give by means of the CAPS LOCK key - but we do not advise it for reasons which will become clear later.

You may like to play around with these ideas. If so, we suggest you try the activities of the next section.

```
100 CLS
110 AT 9,16
120 PRINT "hello"
```

How you enter a program - using lower-case for BASIC

Program
```
100 CLS
110 AT 9,16
120 PRINT "hello"
```

```
100 cls
110 at 9,16
120 print "hello"
```

How the QL displays its program - changing BASIC words to upper-case

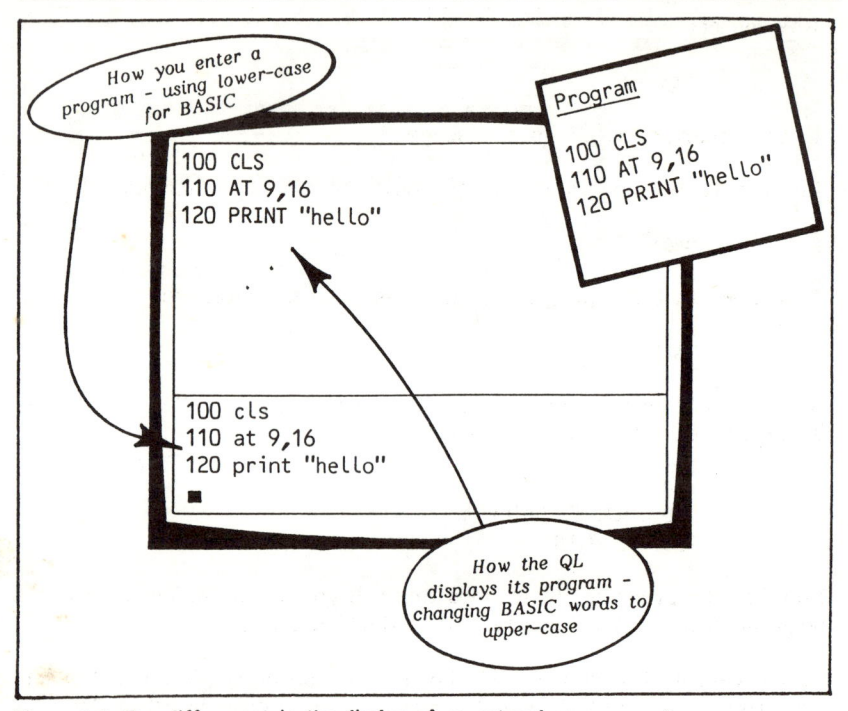

Figure 1.6. The differences in the display of an entered program and a listed program.

1.7 Activities

i. Enter the program which we developed in the previous section. (Remember to use lower-case for the BASIC keywords and let the QL change to upper-case.) Renumber using:

   renum

Does the program appear on the screen with its lines renumbered? Enter:

   run

Does the program perform as you expect?

ii. Clear the screen of all the program lines by entering:

   cls

1   Starting Programming   23

Now enter:

>   list

Is the program listed on the screen?

iii. Remove the program from the QL's memory by entering:

>   new

Now check that the program really has gone by entering:

>   list

Nothing should happen. Now re-enter the program (with BASIC instructions in lower-case) in the following order:

>   100 CLS
>   120 PRINT "hello"
>   110 AT 9,16

Now list the program. What does this tell you about the order in which program lines must be entered? (See Section 1.15.)

iv. Try varying the numbers in the AT instruction so that the message gets printed at the corners of the screen. Vary the message to get your name printed at the bottom of the screen. You may like to add further PRINT instructions in further lines of program. (We comment in Section 1.15.)

1.8   Editing programs

If you have been doing the activities, you will probably feel that the typing has become rather arduous. You almost certainly keep making mistakes and wish that there was some way of editing them without having to retype the entire line. Fortunately the QL is particularly good in its editing provision.

You already know how to delete a single character using the CTRL and cursor keys together. So let us suppose that you want to change part of a line of program that is already complete and entered. You can keep as much of the faulty line as you wish without having to type it all out again. You can merely insert or delete parts.

To edit, say, line 50 enter:

>   edit 50

The line will immediately appear along the bottom of the screen where typed instructions normally appear. You already know what to do next. Merely use the cursor keys to move the cursor to where you want to make the change and use the CTRL key with either the left or right cursor key. Insert additional characters by moving the cursor to the correct position and typing what you want. When you are satisfied with the new version of the line, press the ENTER key to enter it. The new line is now incorporated into your program, just as if you had originally typed it all in properly.

If you use this method to change the line number, a corresponding new line will be entered into your program. The original will remain unaltered.

As an alternative to pressing the ENTER key, you may press the down cursor key, which is on the lower right of the keyboard. This not only enters but also presents the next line ready for editing - a very neat way of moving through the particular parts of a program. The up cursor has a similar effect.

If you want to remove an entire line of program, merely type and enter its line number.

You can delete a number of lines of a program using the 'dline' instruction, followed by the numbers of the first and last lines you want removed. For example, the following removes lines 10 to 30 inclusive:

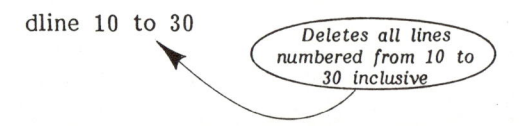

    dline 10 to 30   *(Deletes all lines numbered from 10 to 30 inclusive)*

To remove specific lines, list the numbers of the required lines separated by commas. For example, the following removes lines 90, 95 and 100:

    dline 90,95,100   *(Deletes all these lines)*

You can combine both methods. For example, the following deletes lines 10 to 30, as well as lines 90, 95 and 100, plus those between 150 to 200:

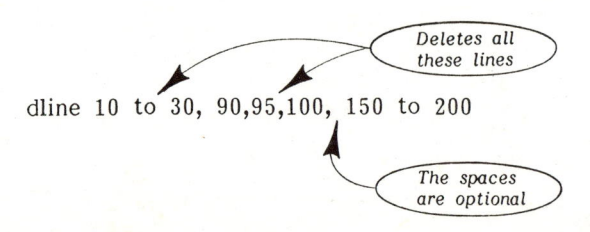

    dline 10 to 30, 90,95,100, 150 to 200

(Deletes all these lines)

(The spaces are optional)

1.9 Activities

i. Practise the editing which we described in the previous section on the program of Section 1.7. For example, change it to the following:

```
100 CLS
110 AT 9,10
120 PRINT "Welcome to the QL"
```

ii. Enter the following program as a basis for practising editing. Incidentally it does nothing as it stands. The colon on each line is a minimum that the QL will accept on a line.

```
1 :
2 :
3 :
4 :
5 :
6 :
7 :
8 :
9 :
```

Now try using various forms of the DLINE instruction. (Remember that, as DLINE is part of the BASIC language, we are giving it in the conventional upper-case, although you should type it in lower case.) Try, for example, the instruction:

dline 2 to 4,6,8 to 100

Does the QL display the revised program with the lines removed?

1.10 First steps in writing a program

An advantage of QL's SuperBASIC is that it makes it easy to write programs in clearly defined and separate blocks. Such programs are described as well-structured, or just 'structured'. You should get into the habit of structuring your programs. When you come back to them later, it is easier to understand what you were doing, and it makes them easier to debug, i.e. to trace any programming errors.

As you progress though the book, we shall be introducing various ways of structuring programs. In this section we introduce a very important way: using what are called 'procedures'.

A procedure is a block of program lines, identified by a name of the programmer's choosing. This usually describes what the procedure does. For example, if the procedure draws a boat, it might be called 'draw_boat', or if it plays a tune, it might called 'tune'. Names in upper-case, like DRAW_BOAT and TUNE are also acceptable, but we shall keep to lower-case in most places in this book, because it is easier to read and cannot be confused with BASIC keywords.

In order for a procedure to be clearly identifiable, BASIC requires that it should start with a line which defines the name of the procedure. This line has to be of the following form:

>DEFine PROCedure name_of_procedure

For example:

>DEFine PROCedure tune

You can enter it in either of the following ways:

>define procedure tune

or

>DEFINE PROCedure tune

or

>def proc tune

For simplicity, you will probably always use the last form, which the QL lists in full.

All procedures must end with the line:

>END DEFine

You can enter it as:

>end def

Optionally you can include the name of the procedure, like this:

>end def name_of_procedure

The QL, of course, lists this as:

>END DEFine name_of_procedure

It normally makes the program easier to read if the procedure is placed at the end of a program. It therefore has to be given line numbers which are safely higher than those of the rest of the program.

As an illustration of the use of procedures, we could turn the program of Section 1.9 into a procedure called 'welcome'. It would be as follows:

1 Starting Programming

```
200 DEFine PROCedure welcome
210 CLS
220 AT 9,10
230 PRINT "Welcome to the QL"
240 END DEFine
```

A procedure can be used in immediate mode, for example, by typing and entering:

welcome

It can also be called as part of a program. The simplest program would need only one line: holding just the newly created BASIC statement 'welcome'.

10 welcome

When you come to complete the program, it is useful to leave a spare line between the main program and the procedure. With a single colon on it, it won't get removed by any renumbering. The complete program, when renumbered, would then be:

```
100 welcome
110 :
120 DEFine PROCedure welcome
130 CLS
140 AT 9,10
150 PRINT "Welcome to the QL"
160 END DEFine
```

The colon stresses the distinction between the main program and the procedure definitions

---

This is how you should enter the program

```
100 welcome
110 :
120 def proc welcome
130 cls
140 at 9,10
150 print "Welcome to the QL"
160 end def welcome
```

This is the minimum you need to type here

This is how the QL displays the program

```
100 welcome
110 :
120 DEFine PROCedure welcome
130 CLS
140 AT 9,10
150 PRINT "Welcome to the QL"
160 END DEFine welcome
```

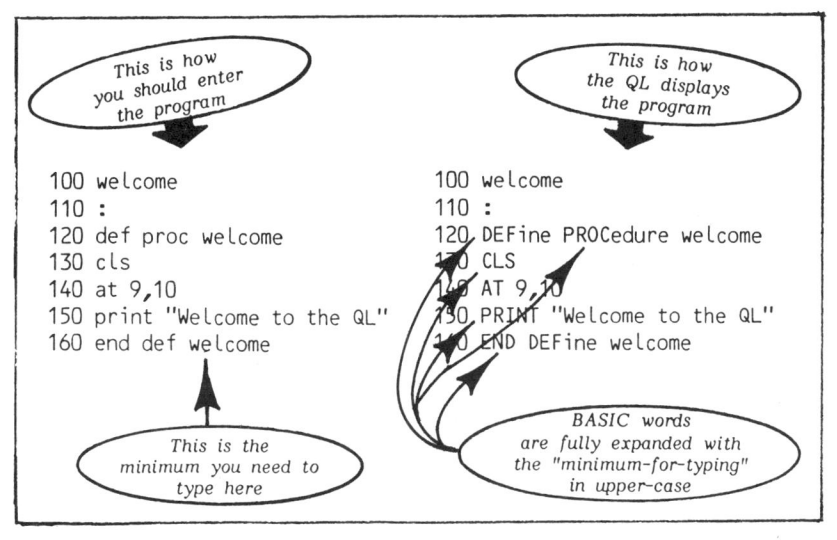

BASIC words are fully expanded with the "minimum-for-typing" in upper-case

Figure 1.7. How the QL expands BASIC words.

You may enter all this program in lower-case.

The QL allows you to save typing time by using a sort-of shorthand for certain BASIC words. It indicates the shorthand equivalents by putting them as capitals in the program listing. Figure 1.7 (on the previous page) shows the idea. On the left is how you should type the listing for entering, and on the right is how we will display programs in this book - which is how the QL will list them. Once again the QL checks for errors and then displays the listing with appropriate BASIC words expanded. The minimum that you may enter is changed to upper-case.

It is helpful to put comments into a program to remind you what the program does. You can do this with a REMark statement. We show this in the following program which is otherwise identical to the one above:

(The colon separates one BASIC statement from another)

(We had to break the line here because of the width of the page. You should type the complete line before pressing ENTER)

```
100 welcome: REMark This program prints a message
             in the centre of the screen
110 :
120 DEFine PROCedure welcome
130    CLS :AT 9,10
140    PRINT "Welcome to the QL"
150 END DEFine
```

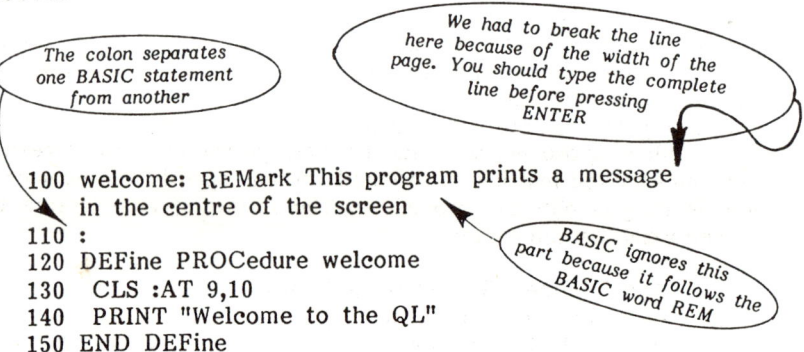

(BASIC ignores this part because it follows the BASIC word REM)

The colon in line 100 separates one BASIC statement, the procedure call 'welcome', from another, REMark. You can use a colon in this way to place as many BASIC instructions as you like on a line. In general we don't recommend this, because it makes programs rather difficult to read. It is appropriate for REMark instructions, though, because it attaches the remark to the line concerned.

Alternatively the REMark could have been placed on a separate line, as in the following version:

```
100 welcome
105 REMark This program prints a message
          in the centre of the screen
```

BASIC will always ignore all the writing which follows the word REMark.

1.11 Some sample procedures

So that you can practise making your own programs, we shall now provide

1 Starting Programming 29

you with some procedures. As you may still be new to typing, we are making them short. Procedures really come into their own when you want to call them more than once, without retyping them each time.

Another reason why we are using procedures stems from our wanting to make early use of the QL's special features of colour, graphics and sound - but it will take time to teach them to you. So we are going to adopt the policy of asking you to use procedures as 'black boxes'. In other words, whereas we will take you gradually through all aspects of programming, and expect you to understand what we and you are doing, we will not - at this stage - expect you to understand what is going on inside the procedures. Our intention is that you should become proficient at writing programs using procedures, but not yet that you should necessarily know how any of the procedures work. So, please, when you come to a set of program lines, surrounded with DEFine PROCedure name-of-procedure and END DEFine, do not worry if you do not understand them. You should still enjoy using them, because they will illustrate what the QL can do!

Now for the sample procedures:

The following procedure prints the message 'hello' on the screen as many times as you instruct it to - and you can specify the number of times when you call the procedure. The following lines define the procedure which we call hello:

```
100 DEFine PROCedure hello(n)
110   FOR num=1 TO n
120     PRINT "hello"
130   END FOR num
140 END DEFine
```

Having entered the program lines into the QL, you can get three hellos printed using the following:

hello 3

You can get five hellos with the following:

hello 5

It is very useful to be able to specify several numbers in a call to a procedure. As an illustration we now give a procedure which will print out a horizontal row of stars. It allows you to specify where the row of stars should start and how many should be printed. We call it 'hstars'. When you call it you must give it three numbers. The first two represent the column and line number, just as in the AT instruction. The third is the number of stars that are to be printed. Thus the following entry prints 20 stars, starting after the tenth line from the top of the screen and the third space from the left:

hstars 3,10,20

The lines which define this procedure are:

```
200 DEFine PROCedure hstars(x,y,n)
210   FOR num=0 TO n-1
220     AT y,x+num :PRINT "*"
230   END FOR num
240 END DEFine
```

vstars is a very similar procedure which will print the stars downwards in a vertical column. It is defined as follows:

```
260 DEFine PROCedure vstars(x,y,n)
270   FOR num=0 TO n-1
280     AT y+num,x :PRINT "*"
290   END FOR num
300 END DEFine
```

It can be called by a line such as the following, which prints 10 stars, starting after the eleventh line down the screen and after leaving three empty spaces at the start of the line.

vstars 3,11,10

1.12 Activities

i. Enter the procedure 'hello' from the previous section, but type your own name instead of the hello in line 120. Decide how many times you would like your name to appear on the screen. Then call the procedure, specifying this number. Do you get what you expect?

ii. Enter the procedure hstars into the QL and call on it by entering:

hstars 2,2,10

Now enter:

hstars 30,20,5

Try other numbers and make sure that you get the stars where you want them. In Section 1.15, we comment on why you may get an error message.

iii. Enter the procedure vstars and call it. Make sure that you can get the

1 Starting Programming 31

vertical line of stars precisely as you want.

iv. We suggest that you now use these procedures, together with what we have already shown you about printing a message and clearing the screen, to build up a program to perform the following tasks:

a. Start by creating a program which clears the screen and writes the message 'Welcome to the QL' across the centre of the screen.

b. Extend the program to surround the welcome message with a box made up from stars.

c. Extend the program to add your own name in the form 'by John' at the bottom right-hand corner of the screen.

d. You may like to add a sound accompaniment with the following procedure which will produce a pleasant series of notes. It needs a single number to be given in the procedure call. For example sound 20 would produce a stream of twenty notes:

```
320 DEFine PROCedure sound(n)
330 FOR num=1 TO n
340    BEEP RND(10000),10+RND(200)
350    PAUSE 10
360 END FOR num
370 END DEFine sound
```

We give a complete program in Section 1.15.

1.13 Some points to ponder

a. How important is it that you type everything exactly as we print it?

1.14 Discussion on the points to ponder

a. This question is difficult to answer precisely. SuperBASIC is very tolerant, especially compared with the BASIC of many other micros. For example when you enter programs in lower-case, SuperBASIC changes all the keywords that it recognizes into upper-case. This means that you can see immediately when it has misinterpreted what you typed. In many places SuperBASIC does not object to extra spaces. In others spaces are critical and produce error messages or prevent BASIC key words from being recognized. As we go along, we will try to indicate where spaces are optional. In general you can take many liberties but do check that what appears in the listing is what we have printed in this book.

1.15 Discussion of activities

Activity 1.2i: When anything is enclosed in quotation marks, the QL prints it as it is. Without the quotation marks, the QL tries to evaluate it.

Activity 1.2iii: Since there were no quotation marks, the QL tried to work out a mathematical answer for the writing. This was not possible. So it responded with a *.

Activity 1.2iv: The QL needs to recognize a BASIC word, like 'print' as distinct and separate from what follows. The separation can be in the form of a space or as quotation marks.

Activity 1.7iii: You don't have to enter program lines in order. The computer stores and lists lines in an order corresponding to the numbers of the lines.

Activity 1.7iv: If, when you add further AT instructions, you get the error message 'out of range' don't worry. It will mean you have chosen a position off the screen. The QL only checks for such errors when the program is run, not at the time of entering the instruction.

Activity 1.12ii: If the numbers you give when calling the procedure hstars try to print the stars at a point that is off the screen, the message "out of range" appears.

Activity 1.12iv: The following is one version of the complete program, which assumes that the procedures hstars and vstars are already in the computer:

```
100 CLS
110 AT 10,11 :PRINT "Welcome to the QL"
120 hstars 6,8,27
130 hstars 6,12,27
140 vstars 6,9,3
150 vstars 32,9,3
160 AT 20,23 :PRINT "By Joe John"
170 sound 20
```

The program could be condensed if yet another procedure was written to include all the calls to hstars etc. This would be particularly useful if it were written in a slightly more general fashion, so that it produced a box of stars to go round any message. The main program would then become:

```
100 CLS
110 AT 10,11 :PRINT "Welcome to the QL"
120 box 8,10,23
```

1 Starting Programming

130 AT 19,23 :PRINT "By Joe John"

The program would rely on the new procedure PROCbox, defined as follows, where w is the number of characters in the message to be enclosed.

```
400  DEFine PROCedure box(x,y,w)
410    hstars x-2,y-2,w+4
420    hstars x-2,y+2,w+4
430    vstars x-2,y-1,3
440    vstars x+w+1,y-1,3
450  END DEFine
```

You can go on redefining new procedures until the whole program becomes one procedure. How far it is profitable to go is eventually a matter of personal choice. The thing to note is that, when writing lines for a procedure, it is advisable to make them as universal as possible. Hence 'box' was not merely the previous lines wrapped up with DEFine PROCedure at the beginning and END DEFine at the end. It was defined so that it would produce a box of variable width and position. In later chapters we will demonstrate that it would even have been possible for 'box' to have been written so that it automatically worked out how long the message was and so automatically drew a box of the correct length, whatever the message. This is how all procedures should work, if possible. Then a minimum of mundane counting is left for the programmer, and - more importantly - a slight change of message would not need a re-write of most of 'box'.

2

Saving, retrieving and joining programs

2.0 Introduction
2.1 Preparing a cartridge for saving a program
2.2 Saving programs
2.3 Getting a directory of a cartridge
2.4 Loading programs
2.5 Activities
2.6 Loading and running with one instruction
2.7 Activities
2.8 Merging two or more programs
2.9 Points to watch with merging programs
2.10 Activities
2.11 More sample procedures
2.12 Activities
2.13 A menu-selection program 'boot'
2.14 Activities
2.15 Discussion of activities

2.0 Introduction

In the last chapter we kept programs and procedures short because you had to keep typing them into the QL every time you used them. In this chapter we shall describe how you can save them on cartridges, using the microdrives on the right of the keyboard. Then we shall describe how you can retrieve them again. This will enable us to be a little more adventurous with our programming, because we won't be inflicting you with the chore of repetitive typing.

2.1 Preparing a cartridge for saving a program

When you first buy blank microdrive cartridges, they come with absolutely nothing on them. (This is not of course true of cartridges supplied as software, which should never be treated in the way we are going to describe!) In the blank, untreated form, cartridges will not record programs. You have to what is called 'format' them.

To format a blank cartridge, take it out of its case, holding it only by the ribbed end, and insert it into microdrive 1. This is the left of the two microdrives. The cartridge has to be the correct way up, i.e. with the edge where tape is visible to the left (see Figure 2.1).

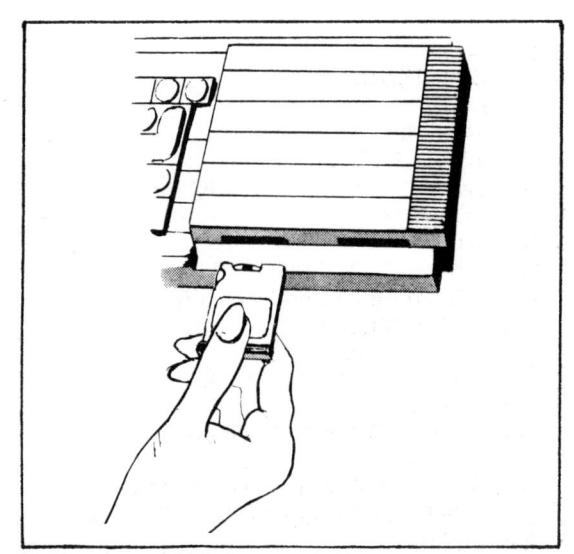

Figure 2.1. The correct way up for inserting a cartridge into a microdrive.

2 Saving, Retrieving and Joining Programs

Enter the following instruction to format the cartridge:

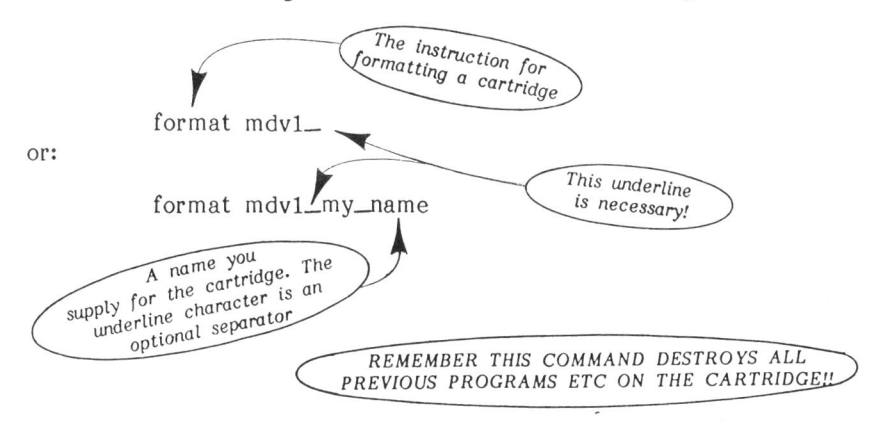

        format mdv1_ ← *The instruction for formatting a cartridge*

or:

        format mdv1_my_name ← *This underline is necessary!*

A name you supply for the cartridge. The underline character is an optional separator

REMEMBER THIS COMMAND DESTROYS ALL PREVIOUS PROGRAMS ETC ON THE CARTRIDGE!!

2.2 Saving programs

We shall describe the process of saving, by assuming that you want to save the following program - which we don't expect you to understand yet:

```
100 MODE 8
110 i=150
120 DIM j(i),k(i)
130 x=1
140 y=1
150 a=10 : FILL 1
160 b=1
170 c=1
180 p=0
190 :
200 REPeat main_loop
210   c=1+c MOD 8
220   p=1+p MOD i
230   INK c
240   x=x+a
250   IF x<1 OR x>165 THEN a=-a
260   y=y+b
270   IF y<1 OR y>100 THEN b=-b
280   LINE x,y TO j(p),k(p)
290   j(p)=x
300   k(p)=y
310 END REPeat main_loop
```

2 Saving, Retrieving and Joining Programs

You have to start by choosing a name for the program. We shall call this one 'patterns' because of the display that it produces - but any other name would do.

Insert the cartridge into one of the microdrives and enter:

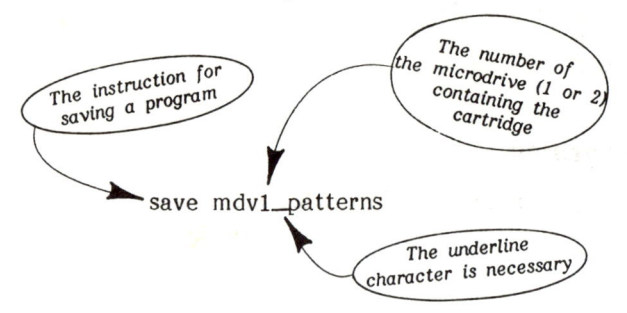

save mdv1_patterns

(The instruction for saving a program)
(The number of the microdrive (1 or 2) containing the cartridge)
(The underline character is necessary)

You will hear the microdrive motor start running, and the light on the microdrive will light up. At the same time the cursor will disappear, to indicate that the QL is busy and will not respond to your instructions. When the program has been saved, the cursor will reappear on the next line. The microdrive will not stop immediately, but you can still go ahead with typing on the keyboard. You should, however, always wait for a microdrive to stop working and its light to go out before removing a cartridge.

2.3 Getting a directory of a cartridge

As you will be able to store several programs on a cartridge, you will need to be able to get a list of what is on it. This is called getting a 'directory'. To get a directory, first clear the screen by entering:

cls

Then enter:

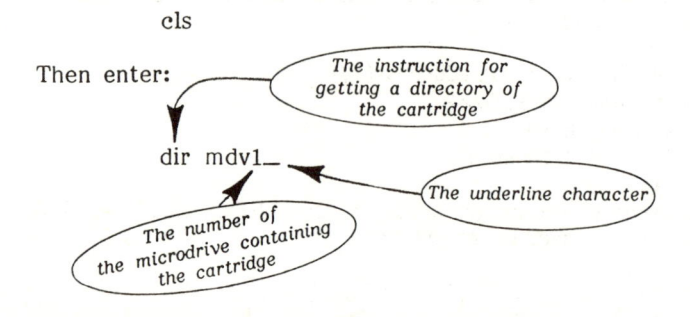

dir mdv1_

(The instruction for getting a directory of the cartridge)
(The number of the microdrive containing the cartridge)
(The underline character)

The microdrive will run for some time and a list of the programs stored on the cartridge will appear on the screen.

You can always simplify the task of getting a directory by defining a

2 Saving, Retrieving and Joining Programs

suitable procedure. Suppose you call it 'cat' (for catalogue). Then you can always bring up a directory merely by entering the single word 'cat'. A suitable definition might be:

```
30000 DEFine PROCedure cat
30010    dir mdv1_
30020 END DEFine cat
```

2.4 Loading programs

To load the program from the cartridge back into the QL, type:

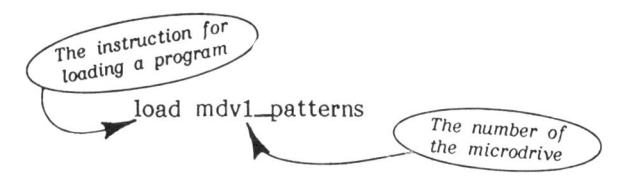

The instruction for loading a program

load mdv1_patterns

The number of the microdrive

Then enter by pressing ENTER. The motor will start up and the microdrive light will appear. The cursor will disappear until the program has loaded.

The program is now in the QL's memory and will run in response to the 'run' instruction and will list up on the screen in response to the 'list' instruction. (Incidentally when you run this particular program, it will go on forever unless you interrupt it by holding the CTRL key down while pressing the SPACE bar.)

If you want to keep saving a program - perhaps every few lines, as you develop it - you will find it arduous to keep typing out the whole of the 'save' and 'load' instructions. SuperBASIC allows a procedure to be defined to do the same job. It could be defined as follows and used by merely entering sv "name":

```
30100 DEFine PROCedure sv(a$)
30110    a$="mdv1_"&a$
30120    SAVE a$
30130 END DEFine sv
```

Appended on the end of the program you are developing, this will allow the latest version to be saved by entering:

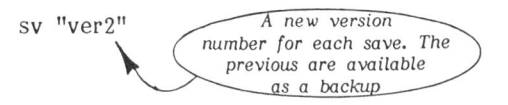

sv "ver2"

A new version number for each save. The previous are available as a backup

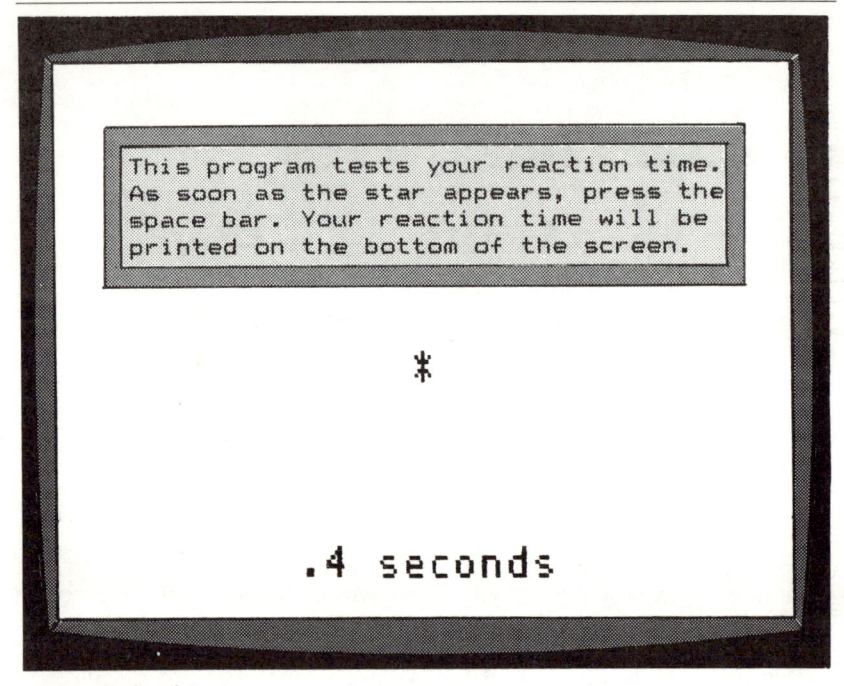

```
This program tests your reaction time.
As soon as the star appears, press the
space bar. Your reaction time will be
printed on the bottom of the screen.
```

```
                    *
```

```
.4 seconds
```

Screen Display 2.1

In the next and the next but one activities sections, we provide two programs which illustrate some of the QL's special features. They are longer than those that you have met so far in this book because, now that you know how to edit, save, and retrieve, you won't find it such a chore to type and enter them. We do not - at this stage - expect you to understand the programming. That will come later. We give them as material on which you can practise saving, and loading - although we expect you to enjoy running them too.

2.5 Activities

Listing 2.1 tests your reaction time by timing how quickly you can press the space bar after a star appears on the screen. In each game, the star appears at a new random position and after a random time delay. Your current reaction time is printed on the screen. The program carries on testing until you hold down the CTRL key and press the SPACE bar. You can get the idea from the Screen Display 2.1 which is opposite Listing 2.1.

Listing 2.1

```
100 REMark A reaction test program
110 display_instructions
120 REPeat mainloop
130   wait_for_a_while
140   display_star
150   wait_for_space_bar
160   rub_out_star
170   display_reaction_times
180 END REPeat mainloop
190 :
200 DEFine PROCedure display_instructions
210   MODE 8
220   OPEN #3,scr
230   OPEN #4,scr
240   OPEN #5,scr :CSIZE #5,0,0
250   WINDOW #3,500,50,12,0:PAPER #3,3:INK #3,0:CLS #3
260   WINDOW #4,480,30,20,210
270   WINDOW #5,500,206,12,50:PAPER #5,2:CLS #5
280   CURSOR #3,20,5
290   PRINT #3," This program tests your reaction time."
300   PRINT #3,"   As soon as the star appears, press the"
310   PRINT #3,"   space bar. Your reaction time will be"
320   PRINT #3,"   printed on the bottom of the screen.";
330   BORDER #3,2,4
340   CSIZE #5,3,1
350 END DEFine display_instructions
360 :
370 DEFine PROCedure wait_for_a_while
380   PAUSE RND(50 TO 250)
390   REPeat off_space_bar
400     IF INKEY$(0)="" THEN EXIT off_space_bar
410   END REPeat off_space_bar
420 END DEFine wait_for_a_while
430 :
440 DEFine PROCedure display_star
450   stary=RND(6)
460   starx=RND(2 TO 30)
470   AT #5,stary,starx :PRINT #5,"*"
480 END DEFine display'star
490 :
500 DEFine PROCedure wait_for_space_bar
                                                    P.T.O
```

Listing 2.1 continued

```
510  count=0
520  REPeat wait_for_space
530     count=count+1
540     k$=INKEY$(5)
550     IF k$=" " THEN EXIT wait_for_space
560  END REPeat wait_for_space
570  END DEFine wait_for_space_bar
580  :
590  DEFine PROCedure display_reaction_times
600     IF count>1 THEN
610        WINDOW #5,200,20,180,220
620        PRINT #5,count/10;" seconds "
630     ELSE
640        WINDOW #5,480,30,20,210
650        CSIZE #5,0,0
660        PRINT #5," Please take your finger off the keys";
670        FOR i=1 TO 1000 :REMark wait a while
680        CLS #5
690        CSIZE #5,3,1
700     END IF
710     WINDOW #5,500,150,12,50
720  END DEFine display_reaction_times
730  :
740  DEFine PROCedure rub_out_star
750     AT #5,stary,starx:PRINT #5," "
760  END DEFine rub_out_star
```

i. Type and enter the program. Error messages are almost certainly due to mistyping (see Section 2.15). Save the program under the name 'react' using the 'save' instruction as explained in Section 2.2.

ii. Retrieve the program from the cartridge using the 'load' instruction, as explained in Section 2.4.

iii. Run the program. We hope you enjoy it! (If you keep the space bar pressed for too long, the program will remind you to remove your finger. Otherwise it can't time your reaction.)

2 Saving, Retrieving and Joining Programs 43

2.6 Loading and running with one instruction

There is an instruction, 'lrun', which allows a program to be loaded from a cartridge and then executed immediately, without anything else being entered. It is therefore equivalent to loading and running. This is particularly useful when you want to load and run one program immediately after another.

We can illustrate the use of the 'lrun' instruction with the reaction-test program 'react' You could load and run it in one go, by entering:

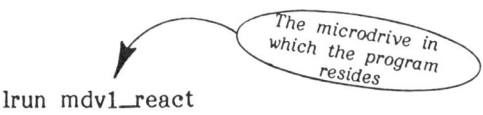

lrun mdv1_react *(The microdrive in which the program resides)*

When you enter this line, the program loads in and then starts running without you typing in anything more.

One of the special advantage of 'lrun' is that you can put it into a program, so allowing one program to 'lrun' another.

2.7 Activities

In order to demonstrate the effect of 'lrun', you need to have at least two programs saved on the microdrive, the first ending with an instruction which 'lrun's the second. We suggest that the first be the 'react' of Listing 2.1, and that the second be the program of Listing 2.2. Again we do not expect you to understand its programming at this stage, but we hope that you will enjoy running it. The program draws a pattern of ever-changing colours, as indicated in Screen Display 2.2.

i. Modify the program REACT by adding the following line:

555 IF k$="n" THEN LRUN mdv1_colours

Resave it under the name REACTE. Save the program of Listing 2.2 (overleaf) under the name COLOURS.

ii. Load and run the program REACTE using the 'lrun' instruction. Does pressing the 'n' key instead of the SPACE BAR cause the reaction test program to cease and COLOURS to load and run?

2.8 Merging two or more programs

When you use the 'load' instruction to load a program into the QL,

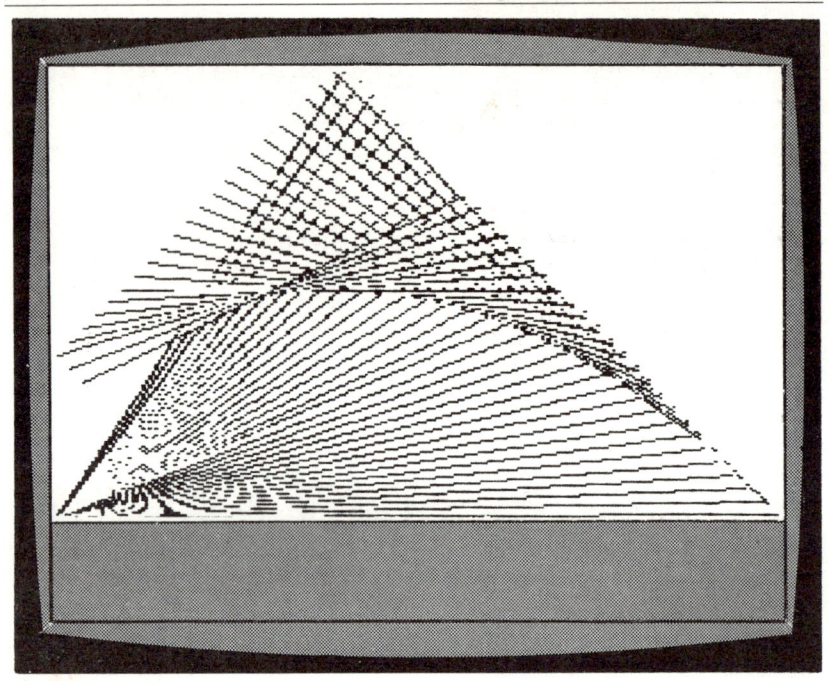

Screen Display 2.2

anything else in its memory is automatically wiped out. This can be irritating, particularly when you want to retrieve several procedures from a cartridge and have them all joined together. In these circumstances, you must use a different method of retrieving - one in which the incoming program does not wipe out anything that already exists in memory. This is achieved with the instruction 'merge'.

A word of caution first! Even using this method, one program will overwrite another where they both happen to have the same line numbers! So if you want to have several programs and/or procedures together in memory as a composite set of program lines, you must make very sure to give them line numbers that do not overlap! This will become clearer when you come to the section of activities.

To merge two sets of program lines type and enter the following, where 'prog1' and 'prog2' are the names of the two sets of program lines which have been previously saved on the microdrive.

        load mdv1_prog1
and
        merge mdv1_prog2

```
Listing 2.2

100 MODE 8
110 s=100 :FILL 0
120 DIM j(s),k(s)
130 x=166 :y=0 :ix=-1 :iy=1:col=1:p=0
140 :
150 REPeat bounce_line
160   col=1+col MOD 8
170   p=1+p MOD s
180   INK col
190   x=x+ix
200   IF x<1 OR x>165 THEN ix=-ix
210   y=y+iy
220   IF y<1 OR y>100 THEN iy=-iy
230   LINE x,y TO j(p),k(p)
240   j(p)=x
250   k(p)=y
260 END REPeat bounce_line
```

Each time you press the ENTER key to enter the instructions, the cursor disappears and the microdrive motor starts up. Once the cursor reappears it means that the QL has done what you asked of it.

2.9 Points to watch with merging programs

Merging two programs has the advantage over loading that previous lines of program are not wiped out. You have to be careful, though, to make sure that there is no overlap of line numbers between the existing program and the incoming program - otherwise the later one does overwrite parts of the earlier one.

Since the 'merge' instruction adds the new program lines to whatever is already in memory, it is a good idea to make sure, before using it, that only the lines you require are in memory. You can delete unwanted lines, by a line like the following, which deletes lines 100 to 140 inclusive:

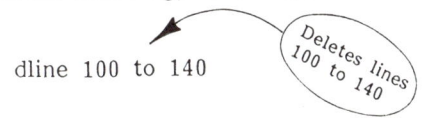

dline 100 to 140 *(Deletes lines 100 to 140)*

2 Saving, Retrieving and Joining Programs

You could then renumber the remaining lines, choosing numbers that are bound not to clash with those which 'merge' is about to add. For this it is useful to know an extended form of the 'renum' instruction, which enables you to stipulate the number at which you want the renumbering to start and the increments in which you want it to go up. For example, the following causes your first line of program to be renumbered as 1 and for the increments to be 2:

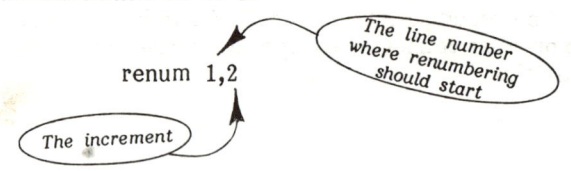

renum 1,2

The line number where renumbering should start

The increment

Either or both of the numbers can be left off. If you don't stipulate a line number, the QL takes it to be 100. If you don't stipulate an increment, the QL takes it to be 10. Renum 10 renumbers from line 10 in increments of 10, and renum ,1 renumbers from line 100 in increments of 1.

```
100 REMark
110 REMark
120 REMark
130 REMark
140 REMark
150 REMark
160 REMark



renum 130 to 500;30000,10
```

```
100 REMark
110 REMark
120 REMark
30000 REMark
30010 REMark
30020 REMark
30030 REMark



renum 130 to 500;30000,10
```

The results of the 'renum' instruction

Renumbering starts by renumbering old 130 to new 30000

If you miss this out, the QL takes it to be 10

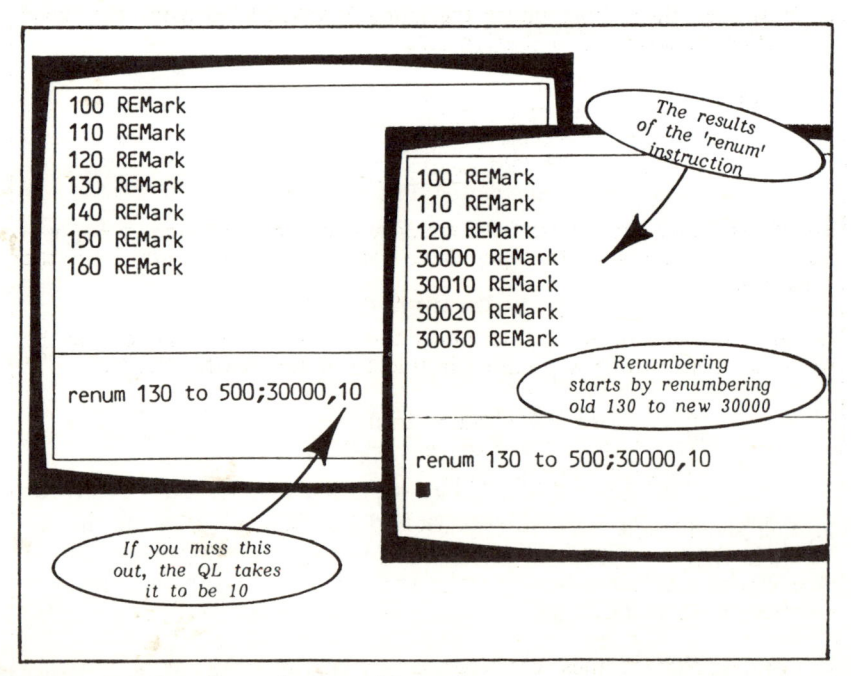

Figure 2.2. The effects of a 'renum' instruction.

2 Saving, Retrieving and Joining Programs 47

There is yet another form of 'renum' which renumbers just a section of program from a specified original starting number to a specified concluding number - which is very useful for renumbering procedures so that their line numbers are safely above those of a program. The instruction allows you to choose the new starting number and the increments. The sequence of the new line numbers must not of course overlap with those of any section of program which is not being renumbered or they will be wiped out. The effect is shown in Figure 2.2.

We advise you to practise retrieving using both 'merge' and 'lrun' by doing the following activities.

2.10 Activities

i. Start by entering the following two lines of program so that you have something to save:

        10 trial
        20 PRINT "end of main prog"

ii. Now save these lines under the name MAIN_PROG using the 'save' instruction, as described in Section 2.2.

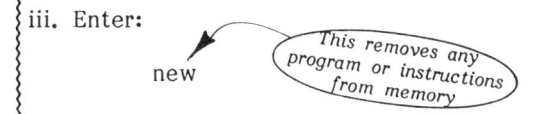

iii. Enter:

        new   *(This removes any program or instructions from memory)*

This is to remove these lines from memory in order to convince you, when you see them again, that you have really retrieved them from the cartridge.

iv. Now save the following lines under the name TRIAL. They define the procedure 'trial' which was called in line 10 of the MAIN_PROG:

        100 DEFine PROCedure trial
        110   PRINT "This is proc trial"
        120 END DEFine trial

v. You should now have two blocks of data saved: under the names MAIN_PROG and TRIAL. Enter 'new' to clear the existing lines of procedure and then retrieve MAIN_PROG using the 'load' instruction as described in Section 2.4.

vi. List the program lines recovered so far. This should confirm that only the first two lines, 10 and 20, have reappeared. Try entering 'run'. Does this produce the following error message?

      at line 10 bad name

vi. Now retrieve TRIAL using the 'merge' instruction. Enter 'list' to confirm that the two sets of lines have been joined to give a complete program. Does the program run now?

vii. Now try the various forms of renum that were described in Section 2.9; and delete blocks of program using the dline instruction.

2.11 More sample procedures

We now give a set of procedures which you may find useful. We certainly find them so, and we shall be using them on various occasions later in the book. Remember, we do not, at this stage expect you to understand the programming of the procedures. We want you to treat them as black boxes, i.e. to know the purpose that they serve, but not to look inside to see how they do it.

The first procedure lets you choose the foreground and background colour for the screen. Like all the procedures in the set, its line numbers are sufficiently high for it to be tacked on to the end of any program with little fear of overwriting. Its definition is as follows:

```
30000 DEFine PROCedure colour(a$,b$)
30010   PAPER ((a$(1 TO 3) INSTR
        "blabluredmaggrecyayelwhi")+2)/3-1
30020   INK ((b$(1 TO 3) INSTR
        "blabluredmaggrecyayelwhi")+2)/3-1
30030 END DEFine colour
```

When you call this procedure, you have to specify the name of the foreground and background colour inside quotation marks, by a line such as:

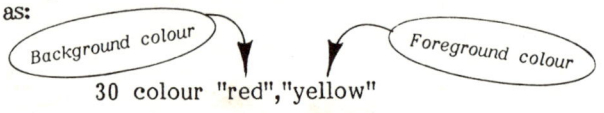

      30 colour "red","yellow"

(Background colour) ↓   ↓ (Foreground colour)

When the QL is first turned on, the following colours are available:

      black
      blue
      red
      magenta
      green

cyan
yellow
white

The procedure will get the colour right if you type in the full colour name or just the first three letters.

The next procedure writes a message on the screen in characters which are larger than the normal height. This is particularly useful for any display at the start of a program. The definition is as follows:

```
30100 DEFine PROCedure lprint(a$)
30110    CSIZE 3,1
30120    PRINT a$
30130 END DEFine lprint
```

You could call it by a line such as:

50 lprint "QL"

The final procedure displays any message of less than 40 characters, symmetrically on a single line of the screen (with as many spaces to the left as to the right). It works with the display that the QL gives when it has just been turned on and f2 has been pressed. The following lines define the procedure:

```
30200 DEFine PROCedure cprint(a$)
30210    PRINT FILL$(" ",18-LEN(a$)/2)&a$
30220 END DEFine cprint
```

A typical line to call this procedure would be:

60 cprint "Noughts and Crosses"

2.12 Activities

i. We suggest that you save the three procedures of the previous section for possible use in future programs.

ii. Try the procedures out, using the call which we gave at the end of each listing.

2.13 A menu-selection program 'boot'

You may find it annoying to have to keep typing out instructions for

```
 1 proc_hello              21 jobs
 2 proc_welcome            22 diary
 3 proc_hstars             23
 4 proc_vstars             24
 5 proc_sound              25
 6 proc_box                26
 7 boxed_welcome           27
 8 patterns                28
 9 listing2_1              29
10 proc display_star       30
11 draw_ellipses           31
12 draw_circles            32
13 histograms              33
14 sine_wave               34
15 clock                   35
16 print_large             36
17 accounts                37

Number of file to load and run?
```

Screen Display 2.3

getting a directory and for loading and running programs. We therefore provide the program of Listing 2.3 which does all three in one go. Screen Display 2.3 shows the appearance of the screen. We describe how to use the program in the next activities.

2.14 Activities

i. Enter the program of Listing 2.3 and save it under the name 'boot'.

ii. Remove the cartridge from the microdrive and press RESET. When the display of Figure 0.2 appears, insert the cartridge into microdrive 1. Press F2 for the television option (although the program also works for the monitor option). The program should now automatically load and run itself. (In Section 2.15 we describe how to use 'boot' at other times.)

2 *Saving, Retrieving and Joining Programs* 51

```
Listing 2.3
100 MODE 8 :PAPER 2 :INK 7 :CLS
120 OPEN_NEW #3,MDV1_qqqqqqqqqq
130 DIR #3,MDV1_
140 CLOSE #3
150 OPEN #3,MDV1_qqqqqqqqqq
160 INPUT #3,A$ :INPUT #3,A$
170 max=40
180 DIM dir$(max,40)
190 count=1
200 REPeat get_directory
210   IF count<=max THEN INPUT #3,dir$(count)
220   IF dir$(count)<>"qqqqqqqqqq" THEN
230     count=count+1
240   ELSE
250     dir$(count)=""
260   END IF
270   IF EOF(#3) OR count >max THEN EXIT get_directory
280 END REPeat get_directory
290 CLOSE #3
300 FOR i=count TO max :dir$(i)=" "
310 DELETE MDV1_qqqqqqqqqq
320 FOR Lin=1 TO 20
330   AT Lin-1,0 :PRINT Lin;" ";dir$(Lin)(1 TO 15)
340   AT Lin-1,19 :PRINT Lin+20;" ";dir$(Lin+20)(1 TO 15);
350 END FOR Lin
360 CLS #0
370 INPUT #0,"Number of file to load and run? ";f
380 f$="mdv1_"&dir$(f)
390 LRUN f$
```

2.15 Discussion of activities

Activity 2.5i: Mistyping is the most likely reason for error messages. Typical mistakes include typing a capital O instead of a zero, and a lower-case L (l) instead of a one (1). Fortunately the QL's error messages are reasonably helpful for indicating the nature of errors. The following error messages are the most likely:

bad line

bad name

At line 100 error in expression

At line 20 bad name

Activity 2.14ii: You can load and run the menu-selection program at any stage with the instruction:

lrun mdv1_boot

3

QL Super BASIC

3.0 Introduction
3.1 Keywords
3.2 Letters, characters and symbols
3.3 Strings
3.4 Activities
3.5 Variables and variable names
3.6 Activities
3.7 Integer variables
3.8 String variables
3.9 Activities
3.10 Some points to ponder
3.11 Discussion on the points to ponder
3.12 Discussion of activities

3.0 Introduction

An ordinary language like English is made up of parts of speech such as nouns and verbs. SuperBASIC too, like all BASICs, can be thought of as being made up of 'parts of speech'. In this chapter, we introduce these and comment on them. The rest of the book is about how to use them.

3.1 Keywords

You will recall that BASIC keywords are the ones which the QL insists in listing in upper-case. They are the words that sound like English words, such as PRINT, LIST and RUN. They give instructions to the computer, and we – so far – have called them instructions. It is usual, though, to distinguish between two sorts of instruction: 'commands' and 'statements'. A command is an instruction which the computer is normally expected to obey immediately it is entered, like RUN and LIST. A statement is an instruction which normally occurs within a program. The computer only acts on it once the program is executed. The only example which we have introduced so far is PRINT, but it is a poor example because it can be used as either a command or a statement. In general commands are what appear on the bottom of the QL's screen, but don't arrive in a program, while statements are what make up a program listing.

3.2 Letters, characters and symbols

You have already worked with letters, characters and symbols. BASIC accepts letters and characters to represent numbers – and we say more about this later. Symbols like + for plus and – for minus are also part of BASIC. Multiplication, however, is a star like * to prevent confusion with the letter x, and division is a slash like this /. An index (or power) is represented by an up-arrow like this ^. So, for example, ten raised to the power 3 has to be written as follows:

    10^3

3.3 Strings

You have already used strings, although we did not use that name when we introduced them. You may remember that in Section 1.2, you separately gave each of the following instructions to the QL:

    PRINT 5+9

and

    PRINT "5+9"

3 QL SuperBASIC

With the first instruction, the QL worked out the answer and printed it as 14. With the second instruction, though, it printed exactly what was inside the quotation marks without altering it, or processing it in any way. When data is inside quotation marks, like this, it is called a 'string'.

You will find that strings are very useful, because you are bound to want the QL to print messages when you come to do more adventurous programming. You may want to instruct a user how to play a computer game, or you may want to ask him to enter something into the computer, or you may just want the computer to remind you what it is doing. Suppose you have asked the computer to add 2 and 3. Rather than a mere 5 appearing on the screen, it would look much nicer if the following could appear:

The sum of 2 and 3 is 5

You could get this message before the 5 using a string as follows, where the number of the program line is arbitrary:

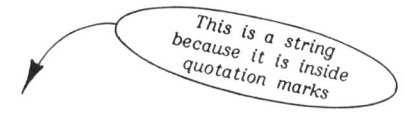

This is a string because it is inside quotation marks

100 PRINT "The sum of 2 and 3 is "

The next step is to get the message and the 5 to appear together on the same line of the screen. The trick is to place a semicolon after the string as shown in line 130 of the following program:

```
100 a=2
110 b=3
120 c=a+b
130 PRINT "The sum of 2 and 3 is ";c
```

The sum of 2 and 3 is 5

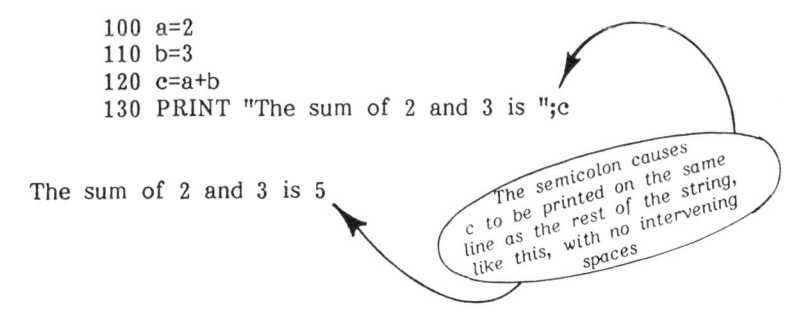

The semicolon causes c to be printed on the same line as the rest of the string, like this, with no intervening spaces

Figure 3.1 (overleaf) shows the general effect of semicolons in a PRINT statement.

Incidentally a semicolon is not the only punctuation mark that can be used with the PRINT statement. A comma (,) has the effect of putting the various parts of the PRINT statement into separate columns, whereas a backslash character (\) forces each part of the printout onto a new line. Figure 3.2 shows the idea.

56   *3 QL SuperBASIC*

```
abcd


print "a";"b";"c";"d"
```

Semicolons in a PRINT statement put separate parts of the printout on the same line

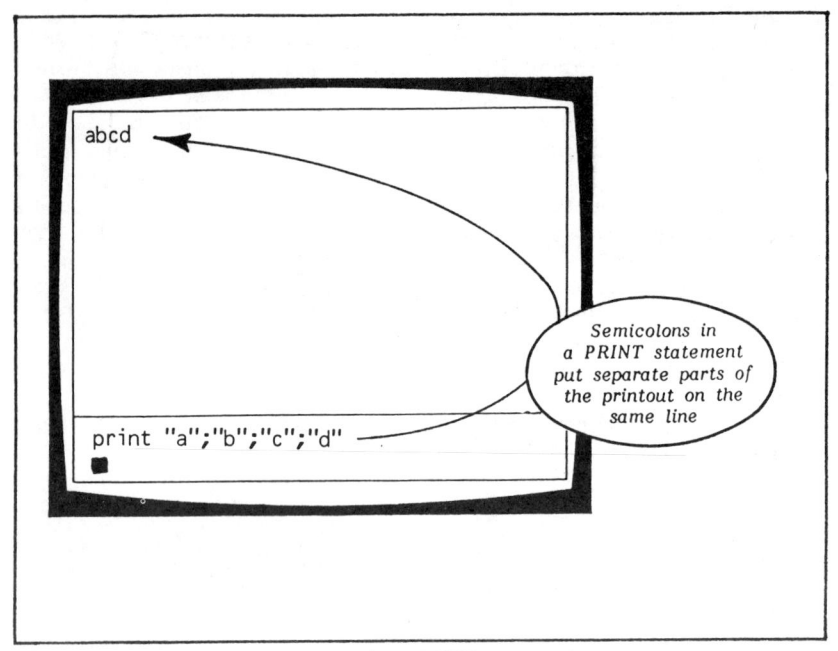

Figure 3.1. The effect of semicolons in a PRINT statement.

Also interesting is the exclamation mark which you can use in a PRINT statement. It provides an 'intelligent space'. The 'intelligence' lies in the fact that the appropriate part of the printout is never split when printed, even if it comes at the end of a screen line. The printout either gives spaces or moves to the next line. You use intelligent spaces in the following way:

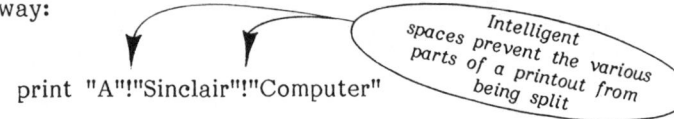

```
            print "A"!"Sinclair"!"Computer"
```

Intelligent spaces prevent the various parts of a printout from being split

You may like to try the following activities, to practise using strings and punctuation marks in the PRINT statement. Now that you are doing more writing and entering of programs, it will save time to start by entering:

```
            auto
```

Provides the next line number automatically, for entering a program, so saving typing.

3 QL SuperBASIC

[Figure showing two screens with PRINT statement examples]

- Commas in a PRINT statement put separate parts of the printout into columns on the same line

```
print "a","b","c","d"
```

- Each backslash in a PRINT statement puts separate parts of the printout onto a new line

```
print "a"\"b"\"c"\"d"
```

Figure 3.2. The effects of commas and backslashes in PRINT statements.

'auto' provides you with the next line number automatically, so that you don't have to type it. You stop the process at the end of the program by pressing CTRL together with the SPACE bar.

3.4 Activities

i. Enter 'auto'. Now enter the following program:

```
100 x=23
110 y=11
120 z=x+y
130 PRINT "The sum of 23 and 11 is";z
```

When the 'auto' command presents you with line 140, just hold the CTRL key down while you press the SPACE bar. Now run the program. Does the result look as nice as you would like? We comment in Section 3.12.

ii. Use the editing facilities to replace line 130 with:

130 PRINT "The sum of 23";" and 11 is";z

Run the program. Is an identical result produced? Does the semicolon cause the two strings to be printed out with no extra spaces between them?

iii. Try replacing line 130 with:

130 PRINT "The sum of ";x;" and ";y;" is ";z

Is an identical result produced?

iv. Try replacing line 130 with:

130 PRINT "The sum of ";x;" and ";y;" is ";x+y

Is an identical result produced?

v. Try removing line 120. Does the program still run?

vi. Try entering the following:

PRINT "cheers","cheers"

Do you see that the effect of the comma is to produce columns?

vii. By using a long string made up of numbers, you can produce a program which more clearly demonstrates the effect of commas. Enter and run the following program:

110 PRINT"1234567890123456789012345678901 2"
120 PRINT 12,345,45
130 PRINT 1,23,345

The first line prints a whole string of numbers across the screen which can be used to count the column position of the numbers printed by lines 120 and 130. Do you see that the effect of the comma is to tabulate them into columns? (We have more to say on this in Section 3.12.)

viii. Using the QL's editing facilities try replacing some of the commas in lines 120 and 130 by semicolons. Run the program each time to see the result.

3.5 Variables and variable names

We have been using symbols like a,b,c and x,y,z to represent numerical values in the computer. As these symbols can take various values or numbers, they are known as 'variables'. For the QL, variables do not need to be just a single character. They can be given names of almost any length and may consist of upper-case letters, lower-case letters, numbers and the underline character. SuperBASIC does, however, require that these variable names start with a letter, not a number. Characters such as & or / are not permitted. Every character is significant. For example, the QL perceives average2 as a different variable from average3. Be careful, though: the QL cannot distinguish between upper-case and lower-case in a variable name. So, for example, it will perceive AVERAGE2 as the same as average2. We recommend that you use lower-case for all variables names. In this way there can be no confusion with BASIC terms in the listings.

Being able to represent variables with names rather than say, x or y, makes a program easier to read and therefore easier to check. To illustrate this, consider the following program which has been written in two ways, the second with the variables as meaningful words and the first as letters. As a variable name cannot contain a space, the words have to be joined in some way. We have used the underline character to join words in a variable name. Apart from in variable names and strings, BASIC ignores extra spaces. So we shall often be putting them in to make programs look more attractive and readable. We do this here in the second version:

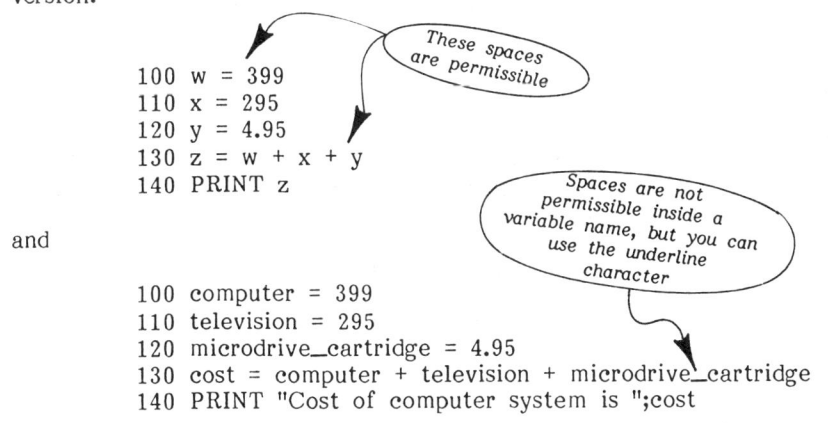

```
100 w = 399
110 x = 295
120 y = 4.95
130 z = w + x + y
140 PRINT z
```
These spaces are permissible

and

```
100 computer = 399
110 television = 295
120 microdrive_cartridge = 4.95
130 cost = computer + television + microdrive_cartridge
140 PRINT "Cost of computer system is ";cost
```
Spaces are not permissible inside a variable name, but you can use the underline character

Anyone can see immediately that the second program is to calculate the cost of three items, a computer, a television and a microdrive cartridge. The first program is nowhere near as clear. If it contained any errors, they would be much more difficult to spot.

3.6 Activities

i. Enter and run the second program in the previous section.

ii. Now try putting more spaces into the program, and see just where they can go without causing error messages when the program is run. For this exercise use the 'edit' command to capitalize on the QL's excellent editing facilities.

iii. See if the following program runs.

```
100 computer                   = 399
110 television                 = 295
120 microdrive_cartridge = 4.95
130 cost=computer+television+microdrive_cartridge
140 PRINT "Cost of computer system is ";cost
```

See Section 3.12 for a comment.

iv. Replace line 120 by:

```
120 microdrive cartridge = 4.95
```

Will it be accepted? (We comment in Section 3.12.)

3.7 Integer variables

The variables that we have used so far can take any value, positive or negative - as long as it is between zero and 10^615 (i.e. 1 followed by 615 zeros!). SuperBASIC has another type of variable, which can take only integers (i.e. whole numbers). It is called an 'integer variable' and is written as a normal variable name followed by a percentage sign, e.g. people%, cars%, num%, g% etc. Such variables can only hold integer values - even if you try to give them non-integer ones. Integer variables may hold any integer numbers between -32767 and +32767.

As an illustration of the use of integer variables, consider the following program:

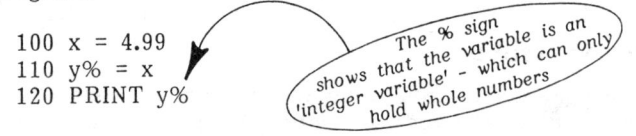

```
100 x = 4.99
110 y% = x
120 PRINT y%
```

The % sign shows that the variable is an 'integer variable' - which can only hold whole numbers

The printout is 4 because the QL rounds any fractional part assigned to an integer variable. This means that 4.99 is rounded to 5.

Integer variables are used when it is important not to have any small fractional parts, or to control the number of decimal places to be printed out. The latter is very useful. Consider the following program:

```
100 x=10/3
110 PRINT x
```

It prints:

3.333333

Printing the answer to only one decimal place could be achieved by the following alternative program:

```
100 x=10/3
110 y%=10*x
120 PRINT y%/10
```

This results in the printout:

3.3

Suppose you should require the integer part of a number without the decimal part. (The integer part is everything to the left of the decimal place.) Then you can use a special part of BASIC called INT, which is short for 'integer'. INT(3.49) or INT(x) where x=3.49, has the value 3. You can print such a value or use it in calculations. In consequence it is possible to put together a procedure which prints numbers to a controlled number of decimal places. One version is:

```
1000 DEFine PROCedure decprint(n,d)
1010   PRINT INT(n*10^d+.5)/10^d;
1020 END DEFine decprint
```

You can use it in the following form, where 3.49 is the number to be printed and 1 is the number of decimal places:

decprint 3.49,1

3.8 String variables

BASIC not only allows variables to represent numbers, it also allows them to represent strings - which is very useful because it enables words to be manipulated. When a variable is used in this way, it is known as a 'string variable'. It can be represented by any letter or name, but SuperBASIC requires that it be immediately followed by a dollar sign, as for example in the following:

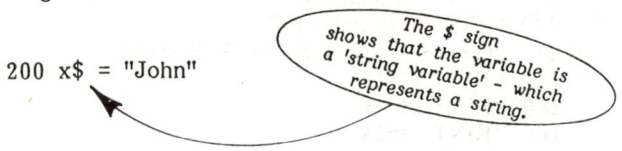

200 x$ = "John"

The $ sign shows that the variable is a 'string variable' - which represents a string.

Line 140 of the program in Section 3.6 caused a message to be printed on the screen by the use of a string in the PRINT statement. Alternatively, a string variable could have been used. The following two lines of program could have replaced line 140:

140 message$ = "Cost of computer system is "
150 PRINT message$;cost

Then everything between the quotes would have been printed exactly word for word and, because of the semicolon, the value of cost would have been printed immediately after the string. So the printout would have read:

Cost of computer system is 698.95

It is sometimes useful to be able to join strings together. On many other dialects of BASIC a plus sign is used, as in "123" + "45" to give "12345". For the QL the plus sign is, quite logically, reserved for arithmetic. The QL will therefore try to interpret an expression such as "123" + "45" as numbers and give a result of 168. To join two strings together separate the two parts with an ampersand (&). Examples of suitable program lines for joining strings together are:

or
    120 a$=b$ & c$ & d$

or
    120 phrase$="QL" & " is a " & "Computer"

    120 ex$="Hello " & B$ & "."

The & allows strings to be joined together

You can practise this type of manipulation in the following activities.

3.9 Activities

i. Try entering and running the following program, where you will notice in lines 100, 110 and 120 that there is a space as the first character of each string:

3   QL SuperBASIC   63

```
100 str1$ = " QL"
110 str2$ = " business"
120 str3$ = " computer"
130 phrase$ = str1$ & str2$ & str3$
140 PRINT str1$
150 PRINT str2$
160 PRINT str3$
170 PRINT phrase$
```

ii. What happens if you edit out the space at the start of each string? See Section 3.12.

iii. Try running the program with line 170 changed to:

```
170 PRINT str1$;str2$;str3$
```

Is there any change in the printout?

iv. Try entering the following:

```
PRINT "123" + "5"
```

Can you see what the QL has done? (We comment in Section 3.12.)

3.10   Some points to ponder

a. Consider the following short program:

```
100 a = 123
110 b = 5
120 PRINT"1234567890123456789012345678901234567890"
130 PRINT a,b,"hello";a
140 PRINT a;b,"hello",a
```

Without running the program, can you work out what the printout would look like?

b. Consider the following two short programs:

```
100 a = 32145      and      100 a$ = "32145"
110 PRINT a,a                 110 PRINT a$,a$
```

Would there be any difference in their displays?

c. How would the printout from the two programs differ if a semicolon replaced the comma in the PRINT statements?

d. Where is it not permissible to include spaces in a program?

e. Which of the following variable names are invalid in BASIC?

> WOOD_price
> 3D
> Y1
> why?
> cost
> TAX$
> TAX$CODE

3.11 Discussion on the points to ponder

a. The appearance of the printout would be as follows:

```
123456789012345678901234567890123456789 0
123     5          hello123
1235    hello   123
```

It is helpful to consider the screen as divided into zones where each zone is an imaginary column eight spaces wide. All numbers and strings are printed to the left of a zone unless you issue some instruction to the contrary.
   The first number to be printed in this exercise is automatically printed aligned on the left of the first eight space zone, i.e. at the edge of the screen. In the PRINT statement the second number '5' is separated from the first by a comma. The comma is an instruction to move onto the next zone and hence the 5 is printed in character position 9. The 'hello' is also separated by a comma in the PRINT statement and hence is also printed in the next zone at character position 17. The last number '123' is separated in the PRINT statement by a semicolon and hence is printed immediately with no intervening spaces.
   On the last line of printing the first and second number '123' and '5' are printed together because of the semicolon separating them in the PRINT statement. The 'hello' is separated by a comma and is hence printed in the next available print zone starting in character position 9. The last number '123' is not separated from the 'hello' by a comma and is hence printed in the next available zone at character position 17.

b. No. Strings and numbers are printed the same way, to the left of a zone.

c. The inclusion of the semicolon in the modified program causes the printout of both numbers and strings to be joined together starting at the beginning of the line like this:

3214532145

d. Spaces can be put anywhere except that:

- Extra spaces in a string are part of it and thus alter how the string reads.
- Spaces are not permissible in variable names.
- Spaces are not permissible within a BASIC keyword, for example as in PR INT for PRINT or RU N for RUN.

e. The underline character is permissible. So WOOD_price is permissible. 3D starts with a number and is invalid. Y1 is valid. why? contains a query which is invalid. cost is valid. TAX$ is valid for a string variable. TAX$CODE is invalid because of the imbedded $.

3.12 Discussion of activities

Activity 3.4i: We purposely left out a space at the end of the string, and this made the 'is' and the '34' appear together. You will need to look out for this sort of thing. You could make the printout look better if you cleared the screen first and incorporated an AT instruction, as described in Section 1.6. The entire program, suitably renumbered, would then be as follows:

```
100 x=23
110 y=11
120 z=x+y
130 CLS
140 AT 10,5
150 PRINT "The sum of 23 and 11 is ";z
```

Activity 3.4vii: It is useful to think of the screen as divided into zones which are eight characters wide. A comma in the PRINT statement causes the number after it to be printed as far to the left as possible in the next available zone.

Activity 3.6iii: The program runs because the QL ignores spaces unless they are in the middle of keywords, variable names, etc.

Activity 3.6iv: You get the following error message:

At line 120 bad name

The mistake occurs because the QL takes the space to mean that microdrive and cartridge are two separate variables, where it expects only one.

Activity 3.9ii: If you edit out the space at the beginning of each string, the final printout becomes:

QL
business
computer
QLbusinesscomputer

Activity 3.9iv: SuperBASIC has a special feature called 'coercion' whereby it endeavours to compensate for what it considers to be a mistake by the programmer. When it comes across what it considers to be the wrong type of variable, such as a string where it expects a number, it will try to compensate - in this case by removing the quotes from the string and interpreting it as a number. Although coercion is very convenient, it can, at times, cause a program to continue to operate past what is indeed a programming error. This will be a particular problem for programmers used to other dialects of BASIC. If this applies to you, you must be especially careful to check that you have indeed written what you intended!

4

Putting data into programs

4.0 Introduction
4.1 Putting data into variables
4.2 Entering data while a program is running
4.3 Activities
4.4 Giving values to more than one variable
4.5 Inputting a lot of data
4.6 Activities
4.7 Some points to ponder
4.8 Discussion on the points to ponder

4.0 Introduction

If the QL is to be of any help to you personally, it has to be able to do things with data (or information) which you supply yourself. In this chapter, we describe the various ways in which you can put data into the QL for it to process.

4.1 Putting data into variables

You have already entered data into the QL by using statements like lines 100 and 110 of the following program:

```
100 x = 5
110 y = 3
120 PRINT x + y
```

When BASIC was first developed, a line like line 100 would have to have been written as:

```
100 LET x = 5
```

In this form its meaning was rather more clear, i.e. as a shorthand for: LET x have the value 5. However, this statement which is called the 'LET statement' is so frequently used that nowadays most BASICs allow the shortened form which we have already introduced - and which we shall still continue to use. Nevertheless, since this chapter is about the various ways of feeding data into the computer, it is probably good for you to realize that the LET statement exists, especially as we shall be comparing it with other methods of putting data into the QL.

As a general method of storing data, the LET statement is very limited. With large amounts of data, it is clumsy to enter, check and edit. Its best use is for setting up a few initial values in a program.

4.2 Entering data while a program is running

In this section, we introduce a method of putting data into a program while it is running. The method relies on what is called the INPUT statement. The INPUT statement causes the computer to stop execution of the program and display the cursor. Anything typed and entered at this stage is given to a variable in the INPUT statement. This is best illustrated by an example:

4 Putting Data Into Programs

```
100 CLS
110 INPUT a$
120 CLS
130 AT 6,6
140 PRINT a$
```

The INPUT statement allows information to be put into a program while it is running

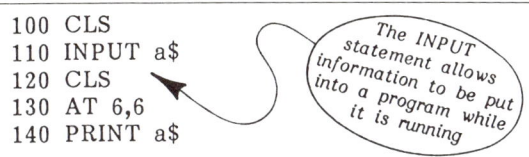

When the program runs, line 110 causes the program to stop execution temporarily with the cursor flashing on the screen. Suppose you then type in:

>   hello there

Once this is entered, the program continues – in this case, with the screen clearing and the message 'hello there' being printed to the screen somewhere in the middle of the screen. After line 110 the string a$ would have a value identical to that from the following statement:

>   110 a$ = "hello there"

Whenever you write a program which requires you or someone else to type and enter information while the program is running, it is a good idea to make the request appear on the screen in the form of a message. One way is to use a PRINT statement just before the INPUT statement. Another way is by means of a small extension to the INPUT statement. The message to be displayed is put within quotes like this:

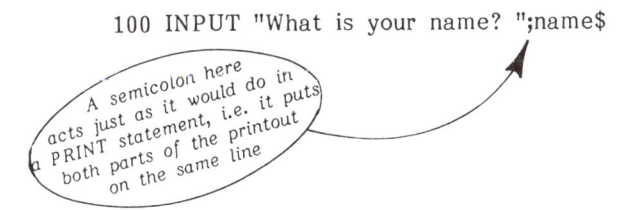

>   100 INPUT "What is your name? ";name$

A semicolon here would do in acts just as it puts a PRINT statement, i.e. it puts both parts of the printout on the same line

As a result of line 100, the following message appears on the screen:

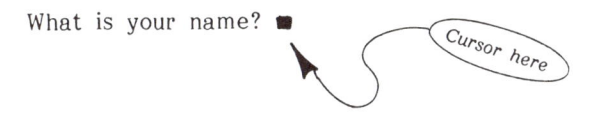

>   What is your name? ■

Cursor here

The QL then waits for a keyboard entry for the string variable name$.

Figure 4.1 (overleaf) shows the effect of the INPUT statement as an immediate action.

The following activities familiarize you with the message facility in the INPUT statement.

```
┌─────────────────────────────────────────────┐
│  ┌───────────────────────────────────────┐  │
│  │ What is your computer? ■              │  │
│  │                                       │  │
│  │               As a result of          │  │
│  │         INPUT, the cursor appears     │  │
│  │          here, ready for you to type  │  │
│  │              and enter a reply        │  │
│  │                                       │  │
│  │ input "What is your computer?";name$  │  │
│  └───────────────────────────────────────┘  │
└─────────────────────────────────────────────┘
```

Figure 4.1. The effects of an INPUT statement.

4.3 Activities

Enter and run the following program, and put in appropriate responses:

```
100 INPUT "Who am I talking to? ";name$
110 PRINT "Thank you ";name$
120 INPUT "How are you feeling today?"!answer$
130 PRINT name$;" I note you are feeling ";answer$
140 INPUT "Please type in anything ";m$
150 PRINT m$
```

4.4 Giving values to more than one variable

The INPUT statement can be used to give values to more than one variable. For example the following line requires values for three string variables:

4 Putting Data Into Programs

```
100 INPUT a$,b$,c$
```

As there is nothing more than the cursor to show that the QL has stopped and is waiting for the user to enter something, it is important that you arrange for a message to prompt him.

Each response must be entered separately by pressing the ENTER key. When the ENTER key is pressed, a number of alternative responses can occur depending on what separates the variables in the list. This is best illustrated by example. Suppose that the program wanted, as data, the first name and surname of the person running the program. The INPUT statement would best be written as:

```
100 INPUT "Please enter your first name ";fname$ \
    " and now your surname ";sname$
```

When it comes across this line, the QL will print the first request on the screen and then a space. It will then wait for the user to type his first name. So, just before pressing the ENTER key, the screen will display:

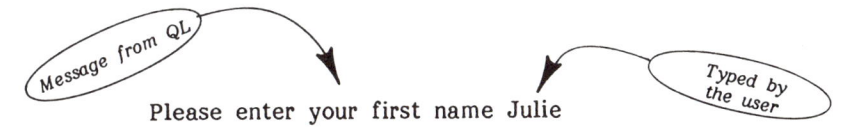

(Message from QL) Please enter your first name Julie *(Typed by the user)*

The backslash (\) after the variable fname$ will cause the printout to move to a new line when 'Julie' presses the ENTER key. The rest of the INPUT statement then causes the message concerning the surname to appear giving a complete dialogue as follows:

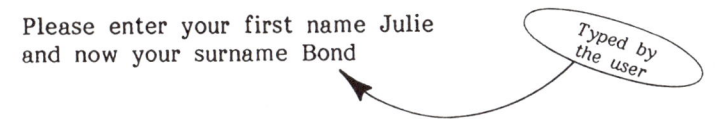

Please enter your first name Julie
and now your surname Bond *(Typed by the user)*

It is perhaps best to consider the INPUT statement as like a special form of the PRINT statement, where the value for all variables is entered on the keyboard by the person running the program. The format on the screen is dictated by appropriate punctuation.

If you type and enter more than the computer expects, the extra will be ignored. If you forget to press the ENTER key, the QL will just continue to wait!

A similar form of the INPUT statement may be used for a numerical input with numerical variables. For example, the following program would ask for two numbers to be typed in, and would then cause their sum to be printed:

```
100 INPUT "Please type a number\";n1"and a second ";n2
110 sum=n1+n2
120 PRINT "Their sum is ";sum
```

Once again the ENTER key should be pressed to enter each number separately.

Although there is no problem with using the INPUT statement with a mixture of numerical and string variables, you must ensure that each variable receives the value expected by the program. If you enter a number for a string, it will be accepted as a string and not give an error message. If, however, you enter a string for a numerical variable, the program will cease execution with the error message:

At line 100 error in expression

4.5 Inputting a lot of data

It is not practical to supply much data to the QL with the LET or the INPUT statements. In this section we introduce a more suitable method, which is particularly useful when the data is the same each time the program is run.

For this method, the data is stored at the end of the program in what are called DATA statements, and data is read from them, as required, in response to a READ statement somewhere in the program. Typing errors within the DATA statements can be corrected very easily using the QL's excellent editing facilities. The DATA statements themselves can be updated in the same way.

The program of Listing 4.1 illustrates the use of DATA statements. It plays a tune. As you can see, the main program is relatively short. This is because the data which defines the notes come outside it, in the DATA statements. (Incidentally you can make the program play your own tune by merely suitably modifying the data in the DATA statements!) We have placed most of the program inside procedures, which we are treating as black boxes. So we shall not explain their operation here. We shall wait until Chapter 7 before explaining the relationship between the numbers and the notes. We shall however, say a few more words here about reading from the DATA statements.

The QL needs to know for each note which note on the scale is to be played and how long it should last. The READ statement in line 150 accomplishes this. It causes the QL to look at the DATA statements where the numbers come in pairs. The first in each pair specifies the pitch of the note while the second specifies the duration. The READ statement causes the QL to take the first item and give it to the variable n, and then to take the next item and give it to d. Each time the program comes across a READ, it behaves in the same way, except that it progresses through the data, i.e. taking the third and fourth items of

4 *Putting Data Into Programs*   73

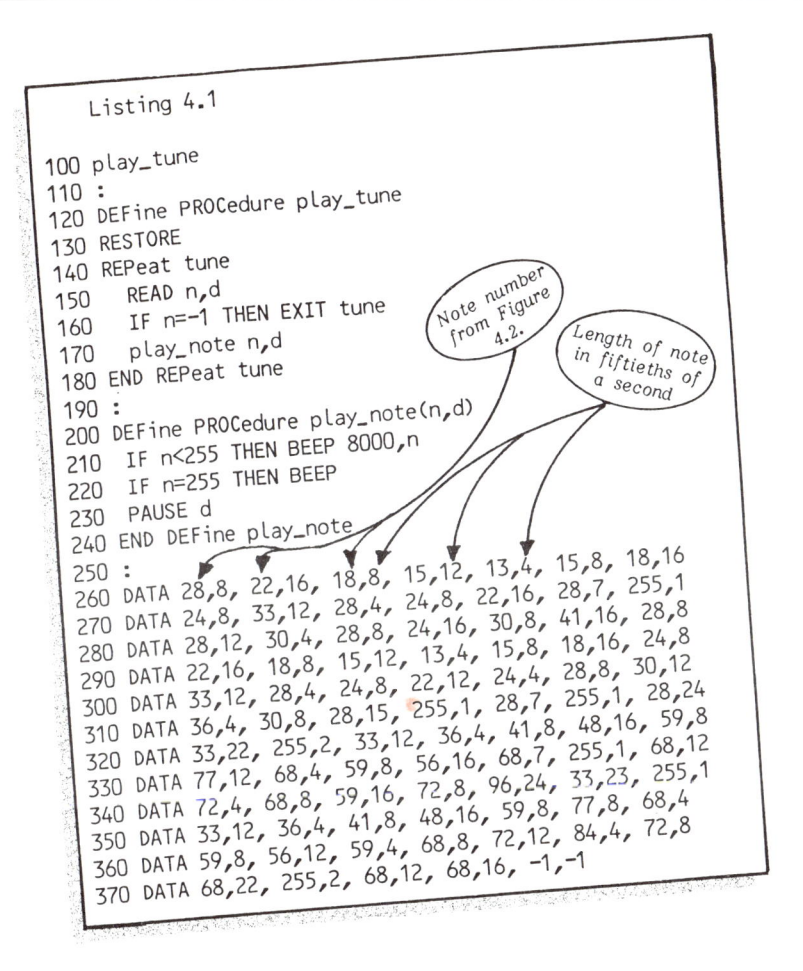

```
Listing 4.1

100 play_tune
110 :
120 DEFine PROCedure play_tune
130 RESTORE
140 REPeat tune
150    READ n,d
160    IF n=-1 THEN EXIT tune
170    play_note n,d
180 END REPeat tune
190 :
200 DEFine PROCedure play_note(n,d)
210 IF n<255 THEN BEEP 8000,n
220 IF n=255 THEN BEEP
230 PAUSE d
240 END DEFine play_note
250 :
260 DATA 28,8, 22,16, 18,8, 15,12, 13,4, 15,8, 18,16
270 DATA 24,8, 33,12, 28,4, 24,8, 22,16, 28,7, 255,1
280 DATA 28,12, 30,4, 28,8, 24,16, 30,8, 41,16, 28,8
290 DATA 22,16, 18,8, 15,12, 13,4, 15,8, 18,16, 24,8
300 DATA 33,12, 28,4, 24,8, 22,12, 24,4, 28,8, 30,12
310 DATA 36,4, 30,8, 28,15, 255,1, 28,7, 255,1, 28,24
320 DATA 33,22, 255,2, 33,12, 36,4, 41,8, 48,16, 59,8
330 DATA 77,12, 68,4, 59,8, 56,16, 68,7, 255,1, 68,12
340 DATA 72,4, 68,8, 59,16, 72,8, 96,24, 33,23, 255,1
350 DATA 33,12, 36,4, 41,8, 48,16, 59,8, 77,8, 68,4
360 DATA 59,8, 56,12, 59,4, 68,8, 72,12, 84,4, 72,8
370 DATA 68,22, 255,2, 68,12, 68,16, -1,-1
```

(Note number from Figure 4.2.)

(Length of note in fiftieths of a second)

data and then taking the fifth and sixth, etc. The end of the data is marked by the two numbers -1,-1, both of which are impossible values for a note or a length. When these are reached, the program automatically stops. Without a method of marking the end of the data, the program would carry on trying to read in more data. This would not be available and would result in the following error message:

    At line 150 end of file

    In a READ statement, just as in any other inputting statement, it is

74   *4 Putting Data Into Programs*

important for a numerical value to be given to a numerical variable and a string to be given to a string variable. If a numerical value is given to a string variable, no computers recognize the error. If a program tries to read a string where a numerical value is required, the following error message will be issued and the program will stop:

> At line xxx error in expression

So you should be careful to avoid this kind of programming error.

There will be times when you would like to alter the starting point from which the computer reads values from DATA statements. The RESTORE statement, as seen in line 130, allows this. For example the following forces the program to read data values starting from the DATA statement of line N:

> RESTORE N

4.6 Activities

i. Enter and run the tune playing program of Listing 4.1.

ii. Enter data of your own construction for playing a tune. The numbers corresponding to the notes above middle C are shown in Figure 4.2.

```
         A
    4    G
    6    F
    7    E
    9    D
   11    C
   13    B
   15    A
   18    G
   22    F
   24    E
   28    D
   33    C
```

Figure 4.2. A stave.

4.7 Some points to ponder

a. The following program line is completely valid:

    100 c=c+1

Explain the apparent confusion.

b. The following short program feeds data into the computer through a LET statement – and with so little data, this method is probably the most sensible. Just as an exercise, though, adapt the program to use the READ and DATA statements instead.

```
100 n$="E"
110 d=4
120 PRINT n$,d
```

4.8 Discussion on the points to ponder

a. The apparent confusion is due to the statement looking like an equation. It is not an equation. It is a LET statement with the LET left out. It actually means: 'Give the variable c the value obtained after calculating a value for the expression on the right of the equals sign'. So it merely commands the QL to take whatever value it holds for c, add 1 to it, and give it to the variable on the left. So, every time the statement is executed, the previous value of c is increased by 1. In practice this type of program line is useful for counting the number of times a statement is executed.

b. The following version would be suitable, although the amount of data is too small to give much advantage in using READ and DATA statements.

```
100 READ n$,d
110 PRINT n$,d
120 DATA "E",4
```

5

Repetition

5.0 Introduction
5.1 Repetition in steps of one
5.2 Repetition in other steps
5.3 Examples of the use of the FOR loop
5.4 Activities
5.5 REPEAT loops
5.6 Activities
5.7 Loops within loops
5.8 Which loop to use
5.9 Activities
5.10 Points to ponder
5.11 Discussion on the points to ponder
5.12 Discussion of activities

5.0 Introduction

There are many occasions when you want the same process to be repeated several times with different numbers. You could just keep repeating the program – but fortunately you don't have to because BASIC has structures, called 'loops', for just this eventuality. In this chapter we introduce two types of loop. One is called a FOR loop and the other is called a REPEAT loop.

5.1 Repetition in steps of one

The FOR loop construction is a simple way of arranging for a group of lines to be repeated a specified number of times within a program. We shall explain by taking you through the operation of a part of a program in which a group of lines is repeated twelve times.

In line 100 below, a variable v, called the loop variable, is set to start with a value of 1. Lines 110 to 130 are normal program lines, which may or may not involve v. They are executed in the normal way. At line 140, the end of the FOR loop is marked by the instruction END FOR v. This causes the loop to begin again – but this time with v increased by one, i.e. equal to 2. The process repeats with v equal to 3, then 4, then 5, etc. It stops after the loop has been executed with v equal to 12 (because the first line gave 12 as the final value).

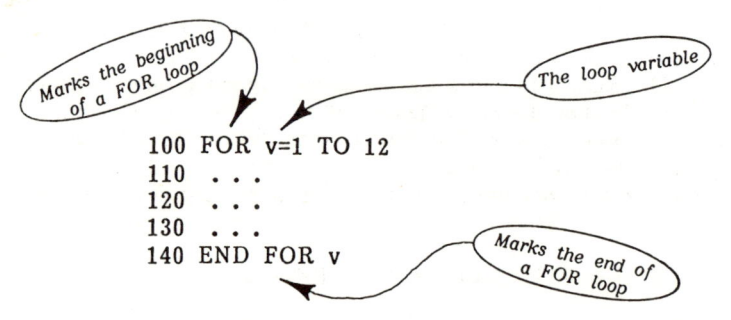

```
100 FOR v=1 TO 12
110 ...
120 ...
130 ...
140 END FOR v
```

Marks the beginning of a FOR loop — points to line 100.
The loop variable — points to v.
Marks the end of a FOR loop — points to line 140.

The following program, for example, would print five lines of 'hello':

```
100 FOR num=1 TO 5
110   PRINT "hello"
120 END FOR num
```

Incidentally, a group of essentially identical lines appears in the first procedure of Section 1.11. The difference is that the variable n is used in place of the 5 in line 100.

If you are used to programming with other dialects of BASIC, you should note that a FOR loop does not necessarily execute. For example the following program produces no printing on the screen:

```
100 FOR i=6 TO 4
110    PRINT "hello"
120 END FOR i
```

You can have as many lines of program as you want in the loop, i.e. between the first line (which starts 'FOR num...') and the final line (which has the form 'END FOR num').

With only a simple instruction to be repeated, the QL allows a shortned form on a single line. For the previous three program lines, it is:

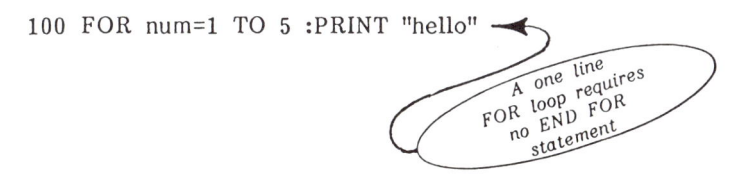

```
100 FOR num=1 TO 5 :PRINT "hello"
```

A one line FOR loop requires no END FOR statement

5.2 Repetition in other steps

In the last section, the loop variable increased by one every time the loop was repeated. This is the 'default' which means that it happens automatically unless you do something to stop it. It is however possible to change the loop variable by any other constant amount. It has to be constant though. So the word 'increment' is preferable to 'increase'.

The loop variable can be incremented by whatever value you choose, by means of a STEP instruction. For example, the following line instructs that the loop variable should start at 1, and go up with a 'loop increment' of 0.3. i.e. the program gives the loop variable the values 1, 1.3, 1.6, ... and finishes when the loop variable has the last allowed value. This is equal to the limit you specify, or less if the next increment would be too large.

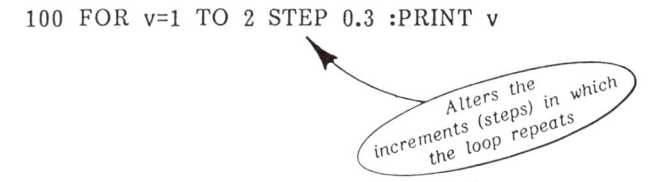

```
100 FOR v=1 TO 2 STEP 0.3 :PRINT v
```

Alters the increments (steps) in which the loop repeats

It produces the following display:

1
1.3
1.6
1.9

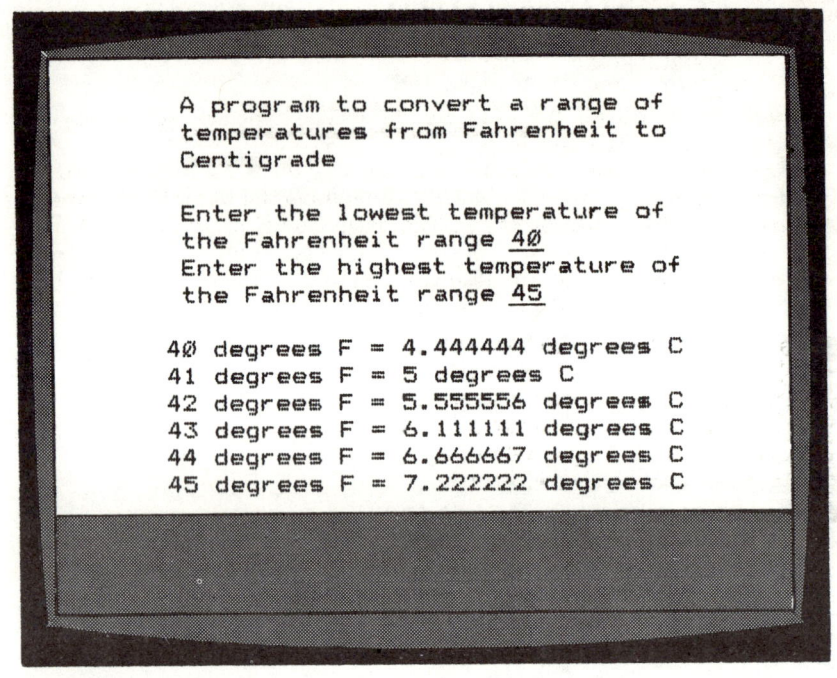

```
A program to convert a range of
temperatures from Fahrenheit to
Centigrade

Enter the lowest temperature of
the Fahrenheit range 40
Enter the highest temperature of
the Fahrenheit range 45

40 degrees F = 4.444444 degrees C
41 degrees F = 5 degrees C
42 degrees F = 5.555556 degrees C
43 degrees F = 6.111111 degrees C
44 degrees F = 6.666667 degrees C
45 degrees F = 7.222222 degrees C
```

Screen Display 5.1

Although it is usual to think of the loop variable as incrementing, it can be made to decrement (or decrease) by assigning a negative value to the loop increment, as for example, in the following line:

100 FOR num=10 TO 1 STEP -1

This causes num to take the values 10,9,8,7,6,5,4,3,2,1

Even more variety is allowed by the SuperBASIC in the QL. The loop variable may be given a whole series of special values as demonstrated in the following sample line

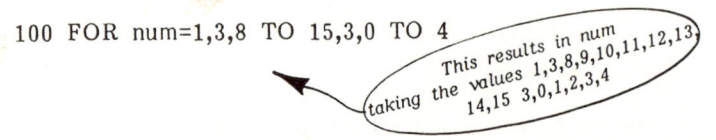

100 FOR num=1,3,8 TO 15,3,0 TO 4

This results in num taking the values 1,3,8,9,10,11,12,13, 14,15 3,0,1,2,3,4

5 Repetition

```
Listing 5.1

100 CLS
110 AT 7,3:PRINT "A program to convert a range of"\
120 PRINT"      temperatures from Fahrenheit to"\
130 PRINT"      Centigrade"\\
140 PRINT"      Enter the lowest temperature of"
150 INPUT"      the Fahrenheit range ";start
160 PRINT"      Enter the highest temperature of"
170 INPUT"      the Fahrenheit range ";range_end
180 PRINT \
190 FOR Ftemp=start TO range_end
200    PRINT;Ftemp;" degrees F = ";(Ftemp-32)*5/9;
       " degrees C"
210 END FOR Ftemp
```

5.3 Examples of the use of the FOR loop

FOR loops are widely used in programming. We shall now give some examples to indicate their scope.

We start with the program of Listing 5.1, which prints a table of temperature conversions from the Fahrenheit scale to the Centigrade scale, as shown in Screen Display 5.1. (In the dialogue, data which the user feeds in are underlined – a convention which we adopt throughout the book.) The program uses the following conversion formula:

Centigrade temp = (Fahrenheit temp – 32)*5/9

The program allows you to print the conversion table over any range. The backslash (\) in some of the PRINT statements cause printing to move onto a new line. Such new lines improve the appearance by separating the program title from the request for data.

As another example of a FOR loop in action, consider the following three-line program which will print the 4 times table:

```
100 FOR i=1 TO 10
110    PRINT i;" times 4 equals ";i*4
120 END FOR i
```

It can also be written as:

```
100 FOR i=1 TO 10 :PRINT i;" times 4 equals ";i*4
```

As a further illustration of the FOR construction, consider a program to list the squares of the numbers from 1 to 10.

```
100 FOR num=1 TO 10
110     square=num*num
120     PRINT num;" squared = ";square
130 END FOR num
```

It is a good idea to inset loops like this to stress their structure

Line 100 sets up the loop variable num as a counter for the number of times the lines 110 and 120 are to be executed. When line 100 is executed, num is given the value 1. Lines 110 and 120 are executed in the normal manner and line 130 causes the loop variable num to be incremented by 1 provided this does not place it beyond the programmed maximum. If it would be the loop finishes. If not, the loop is repeated again.

You may have noticed that all the lines of the loop are inset after the FOR. This is to demonstrate the structure of the program. Although the practice is entirely optional, we recommend it as it helps with program checking and debugging.

5.4 Activities

i. Enter and run the number squaring program of the last section. Does it work as you expect?

ii. Try the following alternative:

```
100 FOR num=1 TO 10
110     square = num * num
120     PRINT num;" squared = ";square
130     num = num-1
140 END FOR num
```

Can you see what is happening? Although the program does not execute like the previous version, why is there no error message? (We comment in Section 5.12.)

iii. Enter the following simple program which illustrates the progress of a FOR loop and, in particular, the value of the loop variable on exit from the loop. Before running it, try to work out the form of the printout. Run the program and see if you are right. If you have previously used other

BASICs, turn to the discussion in Section 5.12 after trying this example.

    100 FOR i = 1 TO 5 :PRINT;i;
    110 PRINT i

iv. Try using a FOR construction to write a program to add all the numbers from 1 to 10. (We give a suitable program in Section 5.12.) Run the program. Does it give the answer 55?

v. Try entering and running the temperature conversion program of the previous section. Does it work as you expect?

vi. Can you think of other conversions that you might like a program to provide?

5.5 REPEAT loops

The REPEAT loop is another way of arranging for a group of lines to be repeated within a program. Whereas a FOR loop causes a specified number of repetitions, a REPEAT loop continues until a condition set by the programmer is met, i.e. the group of lines enclosed in the loop is executed continuously until a condition is exactly as the programmer specified.

By way of illustration, the following program asks for someone to enter the cost of a list of items which it then adds up. The list can be of any length. It ends only when someone enters a zero value. The program then prints out the sum of the amounts:

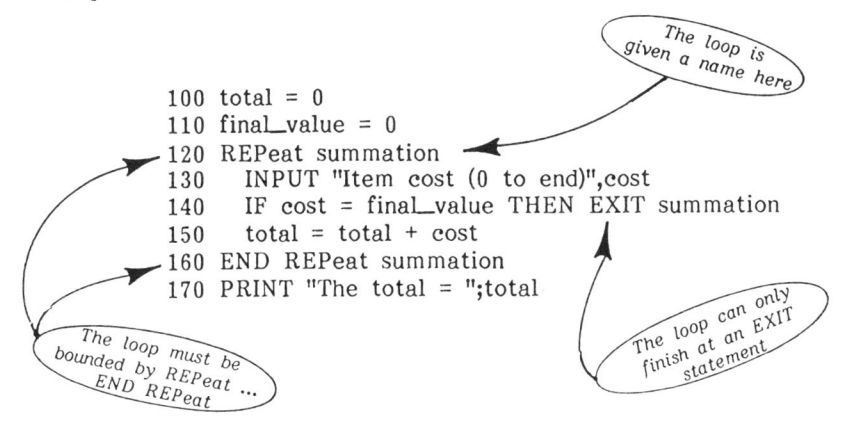

```
100 total = 0
110 final_value = 0
120 REPeat summation
130   INPUT "Item cost (0 to end)",cost
140   IF cost = final_value THEN EXIT summation
150   total = total + cost
160 END REPeat summation
170 PRINT "The total = ";total
```

(The loop is given a name here)

(The loop must be bounded by END REPeat ...)

(The loop can only finish at an EXIT statement)

The group of lines to be repeated is clearly identifiable by the bounding REPeat and END REPeat. Inset lines make the structure clear.

5 Repetition

Many programmers find that the REPEAT loop is the most useful one because the exact situation under which it finishes is so completely under their control. If you use a meaningful name in the EXIT line, such as 'IF cost=final_value THEN EXIT', it is easy to understand how the loop will finish.

Without an EXIT statement a REPEAT loop will carry on executing forever, or until the SPACE bar is pressed while the CTRL key is held down. Such an infinite loop is demonstrated in the following program which requests the current date and time and converts the QL to a digital clock. Incidentally this program uses a new statement CSIZE which alters the size of writing on the screen. For example:

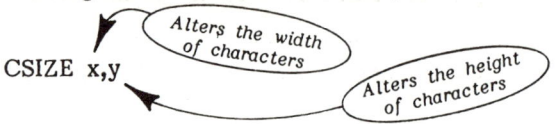

CSIZE x,y

Alters the width of characters
Alters the height of characters

The actual values which CSIZE can take depend on something called 'mode' which we shall not discuss until Chapter 9. The default setting is CSIZE 0,0. Here is the program:

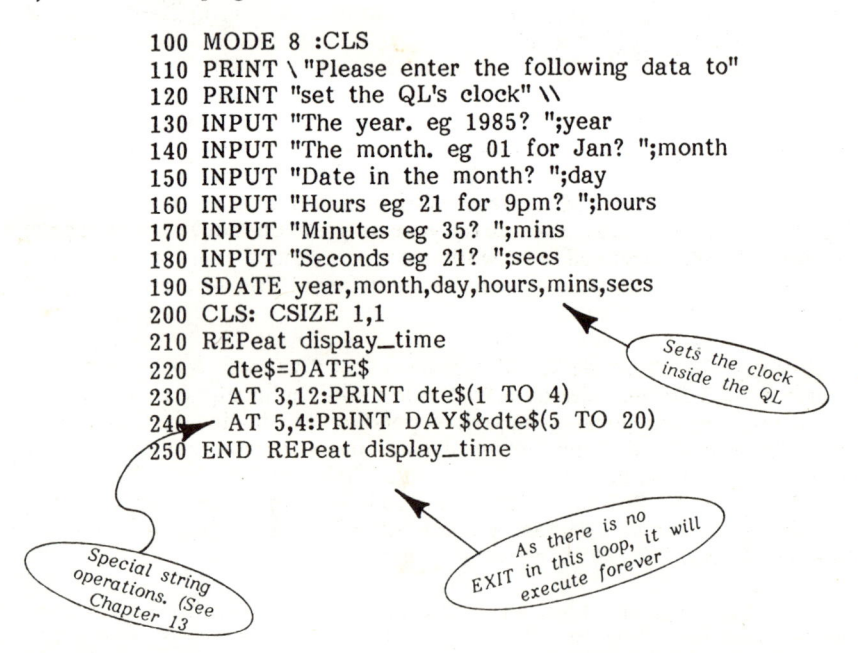

```
100 MODE 8 :CLS
110 PRINT \ "Please enter the following data to"
120 PRINT "set the QL's clock" \\
130 INPUT "The year. eg 1985? ";year
140 INPUT "The month. eg 01 for Jan? ";month
150 INPUT "Date in the month? ";day
160 INPUT "Hours eg 21 for 9pm? ";hours
170 INPUT "Minutes eg 35? ";mins
180 INPUT "Seconds eg 21? ";secs
190 SDATE year,month,day,hours,mins,secs
200 CLS: CSIZE 1,1
210 REPeat display_time
220    dte$=DATE$
230    AT 3,12:PRINT dte$(1 TO 4)
240    AT 5,4:PRINT DAY$&dte$(5 TO 20)
250 END REPeat display_time
```

Sets the clock inside the QL

As there is no EXIT in this loop, it will execute forever

Special string operations. (See Chapter 13)

As many lines of program as you require may appear between the first line of the loop (which starts 'REPeat...') and the last line (which is 'END REPeat').

5 Repetition

If only a short set of instructions are to be repeated, the QL allows a shortened form to be written on one line. A particularly useful single line REPEAT loop is one which waits for a particular key on the keyboard to be pressed. This actually relies on the two BASIC statements INKEY and INSTR which we shall not explain until Chapter 13 on strings. Using them, the following line of SuperBASIC will cause the program execution to stop until the user presses one of the keys Y, y, N or n:

REPeat wt:k$=INKEY$(-1):IF k$ INSTR "YyNn" THEN EXIT wt

Essentially this single line REPEAT loop is of the form:

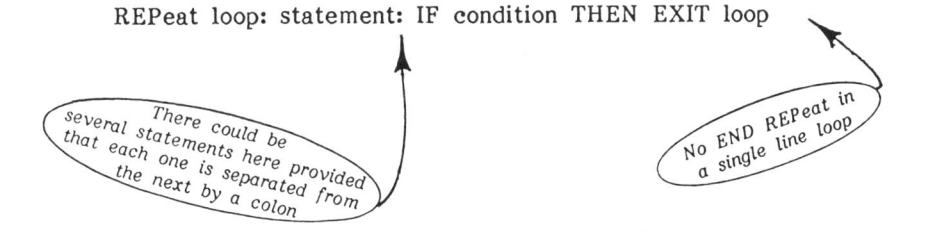

REPeat loop: statement: IF condition THEN EXIT loop

Several statements could be here that each one is separated the next by a colon provided from

No END REPeat in a single line loop

5.6 Activities

i. Use a REPEAT loop in a program to print numbers from 1 to 10, together with their squares. Then try your program on the QL and correct any errors. If you are unable to work out a program of your own, use the one in Section 5.12. It may look very different from yours, but any program is valid if it works.

ii. The program of Listing 5.2 illustrates a REPEAT loop. As you can see overleaf from Screen Display 5.2, it calculates the mortgage still owing on a loan as the years progress, depending on the interest and the monthly repayments. Examine the listing, and when you understand the program, try running it.

The printout of successive lines from such programs may be too rapid to read. Can you suggest and try out two ways of slowing it down? (See Section 5.12.)

iii. Run the program of Listing 5.3 (overleaf) to see a demonstration of the possible variations given by CSIZE. The effects are shown in Screen Display 5.3, which is also overleaf.

```
A PROGRAM TO SHOW THE VARIATION OF
MORTGAGE STILL OWING, ACCORDING TO
TIME - DEPENDING ON MONTHLY REPAYMENT
AND RATE OF INTEREST

Enter original mortgage 8500

Enter monthly repayment 120

Enter percentage interest rate 8

Year 1, Outstanding mortgage 8500
Year 2, Outstanding mortgage 7740
Year 3, Outstanding mortgage 6919.2
Year 4, Outstanding mortgage 6032.736
Year 5, Outstanding mortgage 5075.355
Year 6, Outstanding mortgage 4041.383
Year 7, Outstanding mortgage 2924.694
Year 8, Outstanding mortgage 1718.669
Year 9, Outstanding mortgage 416.163
```

Screen Display 5.2

Listing 5.2

```
100 CLS
110 REMark Mortgage calculation
120 AT 5,0:PRINT "A PROGRAM TO SHOW THE VARIATION OF"
130 PRINT"MORTGAGE STILL OWING, ACCORDING TO"
140 PRINT"TIME - DEPENDING ON MONTHLY REPAYMENT"
150 PRINT"AND RATE OF INTEREST."\\
160 INPUT"Enter original mortgage ";capital
170 INPUT \"Enter monthly repayment ";repayment
180 INPUT \"Enter percentage interest rate ";interest \\
190 year=0
200 REPeat payoff
210    year=year+1
220    PRINT"Year ";year;", Outstanding mortgage ";capital
230    capital=capital+capital*interest/100-12*repayment
240    IF capital<0 THEN EXIT payoff
250 END REPeat payoff
```

5 Repetition 87

```
             A demonstration of CSIZE

    CSIZE 0,0------ Hello there
    CSIZE 1,0------ Hello  there
    CSIZE 2,0------ Hello there
    CSIZE 3,0------ Hello  there
    CSIZE 0,1------ Hello there

    CSIZE 1,1------ Hello  there

    CSIZE 2,1------ Hello there

    CSIZE 3,1------ Hello  there
```

Screen Display 5.3

```
Listing 5.3

100 REMark A demonstration of CSIZE
110 REMark Set the mode in 120 as required
120 CLS
130 AT 2,6 :PRINT "A demonstration of CSIZE"\\\
140 FOR y=0 TO 1
150    FOR x=0 TO 3
160       CSIZE 0,0:PRINT "  CSIZE ";x;",";y;"------ ";
170       CSIZE x,y:PRINT"Hello there"
180    END FOR x
190 END FOR y
200 CSIZE 0,0
```

5.7 Loops within loops

It is possible to have loops within loops. We will illustrate by developing a program to print the following pattern of six lines of crosses, each line with a number of crosses equal to one more than the line number:

XX
XXX
XXXX
XXXXX
XXXXXX
XXXXXXX

A program to print, say, three crosses on a single line could be as follows:

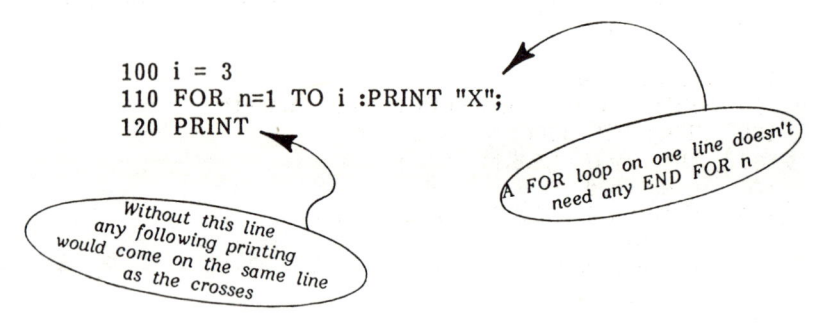

```
100 i = 3
110 FOR n=1 TO i :PRINT "X";
120 PRINT
```

A FOR loop on one line doesn't need any END FOR n

Without this line any following printing would come on the same line as the crosses

You could print six lines with successive numbers of crosses by repeating the above program lines with i increasing successively from 2 to 7. You could use a FOR loop, as shown in the following program:

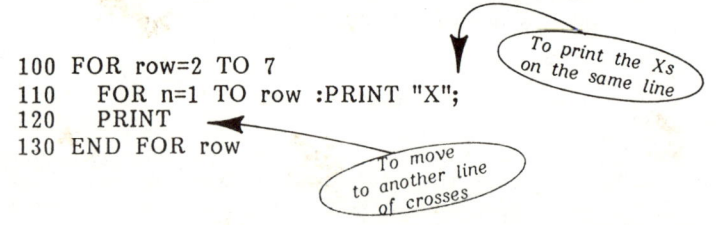

```
100 FOR row=2 TO 7
110    FOR n=1 TO row :PRINT "X";
120    PRINT
130 END FOR row
```

To print the Xs on the same line

To move to another line of crosses

Here there is an outer loop with loop variable line and an inner loop with loop variable n. The value of the outer loop sets the range of values in the inner one.

There can be many inner loops within an outer loop. The process is called 'nesting'. Any type of loop can be nested within or outside any other.

5 Repetition

It is very important that a loop should be either completely within another or completely outside it. In the schematic diagram of Figure 5.1, loop B is entirely within loop A, and is allowable. A good test is to draw a line from each FOR to the corresponding END FOR. None should cross.

```
FOR A =  ─────┐
FOR B =  ───┐ │
....        │ │
....        │ │
END FOR B ──┘ │
END FOR A ────┘
```

Figure 5.1. Properly nested loops.

The schematic diagram of Figure 5.2 represents overlapping loops which are in error.

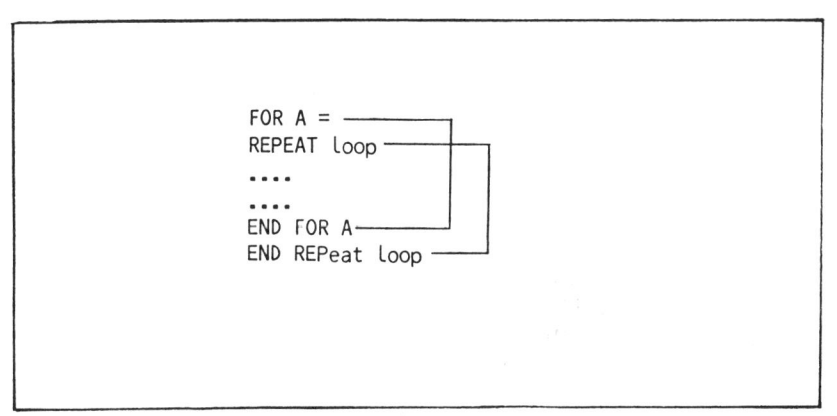

```
FOR A = ───────┐
REPEAT Loop ─┐ │
....         │ │
....         │ │
END FOR A ───┼─┘
END REPeat Loop ─┘
```

Figure 5.2. Overlapping loops which are in error.

5.8 Which loop to use

As a general guideline, you would use a FOR loop for a fixed number of repetitions and a REPEAT loop for most other cases. In some situations, though, it is a matter of individual choice which loop to use, because the same result can be achieved with either. For example, the crosses of Section 5.7, which were obtained with a FOR loop, could equally well have been drawn using a REPEAT loop, as shown in the following program:

```
100 MODE 4:CSIZE 3,1
110 row=1
120 REPeat rows_of_crosses
130   crosses=1
140   REPeat single_crosses
150     PRINT "X";
160     IF crosses=row+1 THEN EXIT single_crosses
170     crosses=crosses+1
180   END REPeat single_crosses
190   PRINT
200   row=row+1
210   IF row=6 THEN EXIT rows_of_crosses
220 END REPeat rows_of_crosses
```

The program with the REPEAT loop has more lines than the one with the FOR loop. It also uses longer names to make the nature of the condition in the EXIT statements as meaningful as possible. Where you can use either loop in a program, you may like to bear in mind that the FOR loop normally executes slightly more quickly.

5.9 Activities

Try writing a program to print the times tables up to ten for numbers from 2 to 10. As a hint, it is most conveniently achieved by a loop within a loop. (Further hints and comments are provided in Section 5.12.)

5.10 Points to ponder

a. In Section 1.9, we used a procedure which contained a FOR loop starting with two lines:

>   DEFine PROCedure hello(n)
>   FOR num=1 TO n

In Section 1.9, we treated this procedure as a 'black box'. Now, though, you should be able to say what value n has when called by a line such as the following:

>   hello 10

b. Is the following grouping of FOR loops allowable?

5 Repetition

```
FOR A= . . 1 TO 10
FOR B= . . 1 TO 10
  . . . . .
  . . . . .
END FOR B
FOR J= . . 1 TO 10
  . . . . .
END FOR J
END FOR A
FOR Z= . . 1 TO 10
  . . . . .
END FOR Z
```

c. Which of the following variable types are suitable for loop variables?

- integer
- numerical
- string

d. What is the value of g after the following loop has completed?

```
100 g = 100
110 REPeat test_loop
120   g = g + 2
130   IF g>139 THEN EXIT test_loop
140 END REPeat test_loop
```

5.11 Discussion on the points to ponder

a. The value supplied as a parameter when a procedures is called, 10 in this case, is transferred to the variable in brackets in the line starting DEFine PROCedure. This n is given the value 10 when the procedure is called.

b. The loops are all allowably nested, because, if you draw a line from each FOR to the corresponding END FOR, none cross.

c. In most BASICs the loop variable may be either numerical or integer. In SuperBASIC it must be numerical.

d. 5.2.

5.12 Discussion of activities

Activity 5.4ii: In the suggested program, an extra line has been inserted which varies the value of the loop variable inside the loop. Consequently the loop variable is reset to its starting value each time this line is executed. The result is a loop which executes forever. It is, from a programming point of view, rather dangerous to alter the loop variable inside a loop. You may use a loop variable at any stage, but it is best not to alter it.

Activity 5.4iii: Some other dialects of BASIC take the loop variable one increment beyond the one set by the programmer in the FOR loop. SuperBASIC retains the last allowed value.

Activity 5.4iv: The following is an example of a program to add all the numbers from 1 to 10 using a FOR loop:

```
100 REMark Program to add all numbers from 1 to 10
110 sum = 0
120 FOR n=1 TO 10 :sum = sum + n
130 PRINT sum
```

Activity 5.6i: The following is a program to print numbers from 1 to 10, together with their squares.

```
100 num=0
110 REPeat numbers_and_squares
120    num=num+1
130    PRINT num;" squared = ";num*num
140    IF num=10 THEN EXIT numbers_and_squares
150 END REPeat numbers_and_squares
```

Activity 5.6ii: One way of slowing down the printing is to program a delay between successive lines. You can do this by forcing the QL to do anything which consumes time. A simple line such as the following FOR loop will do:

```
145 FOR i=1 TO 100 :x=x
```

It does not alter the value of x but, as the QL is forced to calculate, it will take time. How long will depend on the number of times the loop is set to repeat.

A second method is to use the BASIC instruction PAUSE which causes the QL to pause for a given time in fiftieths of a second, for example:

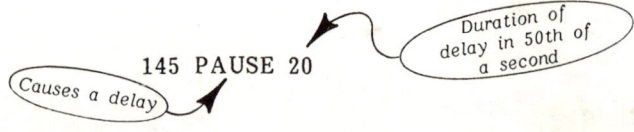

```
145 PAUSE 20
```

(Causes a delay)

(Duration of delay in 50th of a second)

5 Repetition

A third method is to arrange that a new line appears only once you press ENTER. You can do it with a line such as the following:

```
145 INPUT tripe$
```

We use this method when we discuss the next activity, Activity 5.9.

Activity 5.9: A times table program can be written using a double FOR loop as shown below. The outer loop dictates which times table is the current one, while the inner loop prints it. Because the printout from this program is so long, it disappears off the top of the screen before it can be read. So we ask the person running the program if he is ready to move onto the next table before continuing.

```
100 MODE 8:CSIZE 3,0
110 REMark Times-table printing program
120 FOR j=2 TO 10
130   CLS
140   PRINT \\"     The ";j;" times table" \\
150   FOR k=1 TO 10 :PRINT k; " x ";j;" = ";j*k
160   INPUT \\ "Press ENTER to continue";a$
170 END FOR j
```

6

Making decisions

6.0 Introduction
6.1 Comparisons
6.2 Conditional statements
6.3 Activities
6.4 Extending conditional statements
6.5 Activities
6.6 Some points to ponder
6.7 Discussion on the points to ponder
6.8 Discussion of activities

6.0 Introduction

A very important use of computers is to make decisions. You can get the QL to make a decision by instructing that it should do something provided that a certain condition in the program is met. In this chapter we introduce the BASIC instruction which exist for the purpose. In its various forms, it always works by choosing which of alternative sections of program to execute.

6.1 Comparisons

We shall now look at the sorts of decision that you might expect a computer to be able to make.

You might, for example, want the QL to finish taking some action when you enter 'finish'. To achieve this, you would expect some decision of the following form within the program:

if answer$ = "finish" then ....stop or something....

To take another example, the QL might be testing a child in school on his times table. Then when he or she has been asked for the result of, say, 7x9, you would expect the QL to make a test like the following:

if answer = 7*9 then ....congratulations....

You would expect a program to sort a list of numbers into order to need to make a decision of the following form:

if a < b then swop them round

Each of these examples involves a comparison of some sort. They are:

Does answer$ = "finish"?

Does answer = 7*9?

and

Is a < b?

A computer can make several sorts of comparisons. BASIC requires each to be represented by its own symbol as listed in Table 6.1. Each has a result which is either correct or is not correct - in computing terms 'true' or 'false'.

6 *Making Decisions*

COMPARISON	SYMBOL
equals	=
not equal to	<>
less than	<
greater than	>
less than or equal to	<=
greater than or equal to	>=

Table 6.1. Comparisons and their symbols.

6.2 Conditional statements

There is a construction which allows the QL to choose between two alternatives. IF something is true or valid, THEN it should carry out one set of actions. IF that something is not true or valid, THEN it should take the alternative ELSE action. In English the construction follows the following logic:

IF condition is valid THEN do action1 ELSE do action2

In the BASIC equivalent, various parts of the construction have to be written on new lines, in the following way:

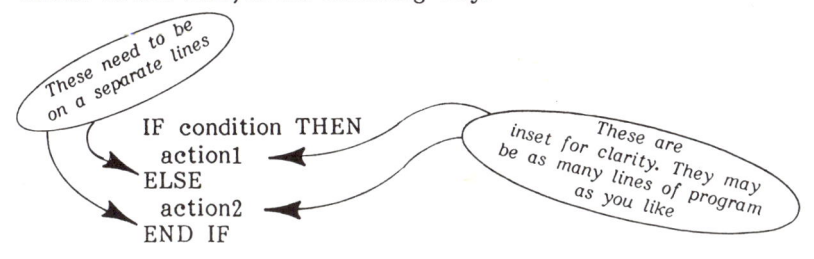

These need to be on a separate lines

```
IF condition THEN
   action1
ELSE
   action2
END IF
```

inset for clarity. These are many lines of program as you like. They may

The construction is called the IF ... THEN ... ELSE ... statement – and is an example of a conditional statement. If the condition following the IF is satisfied, the QL will execute action1 which could be one or a whole set of program lines containing any number of BASIC statements. If the condition is not satisfied, the QL will execute action2 which could also be any number of program lines containing BASIC statements.

As an illustration, the following short program will ask for a number and then report on the size of the number that is entered:

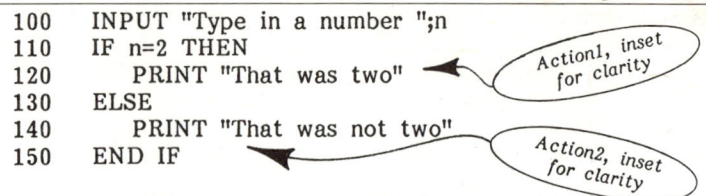

```
100  INPUT "Type in a number ";n
110  IF n=2 THEN
120      PRINT "That was two"          ← Action1, inset for clarity
130  ELSE
140      PRINT "That was not two"      ← Action2, inset for clarity
150  END IF
```

If 2 is entered, the condition n=2 is valid. Then the QL prints the message:

> That was two

However if the number is not two, then the statement following the ELSE is executed. So the QL prints the alternative message:

> That was not two

If you do not want an alternative action, you may leave out the ELSE and write the statement in the alternative form:

> IF condition THEN
>   action
> END IF

Then there is only one possible set of actions, rather than two. The set of actions may still extend to many lines of BASIC program.

There is a short form of conditional statement which can be written on a single line. You can use it where only one possible action is required if the condition is true and where this action is sufficiently simple to express on the same line as the THEN. Colons must separate every BASIC statement following the THEN. No END IF is required. For example the following is perfectly valid and complete:

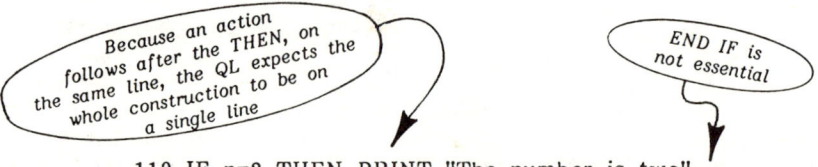

Because an action follows after the THEN, on the same line, the QL expects the whole construction to be on a single line

END IF is not essential

```
110 IF n=2 THEN PRINT "The number is two"
```

If n is 2, then the message gets printed. Otherwise the program execution goes straight to the next line.

Where two or more simple actions are required, they can still be written in a one-line conditional statement by separating each from the

6 Making Decisions

next by a colon. A space helps readability, as you can see in the following example:

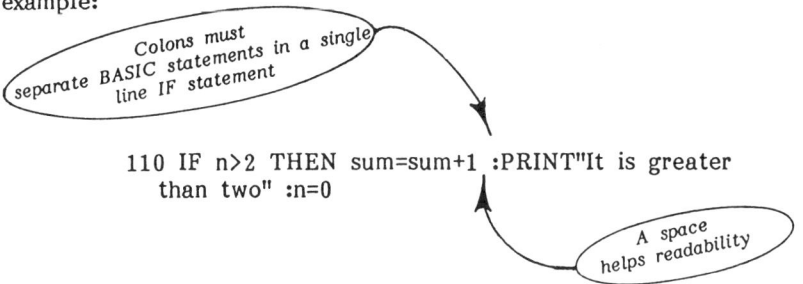

Colons must separate BASIC statements in a single line IF statement

```
110 IF n>2 THEN sum=sum+1 :PRINT"It is greater
    than two" :n=0
```

A space helps readability

Comparisons may involve quite complex expressions which can appear on the left as well as the right of the comparison sign. For instance the following is a valid comparison:

```
1050 IF X*(X^2+Y) = Y^4+6 THEN appropriate_action
```

The QL works out the expression on both sides of the equals sign before performing the comparison. If the comparison turns out to be true then the appropriate action takes place.

String variables may also be used in conditional statements. For example each of the following is allowable, where all hyphenated words represent procedures:

```
110 IF answer$="YES" THEN
120     next_question
130 ELSE
140     explain_answer
150 END IF
```

and

```
200 IF pass$=pw$ THEN accept_user
```

and

```
300 IF name1$ > name2$ THEN swop name1$,name2$
```

Incidentally the last example causes a sort into alphabetical order with, for example, JOHNSON coming before JONES. This is because the QL not only puts numbers in ascending order and letters in alphabetical order. It can also put a mixture of numbers and letters into an order. It treats numbers before letters and upper-case before the corresponding lower-case. This can be represented in the following way:

0<1<2 . . . <9 . . . <A<a<B<b<C<c<D<d . . . <Z<z

Almost any practically useful program contains an IF ... THEN ... ELSE or an IF ... THEN statement. As an example of its use, consider the

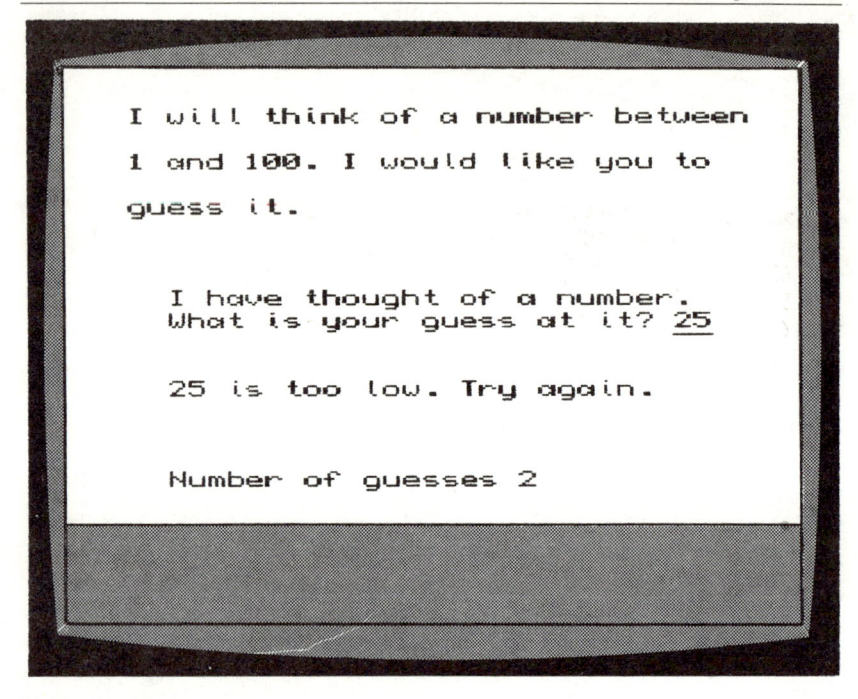

100   6 Making Decisions

```
I will think of a number between
1 and 100.  I would like you to
guess it.


   I have thought of a number.
   What is your guess at it? 25

   25 is too low.  Try again.


Number of guesses 2
```

Screen Display 6.1

---

number-guessing game of Listing 6.1. The QL thinks of an integer between 1 and 100, using its random number generator, in response to the line:

    number=RND(100)

Incidentally there is a more general form, which produces a random integer between any two given numbers. For example, the following gives x an integer value between 12 and 22:

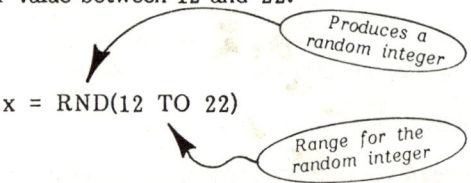

    x = RND(12 TO 22)

Produces a random integer — points to RND

Range for the random integer — points to (12 TO 22)

The program of Listing 6.1 allows you to guess what the number is and it prints up how many attempts you make at that number. Screen Display 6.1 shows the idea.

Listing 6.1

```
100 REPeat guesses
110   MODE 8 :CLS
120   display_start_message
130   number=RND(100)
140   FOR i=1 TO 1000 :REMark wait for realism
150   AT 10,4:PRINT "I have thought of a number."
160   REPeat find_it
170     get_guess
180     IF guess<number THEN AT 14,4:PRINT guess;" is too low. Try again. "
190     IF guess>number THEN AT 14,4:PRINT guess;" is too high. Try again. "
200     IF guess=number THEN EXIT find_it
210   END REPeat find_it
220   AT 14,2:PRINT "Your guess was correct. Would you "
230   INPUT "  like another go";ans$
240   IF ans$="n" OR ans$="no" THEN EXIT guesses
250 END REPeat  guesses
260 :
270 DEFine PROCedure display_start_message
280 PRINT \\"  I will think of a number between"
290 PRINT \"  1 and 100. I would like you to"
300 PRINT \"  guess it."
310 g=0
320 END DEFine start_message
330 :
340 DEFine PROCedure get_guess
350   AT 11,4:INPUT "What is your guess at it? ";guess
360   g=g+1
370   AT 18,4:PRINT "Number of guesses ";g
380 END DEFine get_guess
```

6.3 Activities

i. Enter and run the number-guessing program of Listing 6.1.

ii. Without running the following simple program, can you see that it will only continue to run provided the correct response is entered?

```
100 REPeat trial_loop
110   INPUT "Shall I continue? ";a$
120   IF a$="yes" THEN PRINT "OK I'll continue"
130   IF a$<>"yes" THEN EXIT trial_loop
140 END REPeat trial_loop
150 PRINT "OK then I'll stop"
```

As a check, enter the program and run it.

iii. Try just pressing ENTER in response to the question 'Shall I continue?'. Do you understand why the program stops?

iv. Enter the following program:

```
100 REPeat number_report
110   INPUT "Type a number ";x
120   PRINT "The number was ";
130   IF x<5 THEN PRINT "<5"
140   IF x>=5 THEN PRINT ">=5"
150 END REPeat number_report
```

Study the program to make sure you understand how it operates. Then run it. Can you see other ways of writing a program to give the same results? If so, try writing one, run it and correct any lines in error until it runs correctly. If you feel like a challenge, see how many different versions of the program you could write to give the same results. If you accept this challenge, you will quickly see that your programs vary in length and that some are easier to understand than others. Do you consider clarity or brevity to be most important in your own programming?

6.4 Extending conditional statements

You may want to alter a condition by reversing it or extending it, or you may want to test several conditions at a time.

For example you may want your program to test that something is not happening — when the only BASIC test is for it actually happening. Suppose you want a test for the temperature of a room — when the only test is for 'cold', which can be true or false. There would be no problem with the following:

```
IF cold THEN turn_heater_on
```

Nevertheless, as there is no test for 'hot', you couldn't use the following, even though there might be situations when you would want to:

6 Making Decisions

         IF hot THEN turn_heater_off

It is in situations like these that the BASIC word NOT comes into its own. In our example you could use it as follows:

         IF NOT cold THEN turn_heater_off

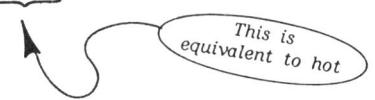

This is equivalent to hot

There are other words which are useful in the same way. For example in an accounting program, you might want to give a discount either on items costing more than £100 or if the customer's total account was over £200. This is a double condition, which could be written fairly recognizably in English as follows:

         IF item costs > £100 OR customer's account is > £200
         THEN give a discount.

BASIC provides the keywords AND and OR for such purposes. They are called 'logical operators'. So, in BASIC, the double condition becomes:

         IF cost >100 OR account>200 THEN give_discount

This will give a discount if:

(a) cost>100
(b) account>200
(c) both (a) and (b)

Such BASIC comparisons can be as complex as you choose, as long as the entire statement goes on a single line of program.
    The condition can be rewritten to include only (c) by using the AND operator, as follows:

         IF cost>100 AND account>200 THEN give_discount

Any number of logical operators may be written on the same line with brackets showing priority. For example the following line arranges for z to be given the value of y^2 if x=A and y=B, or if x=3 and y=4:

         210 IF (x=A AND y=B) OR (x=3 AND y=4)
              THEN z=Y^2

BASIC applies an order of priority when evaluating conditions. In Table 6.2 all the operators in any one group have equal priority and are dealt with from left to right. The groups of operators are listed in order of priority 1 to 7.

PRIORITY	OPERATOR
1	NOT brackets ()
2	raising to a power ^
3	multiplication * division / integer division DIV integer remainder MOD
4	addition + subtraction -
5	= < > < > <= >=
6	AND
7	OR EOR

Table 6.2. Priorities of groups of operators.

So the brackets in line 210 were not essential for correct evaluation of the complicated condition. Nevertheless brackets often help readability which makes them worth putting in. If you are in doubt about whether or not to use them, remember that they have the highest priority. This means that the condition inside each set of brackets will be evaluated before anything else.

We now introduce yet another extension, which is useful when you want to put a lot of IF ... THENs together in a program. Suppose a program needs to work out how many days there are in a particular month. We could do it using write an IF ... THEN statement as follows, where the variable 'month' can take the value 1 to 12. As you can see, though, the result is rather clumsy:

```
200 IF month=9 OR month=4 OR month=6 OR month=11 THEN
210    days=30
220 ELSE
230    IF month=2 THEN
240       days=28
250    ELSE
260       days=31
270    END IF
280 END IF
```

It is difficult to disentangle the conditions on which the various days apply. Fortunately the QL supplies an alternative structure which is much clearer. It is the ON ... SELECT. It is best explained by an example. We shall show its use in the following program which also works out how many days there are in a particular month. The other lines merely enable the program to run.

```
100 CLS :AT 5,0
110 INPUT "Give me a month number ";month
120 SELect ON month
130    ON month=9,4,6,11
140       days=30
150    ON month=1,3,5,7,8,10,12
160       days=31
170    ON month=2
180       days=28
190    ON month=REMAINDER
200       PRINT \"You are not dealing with earth days!"
210       days=-1
220 END SELect
230 :
240 IF days>0 THEN PRINT \"There are ";days;
    " days in month ";month
```

6.5 Activities

i. Look at each of the following statements and see if you can see what would be printed. Then enter the lines and see if you were right.

```
10 IF 1<2 OR 3=4 THEN PRINT "hello"
```

```
10 IF 4=4 OR 3=5 AND 2=1 THEN PRINT "hello"
```

```
10 IF 3<5 AND 2=1 THEN PRINT "hello"
```

```
10 IF 5 MOD 3=2 AND 9 DIV 3=3 THEN PRINT "hello"
```

ii. Could brackets alter any of the above conditions? (See Section 6.8.)

iii. Write a program to accept the entry of a list of numbers so that, when zero is entered, it prints up both the smallest and the largest in the list. (See Section 6.8.)

6.6 Some points to ponder

a. What limits the complexity of the IF ... THEN ... ELSE statement?

6.7 Discussion on the points to ponder

a. There is virtually no limit to the complexity of the IF ... THEN ... ELSE construction with the QL because any number of program lines can be included between IF and THEN etc. The BASICs of many other personal computers limit the whole construction to one line. This is a severe limitation.

6.8 Discussion of activities

Activity 6.5ii: Normally the = is worked out first, then the AND condition and then the OR. This causes 'hello' to be printed. However, if a bracket is put around (4=4 OR 3=5) in the second example, the value would be false. This would make the entire condition false; so resulting in no message.

Activity 6.5iii: The following is a program to accept a stream of numbers. When 0 is typed (or RETURN is pressed) the program ends with a report on the smallest and largest number entered during its run:

```
100 INPUT"Enter your first number ";num
110 smallest=num :largest=num
120 REPEAT test_numbers
130   INPUT"Enter the next number ";num
140   IF num<>0 AND num<smallest THEN smallest=num
150   IF num<>0 AND num>largest THEN largest=num
160   IF num=0 THEN EXIT test_numbers
170 END REPeat test_numbers
180 PRINT "The smallest number was ";smallest
190 PRINT "The largest number was  ";largest
```

7

Adding sound

7.0 Introduction
7.1 Describing sound
7.2 The BEEP statement
7.3 Activities
7.4 Musical intervals
7.5 Musical scales
7.6 Activities
7.7 Extensions to the BEEP statement
7.8 Activities

7.0 Introduction

We have already given you procedures to demonstrate how much more exciting programs can be when you include sound – but we did not expect you to understand the programming. In this chapter we explain how you can program sound for yourself.

7.1 Describing sound

The QL contains a sound generator and a small loudspeaker. You can program to control the 'pitch', the 'quality' and the 'duration' of the resulting sound. In this section, we describe what these terms mean.

Sound is a vibration of the air. When the waveform of the sound is regular, the note is said to be 'pure'.

The rate of vibration is known as the 'frequency'. The faster the vibration, the higher the frequency and the higher the pitch of the note. Figure 7.1 illustrates this by showing the waveform of two pure notes of different frequency. The pitch of the first is the higher.

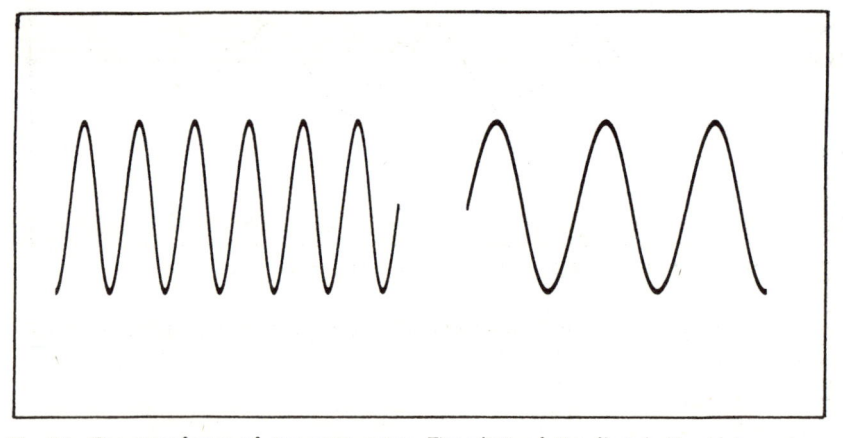

Fig 7.1. The waveforms of two pure notes. The pitch of the first is the higher.

The greatest displacement of a wave is called its 'amplitude'. The greater the amplitude, the greater the intensity and the louder the sound. Figure 7.2 shows the waveform of two pure notes. The first is the louder.

When the waveform is less regular, but the frequency is still constant, as shown in Figure 7.3, the sound is described as containing 'harmonics'. Notes of the same pitch from different musical instruments sound different because of their differing harmonics. They are also described as being of different 'quality'. It is the harmonics that add the pleasing quality to a note.

7 Adding Sound   109

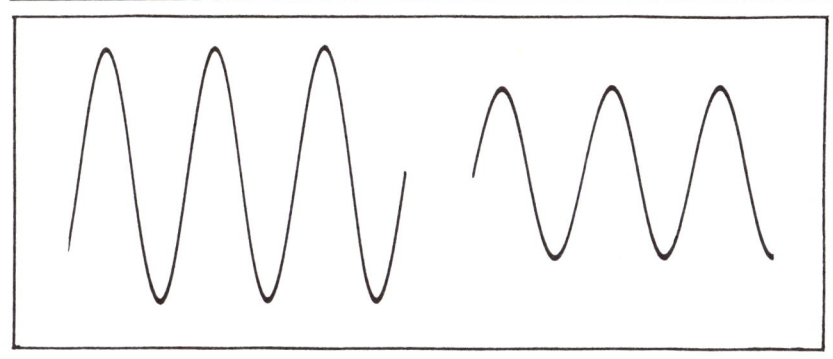

Fig 7.2. The waveforms of two pure notes. The first is the louder.

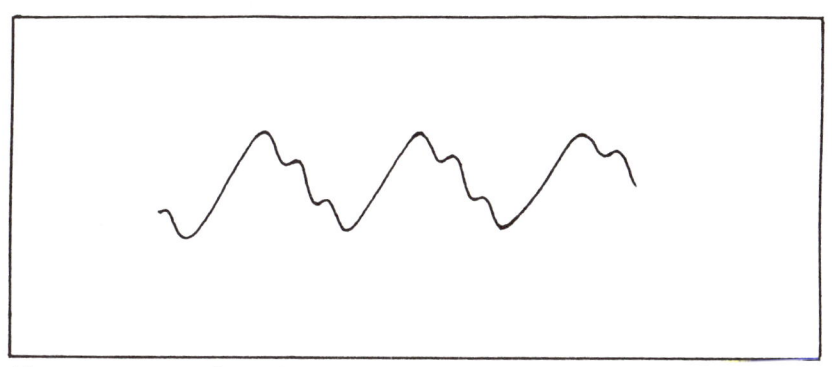

Figure 7.3. The waveform of a note containing harmonics.

A sound is described as 'noise' when there is no discernable pattern to its waveform.

7.2 The BEEP statement

The BEEP statement is the fundamental statement for programming sound. In its simplest form it controls the length and pitch of the note. This simple form is:

BEEP duration,pitch

This controls how long the note lasts

This controls the pitch of the note

The 'duration' of the note has to be a number between 0 to 32767. This specifies how long the note should last in terms of units of - perhaps strangely - 72 microseconds. (A microsecond is a millionth of a second.) So a duration of 10000 causes a note lasting about three quarters of a second - which you can check from the following calculation:

$$10000 \text{ units} = \frac{10000 * 72}{1000000} \text{ seconds}$$

$$= 0.72 \text{ seconds}$$

The various numbers that you can put for 'pitch' in the BEEP statement do not give a close correspondence to pitch on a musical scale. Table 7.1 shows this correspondence, as we found it on our QL. We hope that you will find the table helpful, but do bear in mind that the correspondence may vary slightly from one QL to another.

C	C#	D	D#	E	F	F#	G	G#	A	A#	B
											84
77	72	68	64	59	56	52	48	44	41	38	36
33	30	28	26	24	22	20	18	17	15	14	13
11	10	9	8	7	6	5	4	3			

Table 7.1. The pitch numbers for notes that our QL can produce. (There will probably be slight variations from QL to QL.)

If you are not interested in precise frequencies, it is easy to write a program which produces a series of notes of random pitch. This is what the following program does:

```
100 REPeat random
110    BEEP 10000,RND(254)
120    PAUSE 10
130 END REPeat random
```

Line 120 is necessary because a new BEEP statement will always cut off the previous note and start a new one. The effect of the line is to cause a delay between notes and so control the rate at which notes are sounded. If only one note were sounded, the duration of 10000 in the BEEP statement of line 110 would dictate the length of the note.

A program can test to see if a note is sounding by means of the BEEPING instruction. It can be used in the following form:

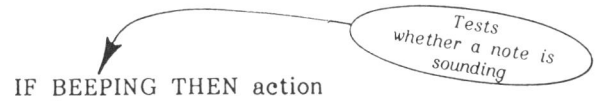

IF BEEPING THEN action *(Tests whether a note is sounding)*

It is often more useful to test that a note is not being emitted, which can easily be done by incorporating a NOT, as follows:

IF NOT BEEPING THEN ...

This causes action if sound is not being emitted, and can be put into a single program line using a REPEAT loop, as follows:

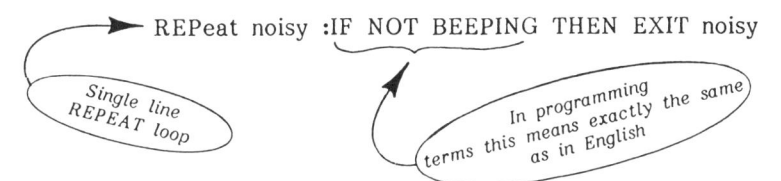

REPeat noisy :IF NOT BEEPING THEN EXIT noisy

(Single line REPEAT loop) *(In programming terms this means exactly the same as in English)*

When a whole series of notes are to be emitted immediately after each other, the delay between them can be produced with a PAUSE statement.

7.3 Activities

i. Listen to the effect of running the random note program of the previous section.

ii. Look back at the tune-playing program of Chapter 4 (Listing 4.1). It used pairs of numbers to represent the pitch and duration of notes. You might like to try altering these to play your own favourite melodies. The first number of each pair is the pitch number of the note in semitones as taken from Table 7.1, the second is the length in fiftieths of a second.

iii. The program of Listing 7.1 (overleaf) composes and plays a tune. You may like to listen to it.

7.4 Musical intervals

So far, we have only considered random notes, but they arc not very pleasing because each one tends to be discordant with the next. To produce more pleasing effects, sequences of notes have to be in harmony

```
Listing 7.1

100 DIM n(19),nte(32)
110 RESTORE 130
120 FOR v=0 to 32 :READ nte(v)
130 DATA 77,72,68,64,59,56,52,48,44,41,38
132 DATA 36,33,30,28,26,24,22,20,18,17,15
134 DATA 14,13,11,10,9,8,7,6,5,4,3
140 ep=0 :r=1
150 n(0)=0 :n(1)=3 :n(2)=7 :n(3)=10
160 FOR i=1 TO 4
170    FOR j=0 TO 3
180       n(j+i*4)=(n(j)+i*12) MOD 32
190    END FOR j
200 END FOR i
210 c=(RND(4)-1)*4 :nl=2 :d=5 :x=15
220 FOR i=0 TO 400
230    REPeat range
240       a=RND(7)-4
250       IF a<>0 AND a+c<=19 AND a+c>0 THEN EXIT range
260    END REPeat range
270    ep=(ep+1)MOD 20
280    BEEP 5000,nte(n(a+c))
290    FOR del=1 TO 40 :REMark wait a bit
300    c=c+a
310 END FOR i
```

with each other. In this connection it is helpful to relate pitch number to the notes on a keyboard. Figure 7.4 shows the arrangement of the black and white keys, covering just more than the one octave from middle C to top C. Above the keyboard is a piece of music showing the note corresponding to each key. Written above each key is the pitch number required to give that note.

The frequency of any note doubles in going to the octave above, as for example from middle C to top C. There are eight notes for an octave, counting only the white ones; twelve, including the black ones. The ratio of frequency between one note and the next in this group of twelve is called a semitone. In the standard system of tuning a keyboard instrument, every semitone is the same size. For the QL there is no simple relationship between pitch number and semitones. In Table 7.1 we gave the pitch numbers for each note in part of the musical scale. Now, in Table 7.2 we give the pitch numbers for each semitone above the note B, 13 semitones below middle C.

7 Adding Sound   113

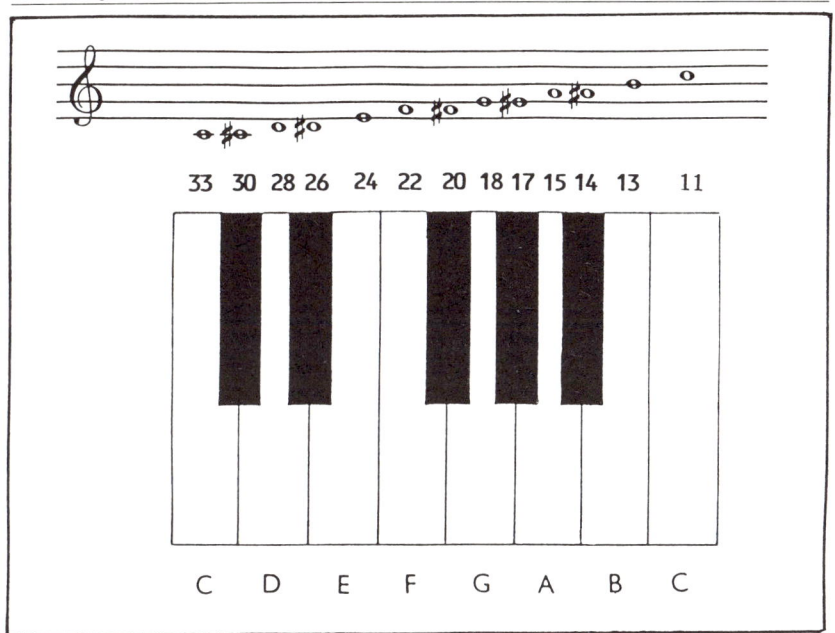

Figure 7.4. The piano keys and their corresponding pitch numbers.

SEMI-TONE	PITCH NUMBER	SEMI-TONE	PITCH NUMBER	SEMI-TONE	PITCH NUMBER
0	84	12	36	24	13
1	77	13	33	25	11
2	72	14	30	26	10
3	68	15	28	27	9
4	64	16	26	28	8
5	59	17	24	29	7
6	56	18	22	30	6
7	52	19	20	31	5
8	48	20	18	32	4
9	44	21	17	33	3
10	41	22	15		
11	38	23	14		

Table 7.2. The pitch numbers for each semitone

To program a particular note, the QL must work with the corresponding pitch number from Table 7.2. We give a procedure, which we call 'tone', to take your pitch in semitones and, using the information of Table 7.2, make the QL sound the note. In some ways 'tone' is an alternative form of the BEEP statement. Before using it though, you need to call on another procedure at the very start of the program. We call it 'initiate_music'. Together these procedures make it much more straightforward to transpose tunes from sheet music to the QL.

Here are the procedures, which we do not expect you to understand fully at this stage.

The procedure 'initiate_music':

```
30000 DEFine PROCedure initiate_music
30010   DIM nte(32)
30020   RESTORE 30040
30030   FOR v=0 TO 32 :READ nte(v)
30040   DATA 77,72,68,64,59,56,52,48,44,41
        ,38,36,33,30,28,26,24,22,20,18
        ,17,15,14,13,11,10,9,8,7,6,5,4,3
30050 END DEFine initiate_music
```

The procedure 'tone':

```
31000 DEFine PROCedure tone(j,p)
31010   BEEP j,nte(p)
31020 END DEFine tone
```

7.5 Musical scales

A scale is a sequence of notes which cover an octave. You might think that there would be twelve notes to a scale but a simple demonstration of such a scale by the following program will convince you that this doesn't sound quite 'right'. (In order to run the program, the procedures 'initiate_music' and 'tone' have to be added.)

```
100 initiate_music
110 FOR p=0 TO 12
120   tone 10000,p
130   PAUSE 20
140 END FOR p
```

For a scale to sound 'right', there have to be fewer notes and therefore larger intervals.

There are a number of different scales. The program of Listing 7.2 plays the C major scale. It relies on the procedures 'initiate_music' and

Listing 7.2

```
100 initiate_music
110 DATA 1,2,2,1,2,2,2,1
120 middlec=13 :finalnote=middlec+12
130 note_value=middlec-1
140 RESTORE
150 REPeat c_major
160    READ stp
170    note_value=note_value+stp
180    tone 10000,note_value
190    FOR w=1 TO 80:REMark wait a while
200    IF note_value=finalnote THEN EXIT c_major
210 END REPeat c_major
```

'tone', which you have to add.
The notes are in the following sequence:

C D E F G A B C

We have gone up the white notes of the keyboard, sounding each one in turn. What is characteristic of the C major scale is the sequence of tonal differences between the notes forming it. The tone differences between the notes in the C major scale are:

tone, tone, semitone, tone, tone, tone, semitone

Since each tone is just two semitones, this can be represented by a series of numbers giving the number of semitones between the notes which characterize the C major scale. These are:

2, 2, 1, 2, 2, 2, 1   (=12 altogether for an octave)

The C major scale is characterized by the sequence of semitone differences between successive notes, rather than by the starting note itself. Table 7.3 lists the semitone differences for various musical scales. Each has its own characteristic mood, which is why composers so carefully choose the scale in which they write their music. The sequence of semitone numbers must add up to 12 in each case.

Listing 7.3

```
100 CLS
110 INK 0
120 initiate_music
130 previous=-1
140 RESTORE 330
150 REPeat scales
160   p=13
170   READ scale$
180   IF scale$="END" THEN RESTORE 340 :READ scale$
190   AT 7,12 :PRINT scale$
200   REPeat one'scale
210     NOTE 10000,p
220     FOR del=1 TO 200 :REMark wait a while
230     READ interval
240     p=p+interval
250     IF interval=-10 THEN EXIT one_scale
260   END REPeat one'scale
270   AT 15,1 :PRINT "Press C to continue, ENTER to finish"
280   reply$=INKEY$(-1)
290   IF reply$<>"c" THEN EXIT scales
300 END REPeat scales
310 STOP
320 :
330 DATA "aeolian mode  ",2,1,2,2,1,2,2,-2,-2,-1,-2,-2,
    -1,-2,-10
340 DATA "dorian mode   ",2,1,2,2,2,1,2,-2,-1,-2,-2,-2,
    -1,-2,-10
350 DATA "major         ",2,2,1,2,2,2,1,-1,-2,-2,-2,-1,
    -2,-2,-10
360 DATA "diminished    ",1,2,1,2,1,2,1,2,-2,-1,-2,-1,-2,
    -1,-2,-1,-10
370 DATA "harmonic minor",2,1,2,2,1,3,1,-1,-3,-1,-2,-2,
    -1,-2,-10
380 DATA "melodic minor ",2,1,2,2,2,2,1,-2,-2,-1,-2,-2,
    -1,-2,-10
390 DATA "pentatonic    ",2,2,3,2,3,-3,-2,-3,-2,-2,-10
400 DATA "whole tone    ",2,2,2,2,2,2,-2,-2,-2,-2,-2,-2,
    -10
410 DATA "END"
```

7 *Adding Sound* 117

SCALE	SEQUENCE OF PITCH NUMBERS
aeolian mode	2 1 2 2 1 2 2
dorian mode	2 1 2 2 2 1 2
major	2 2 1 2 2 2 1
diminished	1 2 1 2 1 2 1 2
harmonic minor	2 1 2 2 1 3 2
melodic minor	
(ascending)	2 1 2 2 2 2 1
(descending)	2 2 1 2 2 1 2
pentatonic	2 2 3 2 3
whole tone	2 2 2 2 2 2

Table 7.3. The semitone differences for various musical scales.

7.6 Activities

i. The program of Listing 7.3 is a modification of the one in Section 7.5, which played the C major scale. It now plays 8 different scales - as given in Table 7.3 - all starting with middle C. Note the marking of the end of any one sequence of intervals by -1. When the program detects this, it waits for the user to press ENTER, before playing the next scale. Enter the program, run it and then try entering your own intervals. Remember that the intervals must add up to 12. Once again this program requires the procedures initiate_music and tone.

ii. The program of Listing 7.4 turns the bottom two rows of the QL's keyboard into a mimic of a musical keyboard. Try entering and running it. Remember to add the procedure 'initiate_music' before running it.

```
Listing 7.4

100 REMark a simple musical keyboard
110 CLS
120 initiate_music
130 REPeat play_keyboard
140   k$=INKEY$(-1)
150   PRINT k$;" ";
160   BEEP 20000,nte(k$ INSTR "ZSXDCFVBHNJM,L.;/")
170 END REPeat play_keyboard
180 REMark requires procedure initiate_music
```

iii. Now try the program of Listing 7.5 which plays a continuously rising musical arpeggio. This program makes use of the procedure 'initiate_music' which must be added:

```
Listing 7.5

100 initiate_music
110 p=0
120 REPeat arpeggio
130   FOR i=3 TO 5
140     p=(p+i) MOD 32
150     BEEP 10000,nte(p)
160     FOR j=1 TO 80:REM wait a while
170   END FOR i
180 END REPeat arpeggio
190 REM requires procedure initiate_music
```

7.7 Extensions to the BEEP statement

There are extensions to the BEEP statement which allow you to vary the pitch of a note even while it is playing. You can stipulate the limits that the note should vary between and you can also program the rate of the variation. The extended form of BEEP statement is as follows, with the relationships between pitch numbers and notes remaining unchanged:

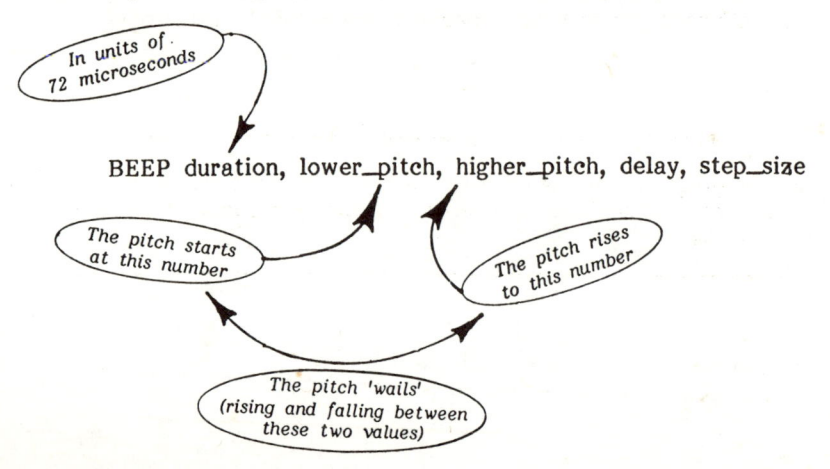

BEEP duration, lower_pitch, higher_pitch, delay, step_size

(In units of 72 microseconds)

(The pitch starts at this number)

(The pitch rises to this number)

(The pitch 'wails' (rising and falling between these two values))

The pitch number holds its initial programmed value for a time given by 'delay', which requires the same units as 'duration'. It then increases by the amount 'step_size'. This new pitch number is then held and the process repeated until the higher pitch level is reached. The whole cycle then repeats, with the overall duration being set, as before, by 'duration'.

We have devised a program to give you some idea of the range of sounds that the BEEP statement can produce. It holds trial values in DATA statements. So you can easily edit in new values to hear their effect on the BEEP statement. The program also illustrates some of the features of the extended form of the BEEP statement.

```
100 CLS
110 RESTORE
120 REPeat trial_beep
130   READ p1,p2,x,y
140   IF p1=-1 THEN EXIT trial_beep
150   PRINT \\"BEEP 30000,";p1;",";p2;",";x;",";y
160   BEEP 30000,p1,p2,x,y
170   INPUT "Press ENTER for the next beep";r$
180 END REPeat trial_beep
190 :
200 DATA 1,254,1,1
210 DATA 1,50,1,1
220 DATA 5,10,1,1
230 DATA 1,50,6,6
240 DATA 1,254,6,6
250 DATA 100,150,6,6
270 DATA -1,-1,-1,-1
```

Remember that, however complex the variations of pitch, the note will only sound for a length specified in the BEEP statement.

7.8 Activities

Run the programs of the previous section. Do you think that they could add interest and realism to some of your own programs? If so, save them for later use.

8

Windows and channels

> 8.0 Introduction
> 8.1 Windows
> 8.2 Channels
> 8.3 Activities
> 8.4 Default channels
> 8.5 Opening channels
> 8.6 Controlling windows
> 8.7 Closing channels
> 8.8 Activities
> 8.9 Resetting windows to their default values
> 8.10 Activities
> 8.11 Discussion of activities

8.0 Introduction

If money and space were no object, you might expect the QL to have several television displays. One might show a copy of commands and error messages; another might be reserved solely for the output from a program; and yet another might display a listing of that program. Figure 8.1 shows the idea.

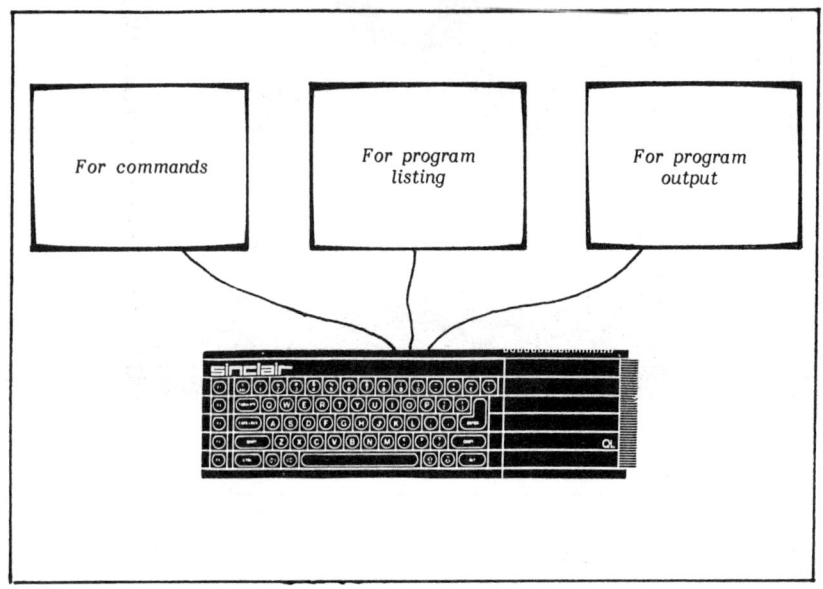

Figure 8.1. The several displays of a futuristic QL.

Actually the QL does have a form of just such a system! - and this is what this chapter is all about.

8.1 Windows

When setting up the multi-displays, Sinclair had to overcome the problem that owners could only reasonably be expected to have one monitor or television. So they compromised by compacting all the QL's displays onto one screen. This is illustrated in Figure 8.2 which represents the display on the QL when monitor, rather than television, is selected.

Each of the areas on the screen is called a 'window', and each displays only its own special-purpose information. In this chapter we shall be explaining how you can program which area of the screen displays what and how large it should be.

8 *Windows and Channels* 123

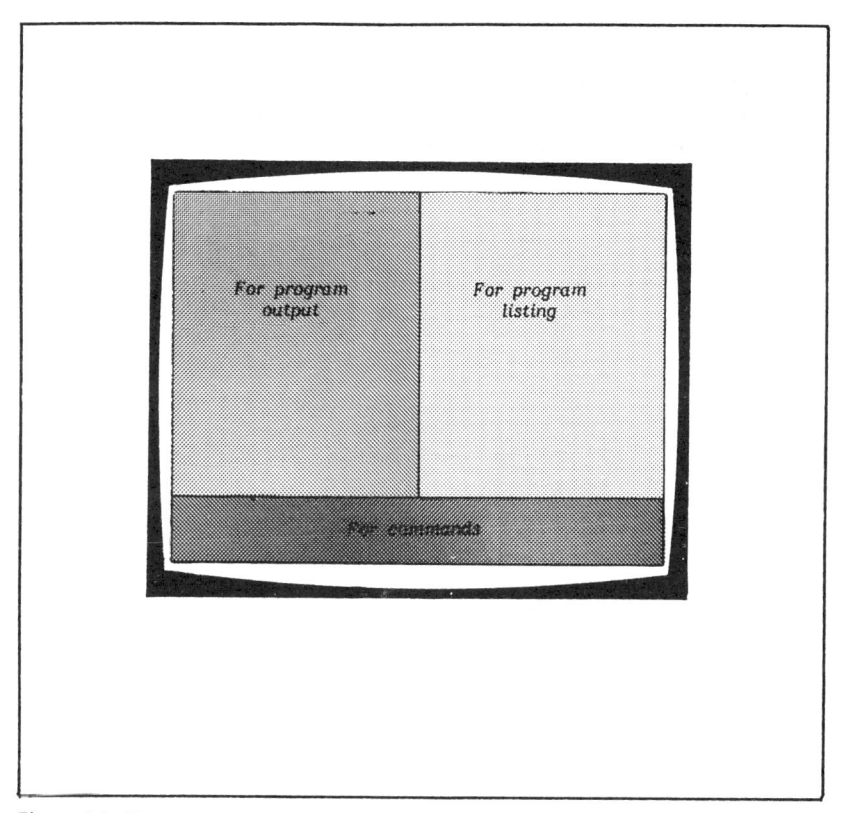

Figure 8.2. The QL and its display when monitor mode is selected.

If you have been using a normal television, you will have been pressing function key f2 when turning on. This gives what appear to be two areas of screen. Actually, though, there are still three, but two of them overlap. Figure 8.3 (overleaf) shows the idea.

The window for displaying program listings has a blue background with white writing, and it overlaps with the window for program output which has a red background with white writing. Figure 8.4 (overleaf) illustrates the effect, as achieved by running the following program:

```
1 CLS
2 PRINT "hello"
3 LIST
```

124   *8   Windows and Channels*

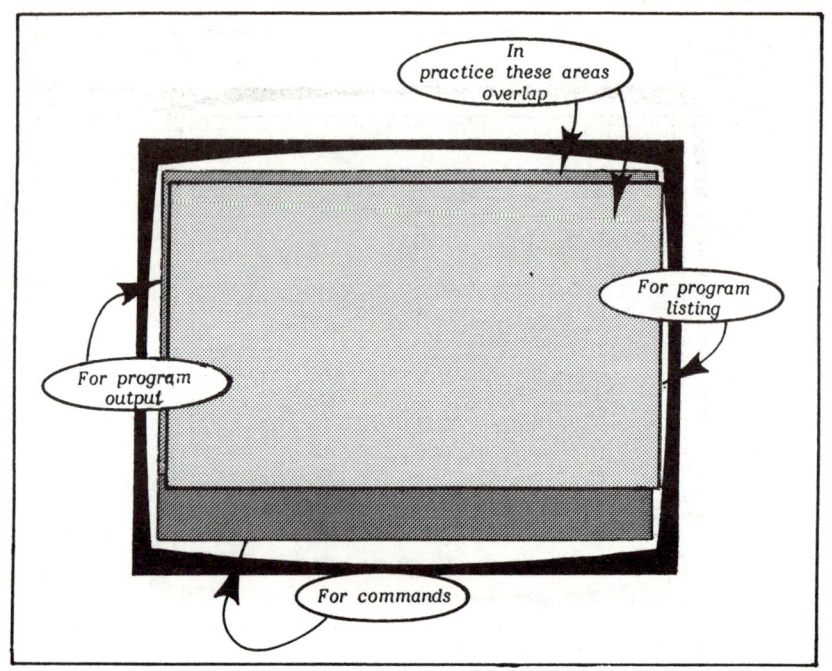

Figure 8.3. The QL and its display when TV is selected.

8.2   Channels

The QL can communicate in many different ways, via many different routes. Each is called a 'channel'. So far you have met the following channels:

1. The television screen - divided into three areas namely:

   - The command window
   - The program output window
   - The listing window

2. The microdrives - for loading and saving programs.

Here are some more communication channels:

3. Other windows on the screen - which you can program as channels.

4. The microdrives - for file-handling (see Chapter 14).

8 Windows and Channels   125

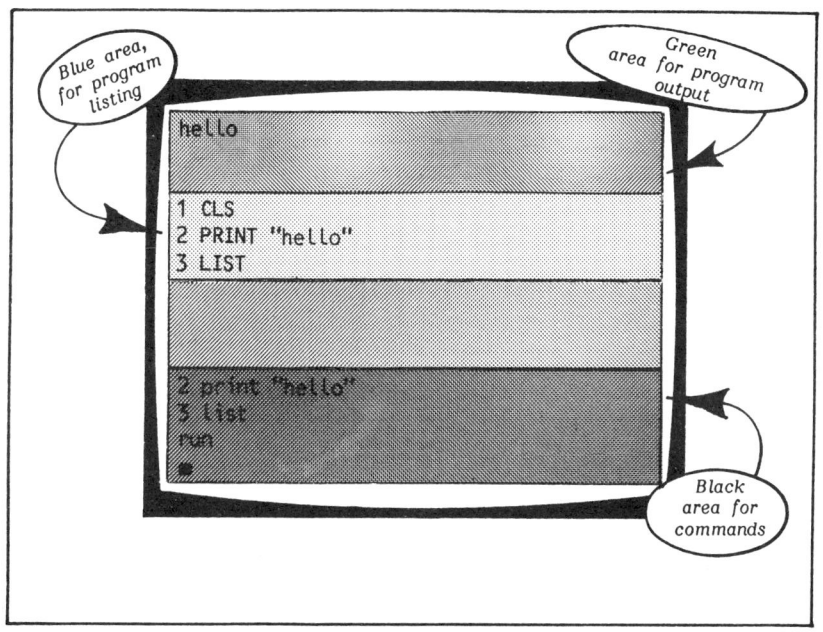

Figure 8.4. A program and its screen display.

5. The serial ports - for connecting printers, etc.

6. The network port - for communicating with other QL's or Spectrum computers.

SuperBASIC allows you to program which device you want to communicate with by specifying a channel number. For example, the complete form of the PRINT statement allows you to send messages to the channel of your choice. In the following example 'hello' is sent to channel 2:

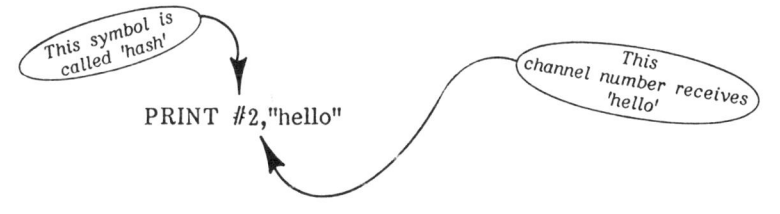

PRINT #2,"hello"

Three channels are available when the QL is first turned on: channels 0, 1 and 2. By way of illustration the following program prints the message 'hello channel' on each of them:

```
10 CLS
20 PRINT #0,"hello channel 0"
30 PRINT #1,"hello channel 1"
40 PRINT #2,"hello channel 2"
```

8.3 Activities

Run the program of the previous section. Do you get one of the displays shown in Figure 8.5? Which one will depend on whether you selected monitor or TV.

```
hello channel 1


hello channel 2                 10 CLS                              hello channel 1
                                20 PRINT #0,"hello channel 0"
                                30 PRINT #1,"hello channel 1"
                                40 PRINT #2,"hello channel 2"

                                hello channel 2

40 print #2,"hello chan
run
hello channel 0
■
                                30 print #1,"hello channel 1"
                                40 print #2,"hello channel 2"
                                run
                                hello channel 0
                                ■
```

The display for a television

The display for a monitor

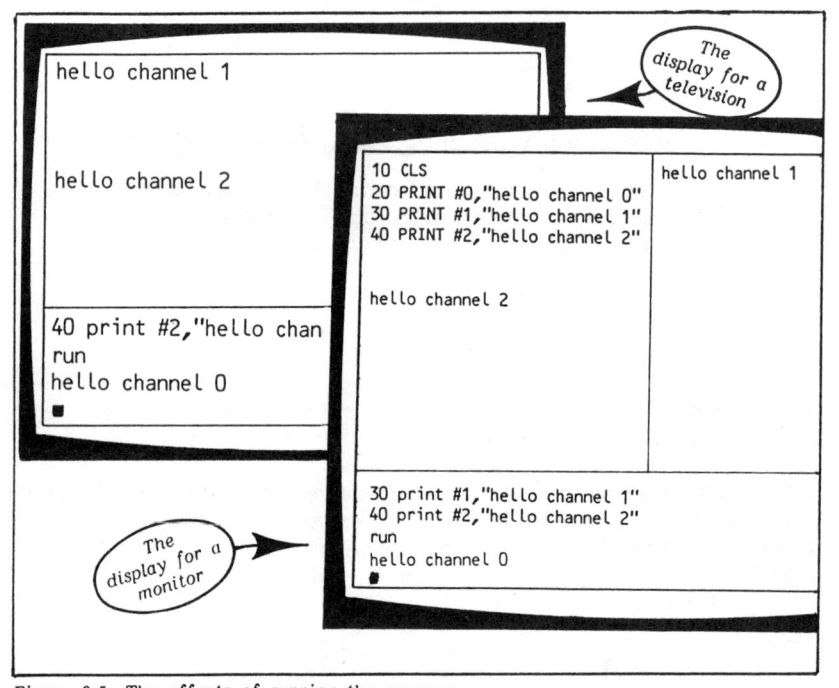

Figure 8.5. The effects of running the program.

8.4 Default channels

Until now you have used the PRINT statement without knowing anything about channels – and you omitted a channel number. In this situation, the QL automatically uses channel 1. Channel 1 is therefore called the 'default' channel for the PRINT statement.

8 Windows and Channels

You have used another keyword to communicate with channels – INPUT. The complete INPUT statement for taking in a value a$ from channel 2 is:

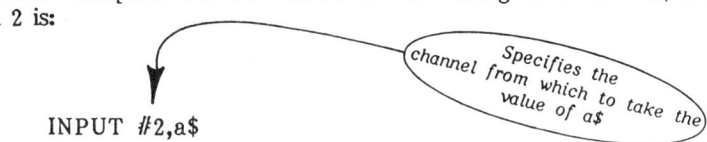

    INPUT #2,a$ *(channel from which to take the value of a$)*

The default channel for the INPUT statement is channel 0.

You have also used CLS to communicate with channels. It is used in the following form to clear the screen associated with channel 3:

    CLS #3   *(Clears the window area associated with channel 3)*

The following is a list of the QL's default channels:

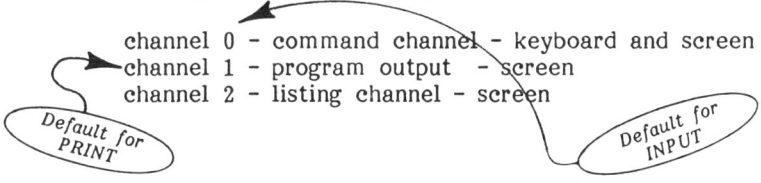

    channel 0 – command channel – keyboard and screen *(Default for PRINT)*
    channel 1 – program output – screen
    channel 2 – listing channel – screen *(Default for INPUT)*

8.5 Opening channels

If you wish a program to communicate with a device, you must arrange for the program to 'open a channel' to that device. You must then use that channel's number in statements such as PRINT or INPUT which refer to that channel.

One of the statements for opening a channel is:

    OPEN #3,SER1   *(Opens channel 3 as a serial port)*

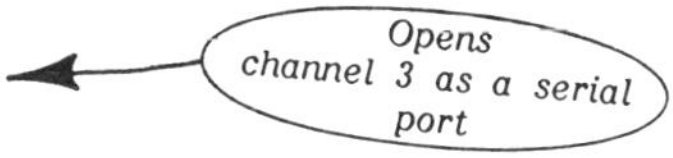

It opens channel 3 as what is called a 'serial port'. This is one of two sockets on the back of the QL, labelled SER1, and one of its uses is for communication with a printer. With the channel open, you can get the printer to print out messages, in response to statements like:

    PRINT #3,"message to printer on channel 3"

You could make the printer list the current program, with a command such as:

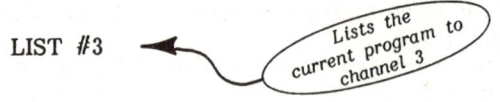

LIST #3 ← *Lists the current program to channel 3*

8.6 Controlling windows

With suitable programming, a window can be placed anywhere on the screen and can be of any size within the screen. It must, however, be rectangular. There are two statements to specify size. The first is the WINDOW statement and is of the form:

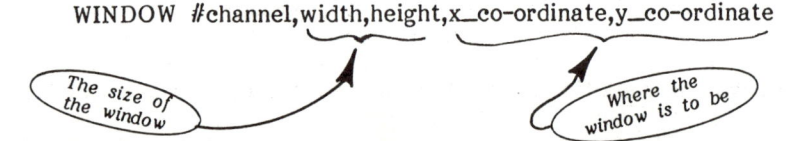

WINDOW #channel,width,height,x_co-ordinate,y_co-ordinate

The size of the window — *Where the window is to be*

The statement requires co-ordinates for specifying the position of the top

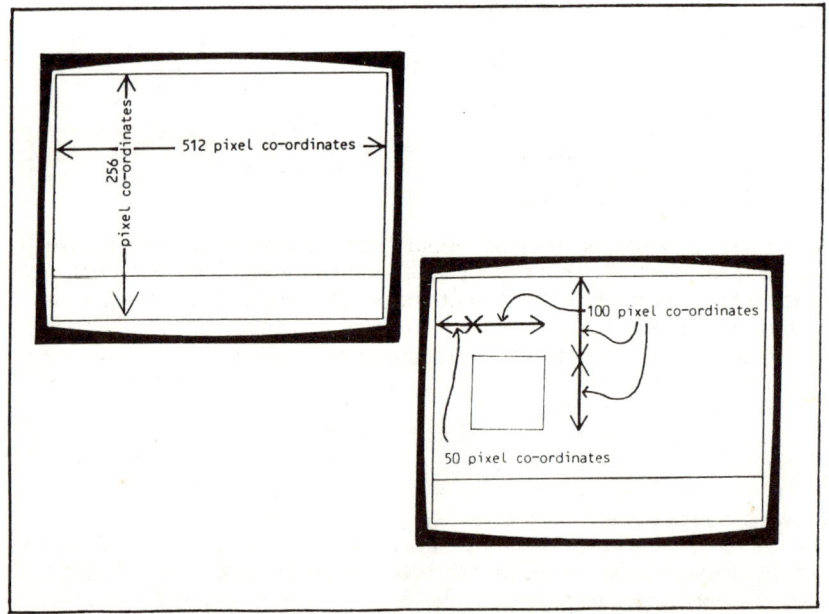

Figure 8.6a. The pixel co-ordinate system for specifying windows.

Figure 8.6b. The window size, as set by WINDOW #3,100,100,50,100.

8 Windows and Channels

left-hand corner of the window. These are called 'pixel co-ordinates' and are shown in Figures 8.6a and b. They refer to the top left-hand corner of the screen. 512 units is equal to the full screen width and 256 units is equal to the full screen height.

The WINDOW statement can alter the size of the window at any stage in a program. Indeed, the size and position can be varied from one PRINT statement to the next. There is no immediate effect. The statement only effects the printing or graphics which will be displayed in that window. A CLS statement will clear the specified window when required. It is used in the following form, where n is the channel number associated with that window:

CLS #n

It is possible to open new channels, each with a corresponding window on the screen. In fact the reaction test program of Listing 2.1 used this as a method to control where the various messages were printed. The program statement for opening a new channel and associated screen window is a variation of the OPEN statement. This one is of the form:

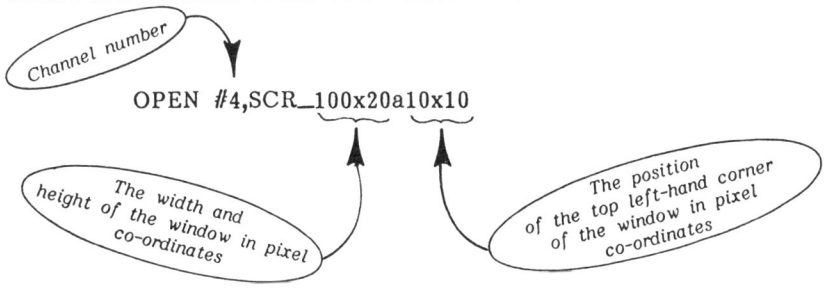

```
                  Channel number
                         ↓
       OPEN #4,SCR_100x20a10x10
```

- height of the window and co-ordinates
- The width and co-ordinates of the window in pixel
- The position of the top left-hand corner of the window in pixel co-ordinates

The 'x' and 'a' must be used as separators between the co-ordinates specifying the window. This is different from the WINDOW statement, in that it requires numbers to represent the width, height, etc. You may not use variables. This means that you cannot allow the program to decide on the size of a window to associate with a particular channel - although you can, of course, alter the window size using the WINDOW statement once the channel has been opened.

In a program which makes extensive use of windows, there may well be the need for an INPUT statement. It would then be elegant to have a window somewhere on the screen associated with the INPUT statement to display the message associated with the INPUT statement, together with a copy of whatever the user types on the keyboard. This form of communication is different from the others we have discussed, in that it is a two-way process, namely from the keyboard and to the screen. The following is the statement for opening such a specialized channel of communication and associating a window with it:

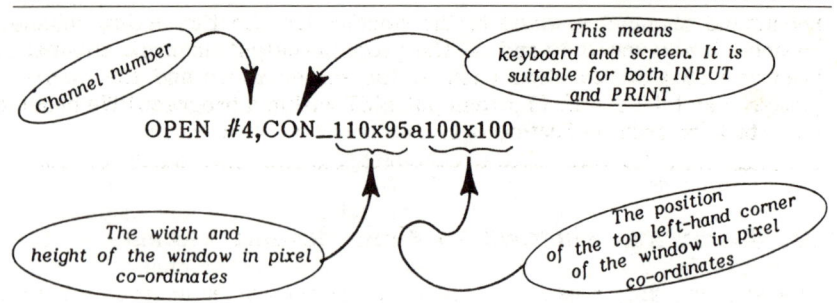

```
                                              This means
                                         keyboard and screen. It is
         Channel number                  suitable for both INPUT
                                              and PRINT
             OPEN #4,CON_110x95a100x100

                                                  The position
     The width and                          of the top left-hand corner
height of the window in pixel                   of the window in pixel
     co-ordinates                                   co-ordinates
```

The form of the window specification in pixel co-ordinates is just the same as for the previous statements. The CON is short for 'console' and is computer jargon for the combination of keyboard and screen. Once this channel has been opened you may PRINT to it using PRINT #4,... or you may ask questions using the INPUT statement in the form INPUT #4,... The rest of the INPUT statement is in the same form as you have used before.

There are many other aspects of the use of channels, but they are either beyond the scope of this book or are dealt with elsewhere. In particular, Chapter 14 is concerned with reading from and writing to the microdrives.

8.7 Closing channels

Once a channel is open, its channel number cannot be used for another purpose - and the channel remains open until you close it (or until you unplug the computer or reset it with the RESET button). A channel can be closed by the following instruction, where, for example, 3 is the channel number:

```
                                           Closes
         CLOSE #3                         channel 3
```

Once closed, the channel number can be re-used for another purpose.
Similarly a channel cannot be referred to by more than one number at a time.

8.8 Activities

It is sometimes useful to set the screen up differently from how it is when it first turns on. So try writing a short program to divide the screen up into, say, three equal horizontal bands. Let the bottom band be the

8 Windows and Channels *131*

command channel, channel 0; the middle band be the listing channel, channel 2; and the top band be the program output channel, channel 1. Get your program to clear each of the screen bands and then write a message and list itself. (You can put LIST within a program.) We provide a suitable program in Section 8.11.

8.9 Resetting windows to their default values

The windows remain as set by one program even after another is loaded in. Yet they may be most unsuitable. The following program resets them to their default values. For convenience lines 110, 150, 160 and 170 also reset colours to their default values, although we do not explain how until Chapter 10. Line 190 will be explained in Chapter 9.

```
100 WINDOW 512,256,0,0
110 PAPER 0 :CLS
120 WINDOW #0,448,40,33,216
130 WINDOW #1,448,200,33,16
140 WINDOW #2,448,200,33,16
150 PAPER #0,0 :INK #0,7 :CLS #0
160 PAPER #2,1 :INK #2,7 :CLS #2
170 PAPER #1,2 :INK #1,7 :CLS #1
180 CSIZE #0,0,0 :CSIZE #1,0,0 :CSIZE #2,0,0
190 SCALE 100,0,0
```

8.10 Activities

We suggest that you save the program of the previous section, so as to have it available for running after any program involve setting windows.

8.11 Discussion of activities

Activity 8.8: Here is our version of a program to divide the screen up into the three equal horizontal bands:

```
100 WINDOW #0,500,85,12,170
110 WINDOW #1,500,85,12,0
120 WINDOW #2,500,85,12,85
130 CLS #0
140 CLS #1
150 CLS #2
160 PRINT "hello this is some program output"
170 LIST
```

9

Beginning graphics

9.0 Introduction
9.1 Pixels
9.2 Scaling windows for graphics
9.3 Drawing points
9.4 Drawing lines
9.5 Activities
9.6 Drawing simple curves
9.7 Activities
9.8 Drawing circles and ellipses
9.9 Drawing arcs
9.10 Positioning writing precisely
9.11 Activities
9.12 Points to ponder
9.13 Discussion on the points to ponder
9.14 Discussion of activities

9.0 Introduction

Computer graphics is about drawing pictures on the screen. You have already seen something of what the QL's graphics can do - but we have put the graphics instructions into procedures, which we treated as black boxes. We didn't explain the programming inside them. In the next few chapters this is what we work towards. We start with some background ideas on how the QL produces shapes on the screen - both for text and for drawing. Then, in the rest of the chapter, we go on to explain how to plot points and to draw lines and curves.

9.1 Pixels

The QL makes up its screen display from small spots of light, called 'pixels'. Most of the time you need not be aware of them. There are always 256 in the vertical direction, although you do have the choice of whether there are to be 512 or 256 horizontally. The larger number gives the crisper picture, with more fine detail, but the smaller number allows you a larger choice of colours.

When you first turn the QL on, your selection of TV or Monitor sets both the window layout and the number of pixels horizontally. Hence it sets the size of writing and the number of available colours. The TV option gives a maximum of 8 colours with 256 pixels across the screen, whereas the monitor option gives a maximum of 4 colours with 512 pixels across the screen.

You may keep the window layout but change to the other pixel/colour arrangement with a MODE instruction. Either of the following commands change to the mode of 512 pixels and 4 colours:

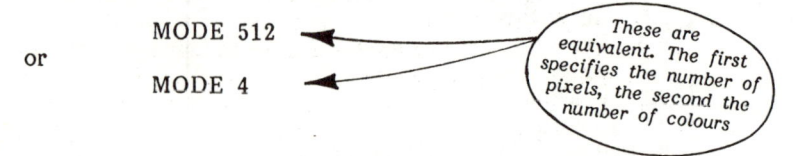

        MODE 512

or

        MODE 4

These are equivalent. The first specifies the number of pixels, the second the number of colours

Any one will do, because one implies the other. Similarly either of the following commands change to the mode of 256 pixels and 8 colours:

        MODE 256

or

        MODE 8

These are also equivalent. One implies the other

The two displays of Figures 9.1a and 9.1b indicate how mode affects the fineness of lines. Each shows a magnified portion of the screen in one of the two modes.

9 *Beginning Graphics* 135

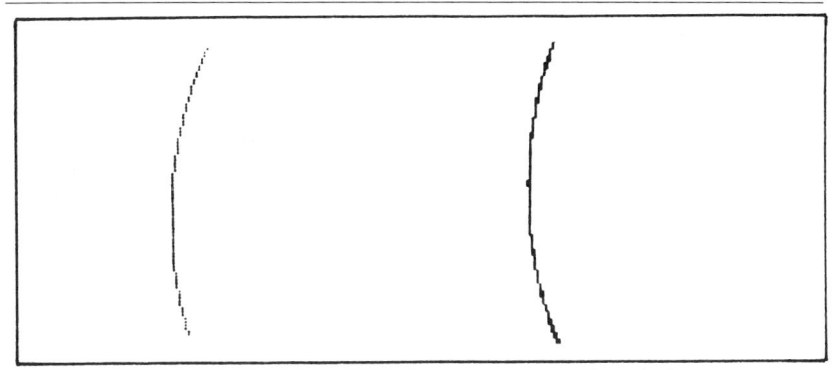

Figure 9.1a. An enlarged view of part of the screen in mode 4.

Figure 9.1b. An enlarged view of part of the screen in mode 8.

MODE also affects the size of writing. When you first turn on, MODE 8 gives 37 characters to the line, whereas MODE 4 gives 74.

9.2 Scaling windows for graphics

As we explained in Chapter 8, the QL divides the screen into windows. Certain windows exist automatically, according to whether you select the television or the monitor option. These are 'default windows' which you don't have to open. You can, however, close them and open others with appropriate instructions at positions of your choice.

The QL can write and draw at any position you choose within a window on the screen. You have to specify the position with what are called 'graphics co-ordinates'. These are not the same as the 'pixel co-ordinates' of Chapter 8. Pixel co-ordinates are for defining the position of a window on the screen, whereas graphics co-ordinates are for defining the position of graphics within a window. The origin of pixel co-ordinates (0,0) is the top left-hand corner of the screen, whereas the origin of graphics co-ordinates (0,0) is the bottom left-hand corner of the window concerned. Figure 9.2 illustrates the idea.

The height of a window in graphics co-ordinates is 100 by default. However, you can alter this using the SCALE statement. With a simple display of one window, such as with the normal television option, SCALE is used in the following form, where 'maxheight' is a number which you want to correspond to the height of the main area of screen:

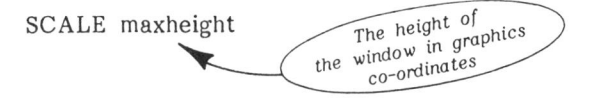

SCALE maxheight ⟵ *The height of the window in graphics co-ordinates*

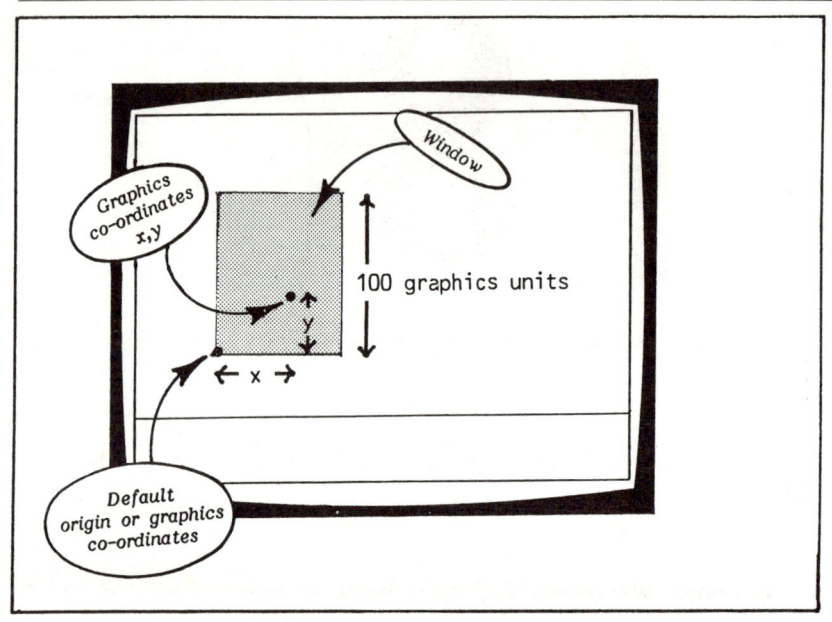

Figure 9.2. Graphics co-ordinates for specifying the position of a point within a window.

An extended form of the statement sets the origin of graphics co-ordinates to anywhere of your choice:

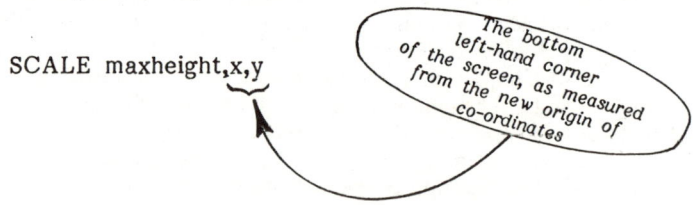

SCALE maxheight,x,y

The bottom left-hand corner of the screen, as measured from the new origin of co-ordinates

If want to program the height of some other window, you use the following form, where n is the channel number of the window concerned:

Channel number of the window concerned

SCALE #n,maxheight,x,y

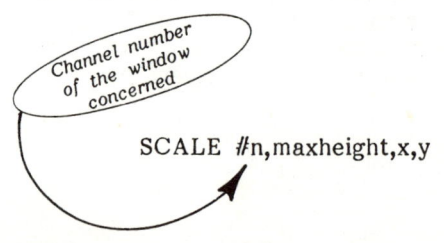

9 Beginning Graphics

When the QL is first turned on, the height of any window is 100 graphics units, by default. You can change the main area of the screen back to this with the following instruction:

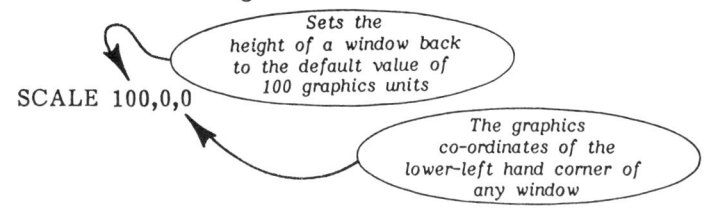

SCALE 100,0,0

- Sets the height of a window back to the default value of 100 graphics units
- The graphics co-ordinates of the lower-left hand corner of any window

For any other window, merely insert a #n after the SCALE, where n is the channel number of the window concerned. Without the x and y co-ordinates of the bottom left-hand corner of the screen, 0,0 is taken by default.

A graphics unit across the screen is automatically identical to a graphics unit down the screen, regardless of scaling. When the QL is first turned on in the television option, the main of the screen (the only open window) is 100 graphics units high by 166 graphics units wide.

The two displays of Figures 9.3a and 9.3b illustrate the effect of SCALE. Figure 9.3a shows the graphics co-ordinates of points on the main screen area when the QL is first turned on in the television option, and Figure 9.3b shows the co-ordinates of these same points after a SCALE statement.

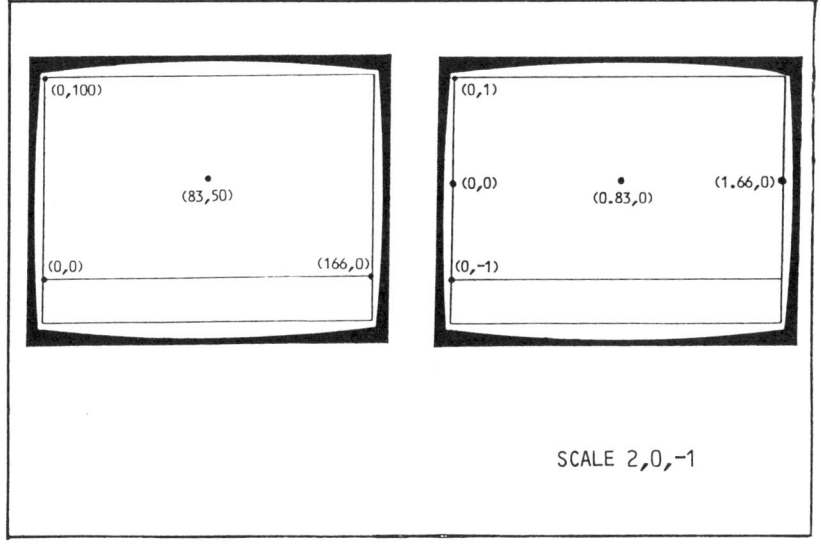

Figure 9.3a. The graphics co-ordinates of points on the main screen area when the QL is first turned on in the television option.

Figure 9.3b. The co-ordinates of these same points after a SCALE statement.

9.3 Drawing points

The QL allows you to draw individual points within a window. The instruction is POINT. You use it in the following form, where x and y are the graphics co-ordinates of the position where the point is to be plotted:

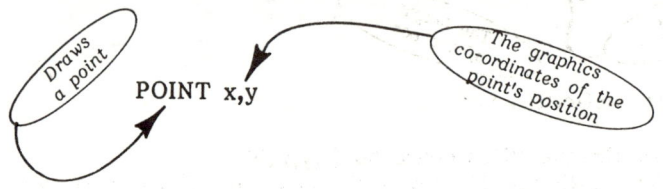

POINT x,y

Draws a point

The graphics co-ordinates of the point's position

9.4 Drawing lines

The QL has a statement called LINE for drawing a line within a window. In its simplest form, it draws the line between two points. You use it, with the graphics co-ordinates of the two points, as follows:

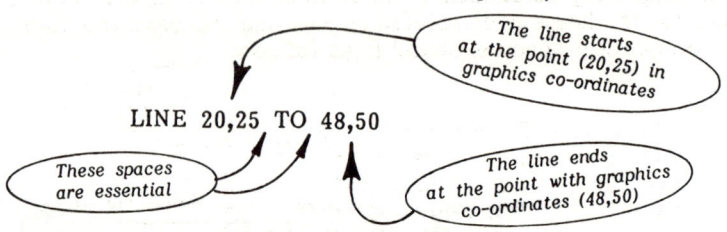

LINE 20,25 TO 48,50

These spaces are essential

The line starts at the point (20,25) in graphics co-ordinates

The line ends at the point with graphics co-ordinates (48,50)

Several lines may be drawn continuously by stringing the graphics co-ordinates of the various points together. As an illustration, the following program draws a square in the centre of the main area of the screen:

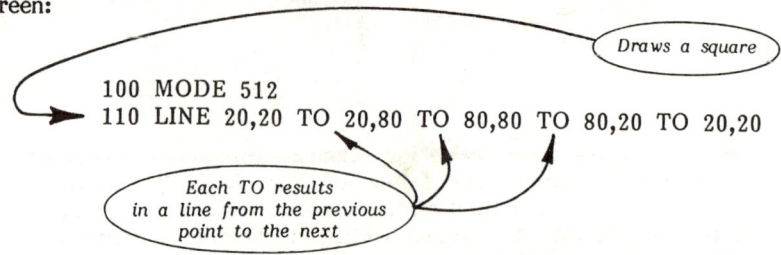

```
100 MODE 512
110 LINE 20,20 TO 20,80 TO 80,80 TO 80,20 TO 20,20
```

Draws a square

Each TO results in a line from the previous point to the next

It is better to write even such simple sections of program in a general form, with variables holding as many of the dimensions as possible. Then you can easily make adjustments like changing the size and shape of the figure. We illustrate with a procedure called 'box' which will draw a box of specified width and height from a specified point. You call it as follows:

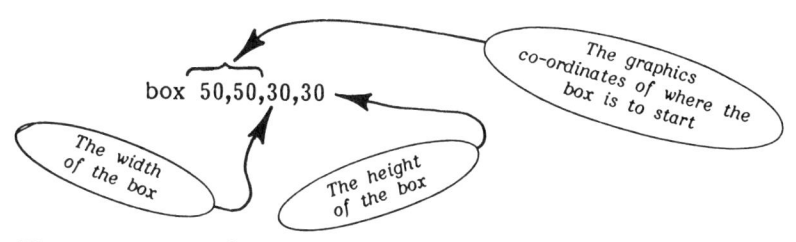

9 Beginning Graphics

box 50,50,30,30

- The graphics co-ordinates of where the box is to start
- The width of the box
- The height of the box

The procedure definition is:

```
320 DEFine PROCedure box(x,y,w,h)
330   LINE x,y TO x+w,y TO x+w,y+h TO x,y+h TO x,y
340 END DEFine box
```

It is simple to combine a number of rectangles together to produce a picture of a house. Then a number of houses can be drawn to give a view like looking down a street. We will now develop such a program. Each house is drawn by a further procedure which makes calls to the procedure 'box' for drawing the general outline, the front door and four windows. The procedure for the house is completed by two lines to make the pitched roof. The complete procedure 'house' is as follows:

```
220 DEFine PROCedure house(x,y,w,h)
230   box x,y,w,h
240   box x+w/6,y+h/8,w/5,h/3
250   box x+.7*w,y+h/8,w/5,h/3
260   box x+w/6,y+.6*h,w/5,h/4
270   box x+.7*w,y+.6*h,w/5,h/4
280   box x+.45*w,y,w/6,h/2
290   LINE x,y+h TO x+w/2,y+1.3*h TO x+w,y+h
300 END DEF house
```

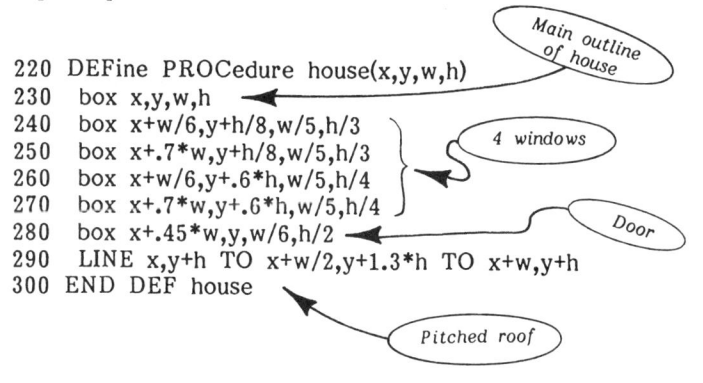

- Main outline of house
- 4 windows
- Door
- Pitched roof

A REPEAT loop produces the series of houses with a size which tends to decrease progressively. By the completion of the loop, the size is so small as to be little more than a dot on the window. The program introduces a random element into the actual width and height of each house, so producing a variety of different houses. Each one butts onto its neighbour to give a terraced effect, and each one is drawn progressively higher up the window and smaller, to give an apparent effect of increasing distance. The houses on the right and left of the street are of different heights but are identical in all other respects. The complete program is given in Listing 9.1 (overleaf).

Screen Display 9.1

9.5 Activities

i. Run the street-drawing program of Listing 9.1.

ii. Try altering the proportions of the houses by playing around with the last number in lines 140 and 150. If you want just one side of the street, remove either line 160 or 170. The street can then be extended right across the window by altering the variable 'length' in line 120.

9.6 Drawing simple curves

The QL allows you to draw a curve in two ways. Either you can make it up from separate points which are left unjoined, or you can join up the points with straight lines. Figure 9.4 (ahead) shows these effects.

9 Beginning Graphics

Listing 9.1

```
100 MODE 4 :CLS
110 SCALE 100,0,0
120 x=166 :y=10 :length=82
130 REPeat houses
140   w=RND(4 TO 8)*(x-length)/20
150   h=RND(4 TO 8)*(x-length)/14
160   house 166-x,y,w,h*1.5
170   house x,y,-w,h
180   x=x-w :y=y+1
190   IF x<length+4 THEN EXIT houses
200 END REPeat houses
210 :
220 DEFine PROCedure house(x,y,w,h)
230   box x,y,w,h
240   box x+w/6,y+h/8,w/5,h/3
250   box x+.7*w,y+h/8,w/5,h/3
260   box x+w/6,y+.6*h,w/5,h/4
270   box x+.7*w,y+.6*h,w/5,h/4
280   box x+.45*w,y,w/6,h/2
290   LINE x,y+h TO x+w/2,y+1.3*h TO x+w,y+h
300 END DEFine house
310 :
320 DEFine PROCedure box(x,y,w,h)
330   LINE x,y TO x+w,y TO x+w,y+h TO x,y+h TO x,y
340 END DEFine box
```

We now develop a program to produce the effects of Figure 9.4. For obtaining alternating values, we rely on the mathematical function SIN(12*x). As x increases, it produces values which alternate between −1 and +1. To make these fill the whole height of the main window and to place the origin half-way up it, we use the extended form of the SCALE statement, as follows:

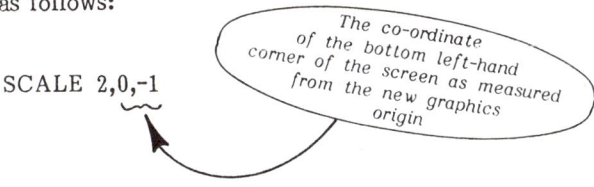

SCALE 2,0,−1

The co-ordinate of the bottom left-hand corner of the screen as measured from the new graphics origin

142 9 *Beginning Graphics*

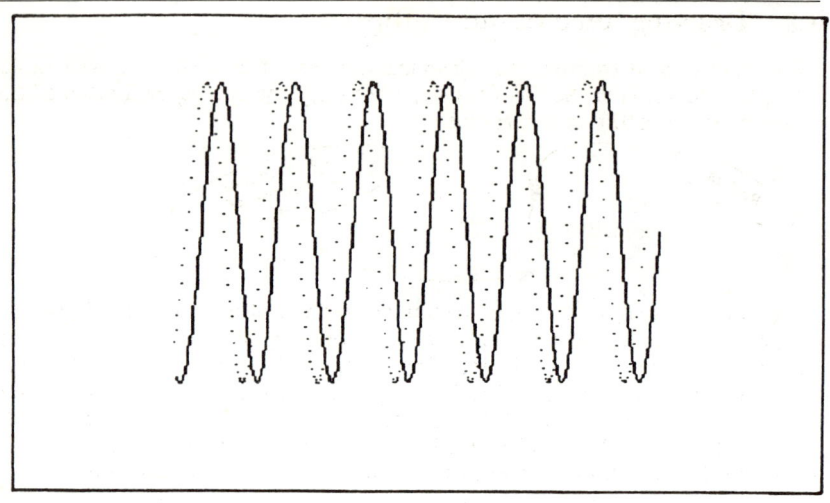

Figure 9.4. Two waves, one produced as a series of points and the other as the points joined by straight lines.

By varying x from 0 to 3.3, slightly more than six cycles will fill the majority of the available width. The complete program is given below.

```
100 MODE 4
110 SCALE 2,0,-1
120 xp=0:yp=0
130 FOR x=0 TO 3.3 STEP 1E-2
140    LINE xp,yp TO x,SIN(12*x)
150    POINT x+.1,SIN(12*x)
160    xp=x:yp=SIN(12*x)
170 END FOR x
```

With these techniques, you can display the shape of any mathematical function - but do remember to alter the value in the SCALE statement to suit the maximum vertical size. Also watch out for expressions which may result in a division by zero, such might occur in an expression like 1/SIN(x).

9.7 Activities

i. Run the curve-drawing program of Section 9.6.

ii. Try to adapt the program to draw some other curve.

9.8 Drawing circles and ellipses

The QL has a statement for drawing circles. It is CIRCLE, and in its simplest form, it is used as follows, where x,y are the co-ordinates of the circle's centre and r is its radius:

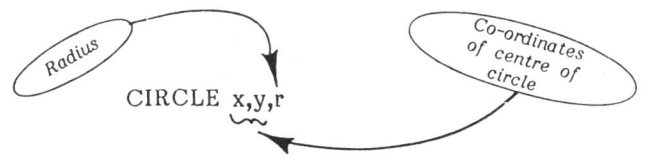

CIRCLE x,y,r

- Radius
- Co-ordinates of centre of circle

The CIRCLE statement can be extended to draw ellipses (ovals). Firstly it requires an additional value for what can be regarded as the amount by which to squash the circle. The technical term is 'eccentricity'. Eccentricity is the ratio of the largest distance across the ellipse (called the major axis) to the smallest distance (called the minor axis). Secondly you must specify the angle at which the major axis should be set. The following is the extended form of the CIRCLE statement for ellipses:

CIRCLE x,y,r,eccentricity,angle

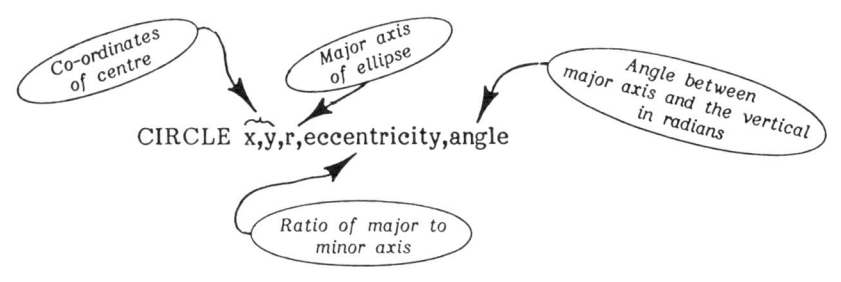

- Co-ordinates of centre
- Major axis of ellipse
- Angle between major axis and the vertical in radians
- Ratio of major to minor axis

Figure 9.5 shows the results of several CIRCLE statements with different parameters.

9.9 Drawing arcs

The last of the graphics drawing statements is for drawing an arc. It is ARC and it draws an arc of specified radius between the two specified points. It is used in the following form:

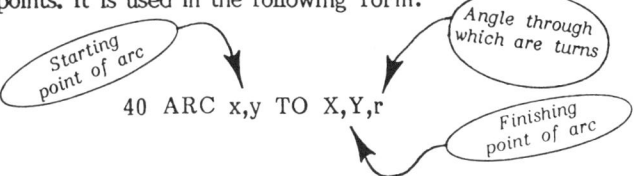

40 ARC x,y TO X,Y,r

- Starting point of arc
- Angle through which arc turns
- Finishing point of arc

CIRCLE 20,80,18

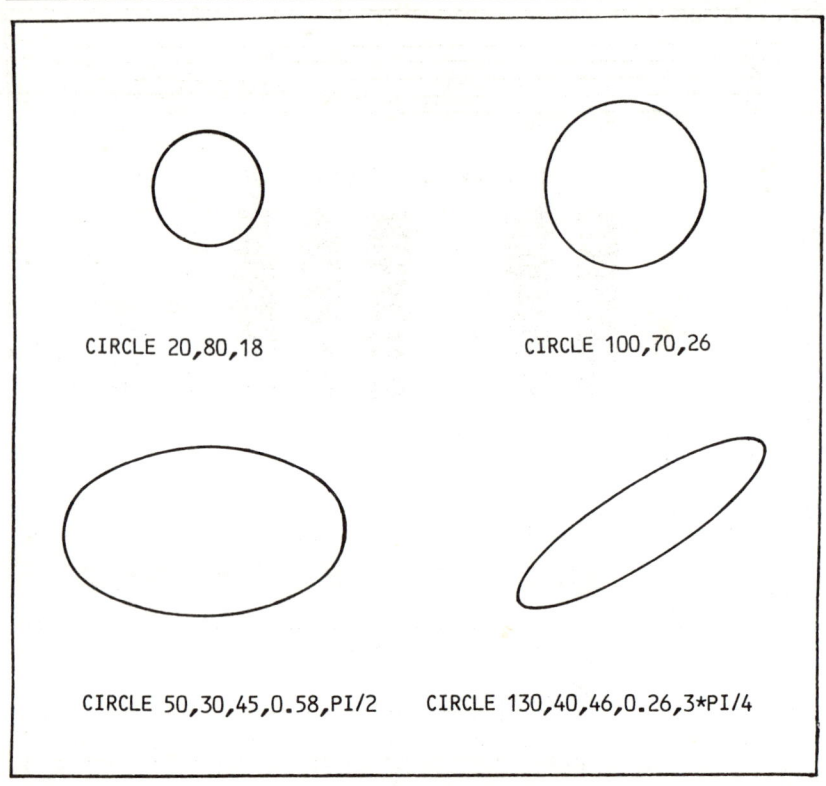

CIRCLE 100,70,26

CIRCLE 50,30,45,0.58,PI/2

CIRCLE 130,40,46,0.26,3*PI/4

Figure 9.5. Some of the ellipses and circles produced by the CIRCLE statement.

The direction in which the arc bows is dictated by the direction in which it is drawn, i.e. by which of the two points comes first in the ARC statement. The arc is always drawn so that it turns towards the left.

9.10 Positioning writing precisely

For most purposes, it is accurate enough to use AT to control where any message is to be printed. However, for programming graphics, there will be times when you will want to position writing more precisely. This will be particularly true for writing titles to graphs and messages along lines of graphics. Fortunately the QL allows you to start printing at a point specified by graphics co-ordinates. The instruction is CURSOR. Its full form is as follows:

9 Beginning Graphics   145

CURSOR x,y,0,0

Graphics co-ordinates

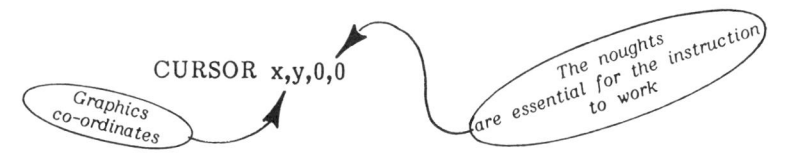

The noughts are essential for the instruction to work

We will wait until the next chapter, which introduces colour, before illustrating what you can do with the graphics cursor.

9.11   Activities

i. See if you can write a program which uses the ellipse-drawing form of the circle statement to produce the display of Figure 9.6. We give a suitable program in Section 9.14.

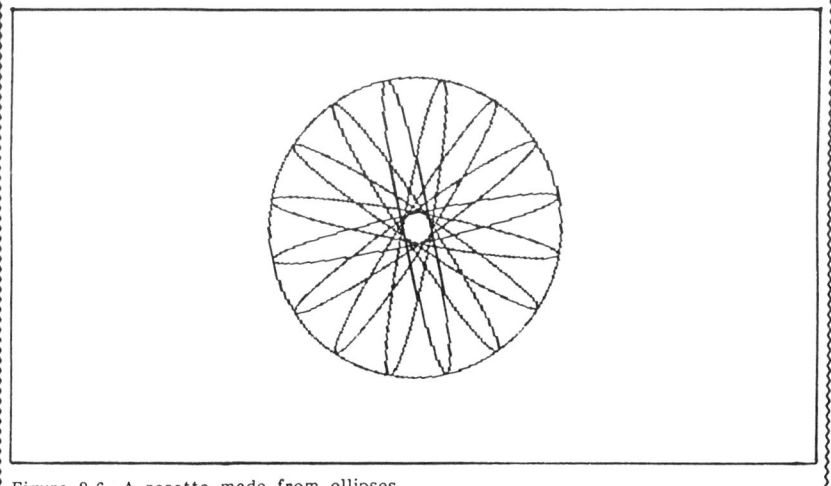

Figure 9.6. A rosette made from ellipses.

9.12   Points to ponder

a. How could a program work out its own optimum scaling so as to keep the graphics on the screen, whatever the values?

9.13   Discussion on the points to ponder

a. The SCALE statement, with an appropriately chosen number, can remove any need to worry about scaling. All you, as programmer, need do is make sure that the maximum range of values your program will try to plot is declared in a SCALE statement. This requires a few program lines to find what the maximum 'y' value is. This could be performed by a set of lines such as the following, which assume that values representing points to be plotted reside in DATA statements at the end of the program:

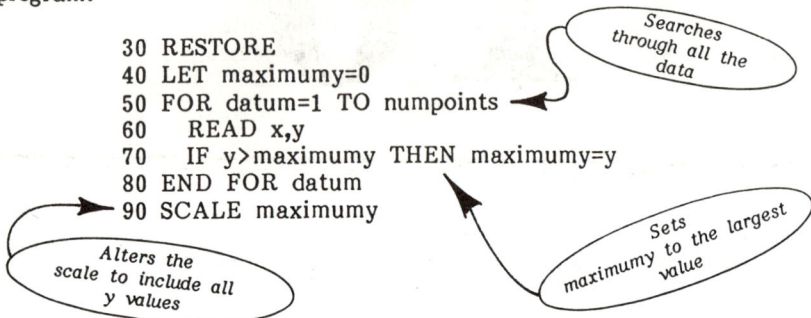

```
30 RESTORE
40 LET maximumy=0
50 FOR datum=1 TO numpoints
60    READ x,y
70    IF y>maximumy THEN maximumy=y
80 END FOR datum
90 SCALE maximumy
```

Searches through all the data

Sets maximumy to the largest value

Alters the scale to include all y values

9.14 Discussion of activities

Activity 9.11i: Here is our version of a program to produce the rosette of Figure 9.6.

```
100 MODE 4
110 CIRCLE 82,50,50
120 FOR angle=0 TO PI*(1-1/16) STEP PI/16
130    CIRCLE 82,50,50,.1,angle
140 END FOR angle
```

10

Introducing colour

10.0 Introduction
10.1 Available colours
10.2 Setting foreground and background colours
10.3 Activities
10.4 Filling with colour
10.5 Activities
10.6 Bordering a window in colour
10.7 Activities
10.8 Mixing colours
10.9 Activities
10.10 An example of colour graphics: a pie chart program
10.11 Activities

10.0 Introduction

Colour livens up any graphics display! It makes the display more attractive and it adds meaning by making features stand out. The QL is particularly good on its colour graphics, and this chapter shows how to capitalize on them. You will of course find it best to have a colour television or monitor, but even with a black and white one, displays should be improved by being in various shades of grey, rather than just black and white.

10.1 Available colours

The QL offers a choice of eight different colours in mode 8 or four colours in mode 4. You will recall that mode 8 gives only 256 pixels across the screen while mode 4 gives 512. Thus the larger number of colours is at the expense of a smaller number of pixels to make up the picture. Many pixels as well as many colours would take up more memory than the QL has available for its screen display.

Table 10.1 gives the colours available in the two modes when you first turn on. It also gives a number, the 'colour number' by which BASIC recognizes each colour. Do notice that the same number can represent more than one colour, depending on mode.

```
MODE 8              MODE 4
(8 colours)         (4 colours)
(256 pixels)        (512 pixels)

0=black             0=black
1=blue              1=black
2=red               2=red
3=magenta           3=red
4=green             4=green
5=cyan              5=green
6=yellow            6=white
7=white             7=white
```

Table 10.1. The colour assignments when a mode is first selected.

10.2 Setting foreground and background colours

When setting the colours of displays, SuperBASIC requires you to distinguish between foreground and background colours.

Foreground colour means the colour of text and graphics. The

10 Introducing Colour

statement for setting it is INK. It has to be used in the following form, where c is the colour number, as given in Table 10.1:

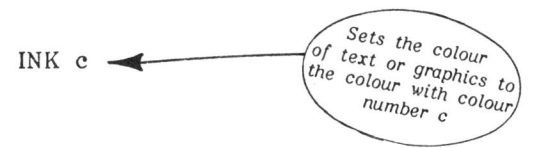

INK c ← (Sets the colour of text or graphics to the colour with colour number c)

There can be as many foreground colours as you wish to program - provided of course that you keep within the allocation of available colours.

In a manner of speaking there can be two background colours. One is the broad, overall background of the window, set by the instruction PAPER. The other is an optional band of background to highlight text characters. Figure 10.1 illustrates the different effects.

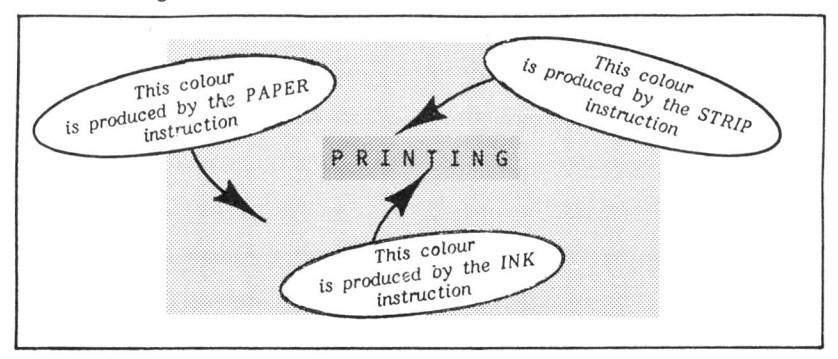

Figure 10.1. The different effects of PAPER and STRIP.

PAPER is used in the following way, where c is the colour number:

PAPER c ← (Sets the broad background to the colour with colour number c)

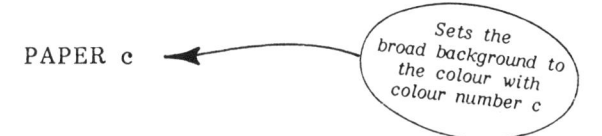

STRIP is used in the following form:

STRIP c ← (Sets a band of colour behind the text to the colour with colour number c)

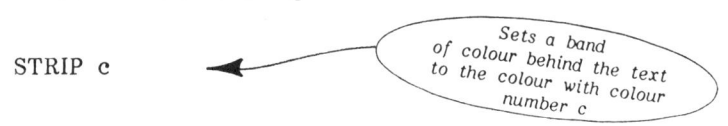

You use STRIP to set the banded background to text after you have used PAPER to set the broad background. By way of illustration, the following lines of program set 8 as the graphics mode, black (colour number 0) for any graphics or writing, magenta (colour number 3) as the overall background colour and green (colour number 4) as the band of background for the text.

```
100 MODE 8
110 INK 0    :REM writing and graphics = black
120 PAPER 3 :REM overall background = magenta
130 CLS
140 STRIP 4 :REM text background = green
150 AT 10,5 :PRINT"Black on green over magenta"
```

Line 100 sets the mode and, in so doing, clears the screen to blue. Line 110 sets the colour of any graphics or text to follow. Line 120 defines the background colour, which only appears on the screen when it is cleared by line 130 or when text is written to the screen.

There are times when it is attractive for writing to be on a transparent background, so as not to block out what is already there. You can turn this effect on with the instruction:

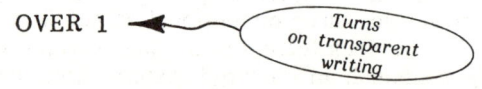

OVER 1 ← *Turns on transparent writing*

To turn it off again, use:

OVER 0 ← *Turns off transparent writing*

10.3 Activities

i. Enter each of the following instructions in the direct mode and note the resulting colour effects.

```
ink 0:print "ink 0"
ink 1:print "ink 1"
ink 2:print "ink 2"
ink 3:print "ink 3"
ink 4:print "ink 4"
ink 5:print "ink 5"
ink 6:print "ink 6"
ink 7:print "ink 7"
```

Keep referring to Table 10.1 to make sure that you can explain the colours of each of the lines of writing. Do you see that the colour numbers affect only the writing which is to follow? They leave previous writing unaltered. With a black and white television, you may need to adjust the contrast to distinguish the various shades of grey which correspond to the colours.

ii. Run the following program to experiment with the various foreground and background colour effects.

```
100 MODE 8:CLS
110 FOR strip_effect=0 TO 7
120   FOR ink_effect=0 TO 7
130     STRIP strip_effect :INK ink_effect
140     PRINT "STRIP = ";strip_effect;", INK = ";
        ink_effect
150     PAUSE 100
160   END FOR ink_effect
170 END FOR strip_effect
```

iii. As an illustration of the use of CURSOR, the program of Listing 10.1 (overleaf) displays attractive, three dimensional effect writing. This is achieved by writing first in black letters to produce a black shadow and then again, slightly displaced, in coloured letters. Run the program. Does it produce the effect you expect?

iv. You may like to modify the program to produce other messages in other colours.

v. Run the following program to see the effects of OVER:

```
100 MODE 8 :PAPER 2 :INK 7 :CLS
110 LINE 20,20 TO 20,80 TO 80,80 TO 80,20 TO 20,20
120 CIRCLE 50,50,30
130 OVER 1
140 AT 5,1 :PRINT "Transparent writing"
150 OVER 0
160 AT 14,4 :PRINT "Normal writing"
```

10.4 Filling with colour

The FILL statement is very useful for attractive colour displays. It colours in a horizontally bounded area between the lines making up any shape (see Figure 10.2).

152   10 Introducing Colour

Screen Display 10.1

Listing 10.1

```
100 PAPER 1
110 OVER 1
120 INK 0
130 CSIZE 3,1
140 CURSOR 44,44,0,0
150 PRINT "Hello in shadow"
160 INK 2
170 CURSOR 45,45,0,0
180 PRINT "Hello in shadow"
190 OVER 0
```

10 Introducing Colour

You use FILL in the following way:

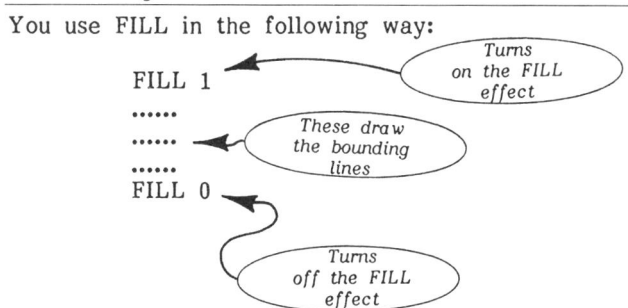

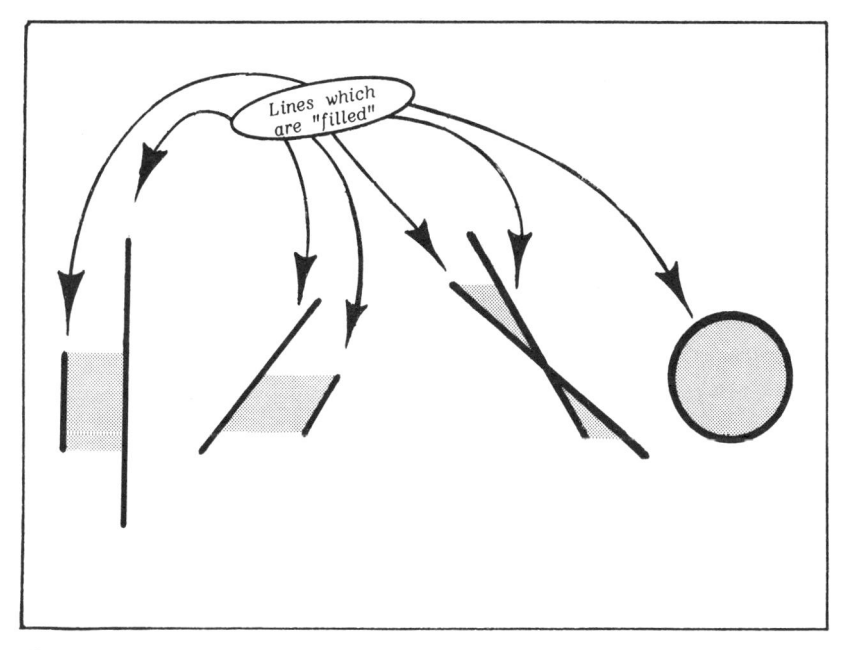

FILL 1 ← *Turns on the FILL effect*

......
...... ← *These draw the bounding lines*
......

FILL 0 ← *Turns off the FILL effect*

Figure 10.2 'FILL's - always bounded by horizontal edges.

10.5 Activities

The program of Listing 10.2 demonstrates what can be done by using colour with the FILL instruction. Run it. The display is different every time. Screen Display 10.2 is an example.

Screen Display 10.2

10.6 Bordering a window in colour

You can place a border round a window in the colour and width of your choice. You use the BORDER statement in the following way:

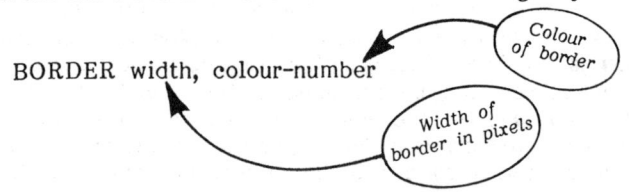

BORDER width, colour-number

Colour of border

Width of border in pixels

10.7 Activities

The following program is an alternative to the one of Section 1.12 which bordered a message with stars, this illustrates the use of the BORDER instruction. It redefines a window for the message and then borders it:

10 Introducing Colour

Listing 10.2

```
100 MODE 8
110 colour=1
120 FOR cir=1 TO 14
130     INK colour
135     FILL 1
140     CIRCLE RND(30 TO 120),RND(10 TO 80),RND(10 TO 40)
145     FILL 0
150     colour=(colour+1) MOD 8
160 END FOR cir
```

```
100 REMark (c) Tony Brain 1984
110 CLS
120 WINDOW 300,100,100,60
130 PAPER 0:CLS
140 BORDER 10,6
150 AT 2,2:PRINT "Welcome to the QL"
160 AT 6,10:PRINT "By Joe John"
```

Run the program to see the effect.

10.8 Mixing colours

It is possible to get more than the eight colours which are normally available. The method is to mix them by placing alternately coloured pixels together. The effect is called 'stippling'. You can use it with any of the normal colour-setting instructions, but three numbers replace the single one that you used for the colour number. The first two represent the colours of the pixels you are mixing and the last (a number btween 0 and 3) dictates how they are to be mixed. For example, the following instruction mixes blue and red:

120 PAPER 1,2,3

The precise effects of the four possible mixes may depend on your television. So we give the following program to illustrate the effects:

```
100 MODE 8 :PAPER 2: INK 7 :CLS
110 AT 1,2 :PRINT"A demonstration of stipple effect"
120 xstart=70 :xsize=90
130 yoff=80 :ystep=20 :ysize=18
140 FOR stipple=0 TO 3
150   INK 7
160   AT 5+stipple*4,0 :PRINT"With ink 3,5,";
      stipple\"i.e. stipple=";stipple
170   INK 3,5,stipple
180   FILL 1
190   LINE xstart,yoff-stipple*ystep TO xstart,
      yoff-stipple*ystep-ysize
200   LINE xstart+xsize,yoff-stipple*ystep TO
      xstart+xsize,yoff-stipple*ystep-ysize
210   FILL 0
220 END FOR stipple
```

10.9 Activities

i. Run the program of the previous section to see the four types of stipple.

ii. To allow you to choose what colours to mix with any type of stipple, run the following program which gives all the combinations of colour and stipple:

```
100 REMark program to show stipple effects
110 REMark (c) Tony Brain 1984
120 MODE 8
130 set_up
140 REPeat loop
150   get_numbers
160   display_effect
170   hold
180   CLS #1:PAPER #2,0:CLS #2
190 END REPeat loop
200 :
210 DEFine PROCedure set_up
220   WINDOW #1,480,125,16,0
230   PAPER #1,0:CLS #1:CSIZE #1,3,1
240   WINDOW #2,480,130,16,125
250   PAPER #2,0:CLS #2:CSIZE #2,3,1:INK #2,0
260 END DEFine set_up
270 :
280 DEFine PROCedure get_numbers
```

10 *Introducing Colour*   *157*

```
290 CLS #0:AT #0,2,4:INPUT #0,"Enter colour
    number (0 to 7) ";colour
300 CLS #0:AT #0,2,4:INPUT #0,"Enter contrast
    number (0 to 7) ";contrast
310 CLS #0:AT #0,2,4:INPUT #0,"Enter stipple
    number (0 to 3) ";stipple
320 END DEFine get_numbers
330 :
340 DEFine PROCedure display_effect
350 CLS #1:INK #1,colour,contrast,stipple
360 AT #1,3,9:PRINT #1,"INK ";colour;",";
    contrast;",";stipple
370 PAPER #2,colour,contrast,stipple:CLS #2
380 AT #2,3,9:PRINT #2,"PAPER ";colour;",";
    contrast;",";stipple
390 END DEFine display_effect
400 :
410 DEFine PROCedure hold
420 PAUSE
430 END DEFine hold
```

iii. The following program demonstrates the complete range of colours that can be obtained by mixing every colour combination. If the MODE is changed to 4 in line 100, the range of colours available in mode 4 can be demonstrated as well.

```
100 MODE 8 :PAPER 0 :INK 7 :CLS
110 stepx=18 :stepy=10
120 xoff=25 :yoff=76
130 xsize=14 :ysize=8
140 CSIZE 3,1 :PRINT"          paper c1,c2,3"
150 CSIZE 0,0 :AT 3,4 :PRINT
    "c2=0   1   2   3   4   5   6   7"
160 FOR col1=0 TO 7
170   INK 7:AT 5+col1*2,0:PRINT "c1=";col1
180   FOR col2=0 TO 7
190     INK col1,col2,3
200     FILL 1
210     LINE col2*stepx+xoff,yoff-col1*stepy TO
            col2*stepx+xoff,yoff-col1*stepy-ysize
220     LINE col2*stepx+xoff+xsize,yoff-col1*stepy TO
            col2*stepx+xoff+xsize,yoff-col1*stepy-ysize
230   END FOR col2
240 END FOR col1
```

iv. It is possible to get the effects of mixing colours and stippling by using a colour number greater than 7. The following program shows the results. It clears the screen to the colour represented in the PAPER statement which forms part of the display:

```
100 REMark display all paper colours
110 REMark (c) Tony Brain 1984
120 setup
130 REPeat show_colours
140    display_colour(colour)
150 END REPeat show_colours
160 STOP
170 :
180 DEFine PROCedure setup
190    WINDOW #2,112,20,200,110:CSIZE #2,2,1:
       PAPER #2,0:CLS #2
200    CLS #0:PRINT #0,"Press 'up arrow' for larger
       number"\"Press 'down arrow' for smaller number"
210    colour=0
220 END DEFine setup
230 :
240 DEFine PROCedure display_colour(c)
250    PAPER #1,c:CLS #1
260    CLS #2:PRINT #2,"PAPER ";c;
270    cd=CODE(INKEY$(-1))
280 IF cd=216 AND colour>0 THEN colour=colour-1
290 IF cd=208 AND colour<254 THEN colour=colour+1
300 END DEFine display_colour
```

10.10 An example of colour graphics: a pie chart program

As an example of the the various graphics statements, we will develop a program for displaying what are called 'pie charts'. A pie chart is a means of showing the relative proportions of anything. For example Figure 10.3 is a pie chart showing the relative areas of England, Northern Ireland, Scotland and Wales.

We will develop the program in two parts. First we will develop a procedure for drawing segments of a pie chart. Then we will put this into a complete program to display a pie chart with the facility to mark one specific segment by allowing it to be displaced from the rest.

First the procedure 'segment' for drawing a single segment. The call requires the following notation:

  x,y is the coordinate of the centre
  sa is the starting angle for the segment
  fa is the finishing angle for the segment
  rds is the radius of the circle.

10 Introducing Colour 159

area of Wales

area of England

area of Scotland

area of Northern Ireland

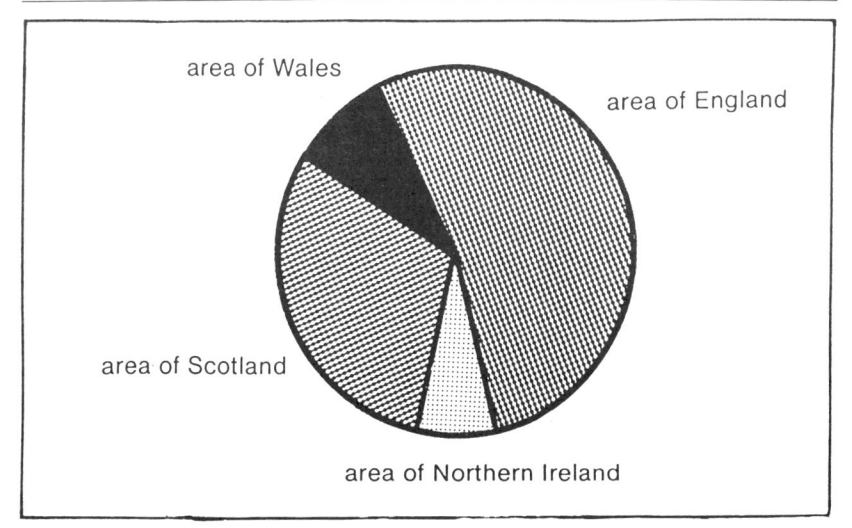

Figure 10.2. An example of a pie chart. It shows the relative sizes of England, Northern Ireland, Scotland and Wales.

The call itself could be a line such as:

    10 segment x,y,sa,fa,rds

Below is a procedure which achieves this:

    400 DEFine PROCedure segment(x,y,sa,fa,rds)
    410 LINE x,y TO x+rds*COS(sa),y+rds*SIN(sa)
    420 LINE x,y TO x+rds*COS(fa),y+rds*SIN(fa)
    430 ARC x+rds*COS(sa),y+rds*SIN(sa),x+rds*COS(fa),
         y+rds*SIN(fa),fa-sa
    440 END DEFine segment

You can check it by entering the procedure definition, followed by a line such as:

    160 segment 50,50,0,PI/2,30.

Line 410 draws one radius from the centre of the circle to the circumference, and line 420 draws the other. Line 430 draws the arc of the circle to join the ends of the radii drawn, by lines 410 and 420.

    To enhance the program and prevent it from being just any old pie chart routine, we decided to add the option of emphasizing one of the segments by moving it out from the rest. The following program achieves

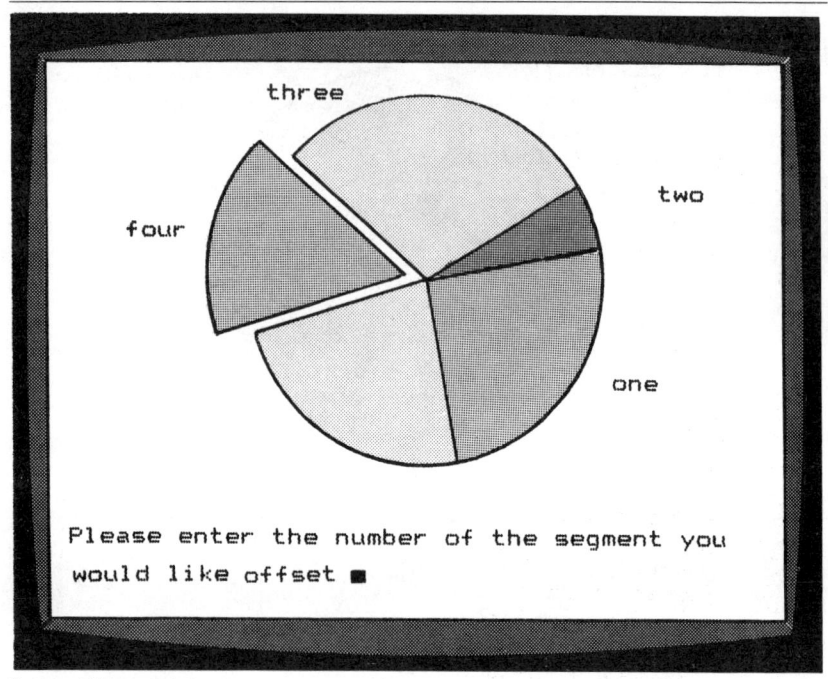

Screen Display 10.3

all this. It starts by selecting mode 4 to give the best definition for the arc-drawing. It also sets a suitable size of writing. Then come DATA statements in lines 120 and 130 which hold the sizes and labels for the segments of the pie chart. You can edit in your own data. Line 120 specifies how many segments are to be drawn, and line 130 holds the labels and relative sizes for the segments. The program scales the size of each segment relative to the aggregate. So there is no need to be concerned about the units of size, provided they are all the same.

Up to line 210 the data is being read into the arrays t$() for the labels and v() for the segment sizes (see Chapter 11). The REPEAT loop between lines 240 and 350 then represents the main program loop, drawing up one pie chart for each execution. The FOR ... END FOR loop between lines 270 and 310 calls upon 'segment' for each of the segments in turn, to draw the complete pie chart. This procedure is a slightly extended version of the earlier one: lines 400 and 410 provide for the offset of one of the segments and line 470 prints a label for each segment at the position of the graphics cursor set by line 460. With two extra tasks to perform, 'segment' has to have two extra parameters in its call: the offset for the segment (of) and the label for the segment m$.

Listing 10.3 gives the complete program for drawing the pie chart. Screen Display 10.3 illustrates its effect.

Listing 10.3

```
100 REMark (c) Andrew Cryer 1984
110 PAPER 0 : MODE 4 :CSIZE 1,1 :CSIZE #0,1,1
120 DATA 5
130 DATA "one",1,"two",2,"three",3,"four",4,"five",5
140 RESTORE 120
150 READ num
160 tot=0
170 DIM t$(num,5),v(num)
180 FOR i=1 TO num
190    READ t$(i),v(i)
200    tot=tot+v(i)
210 END FOR i
220 n=0:q=0
230 :
240 REPeat display
250    CLS
260    gone=0
270    FOR i=1 TO num
280       INK (1+ i MOD 3)*2
290       segment 76,52,2*PI*gone/tot,2*PI*
              (gone+v(i))/tot,q*(n=i),30,t$(i)
300       gone=gone+v(i)
310    END FOR i
320    CLS #0
330    INPUT #0,"Please enter the number of the segment
              you would like   offset ";n
340    q=10 :REMark The offset for the segment
350 END REPeat display
360 :
370 DEFine PROCedure segment(x,y,sa,fa,of,rds,m$)
380    LOCal i,incs,loop
390    FILL 1
400    x=x+of*COS((fa+sa)/2)
410    y=y+of*SIN((fa+sa)/2)
420    LINE x,y TO x+rds*COS(sa),y+rds*SIN(sa)
430    LINE x,y TO x+rds*COS(fa),y+rds*SIN(fa)
440    ARC x+rds*COS(sa),y+rds*SIN(sa) TO
              x+rds*COS(fa),y+rds*SIN(fa),fa-sa
450    FILL 0
460    CURSOR x+(rds+5)*COS((fa+sa)/2)-(LEN(m$)*4+2)*
              (COS((fa+sa)/2)<0),y+(rds+5)*SIN((fa+sa)/2),0,0
470    OVER 1 :PRINT m$
480 END DEFine segment
```

10.11 Activities

i. Try loading and running the pie chart program. Experiment with the offset for any of the segments. The units are the screen co-ordinates and a value of 10 seems generally suitable.

ii. Try looking at your outgoing expenses and divide the money up into about six categories. Enter the amounts for each as the size of the segments, with appropriate strings to describe each entry. Run the program and see how the money goes. Does this make you think about the importance of the various categories?

11

Handling tables

11.0 Introduction
11.1 Array variables
11.2 Arrays of one dimension
11.3 Introducing an array variable into a program
11.4 Putting data into an array
11.5 Manipulations using arrays
11.6 Activities
11.7 Arrays of two dimensions
11.8 Activities
11.9 Points to ponder
11.10 Discussion on the points to ponder
11.11 Discussion of activities

11.0 Introduction

Large amounts of information, such as numbers or names, are often best presented in the form of tables of various kinds. Fortunately SuperBASIC has a special facility for handling tables. It uses what is called an 'array'. This chapter introduces the idea of arrays and explains how to use them in programming.

11.1 Array variables

An array allows a table to be referred to and manipulated by a single name. This is very useful indeed! Without it, the manipulation would be very complex, because separate variables would be required for each item in the table. We can illustrate the idea by referring to the tabular data of Table 11.1, which is a monthly record of some household accounts.

month	house keeping	school dinner +pocket money	sundry bills	savings
1	80	24	102	0
2	80	24	20	20
3	80	24	80	0
4	80	24	43	10
5	100	24	13	90
6	120	24	13	0
7	120	26	64	55
8	120	10	20	0
9	120	26	73	50
10	120	26	41	50
11	120	26	77	0
12	120	26	0	80

Table 11.1

You might be tempted to handle the numbers in the table with separate variables for each – but this would be of little help if you wanted to ask the computer to sort the information in any way. What is needed is some general name which will refer to the table as a whole. BASIC provides one in what is called an 'array variable'. This is a variable which stores not just one number or string but a whole table. For example, to store the data in Table 11.1, you could use an array variable with the general name 'accounts'. As we will shortly describe in some detail, each item is referred to by its position in the table.

11.2 Arrays of one dimension

We shall begin our explanation of arrays by considering a table in the form of just one column. This is equivalent to a list and is called an array of one dimension. We shall consider the list of Table 11.2. It contains a list of prices, which incidentally refer to bottles of wine.

price
2.65
3.83
3.86
7.82
1.94
2.33
4.76

Table 11.2

With such a simple list and for some purposes, you could get away with handling the prices of the wines with variables such as the name of the wine: 'Reisling', 'Sekt' etc. This would be of little help for anything more complex. The answer is to use an 'array variable'. This is like any other variable in that it can be given a name, but it is different in that it refers to a whole list. So a general name like 'wine' is appropriate. In order to specify the list item that the variable is referring to, a number has to be written after the name. We can illustrate with the array variable 'wine' for each item, as follows:

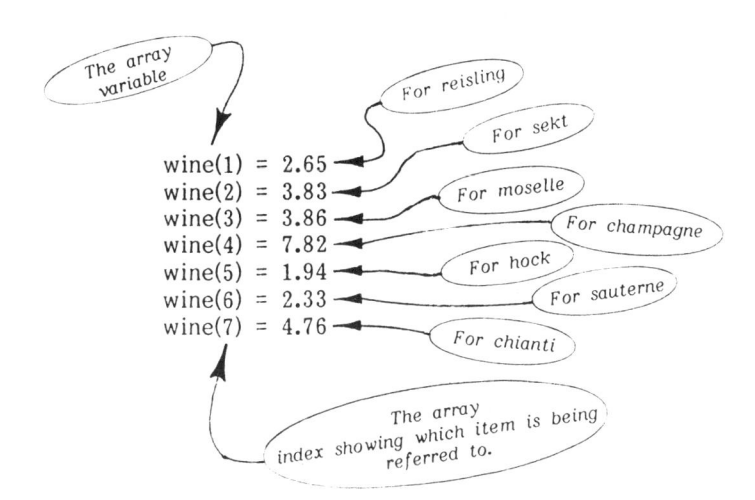

```
                                For reisling
The array variable
                                        For sekt
        wine(1) = 2.65
        wine(2) = 3.83          For moselle
        wine(3) = 3.86
        wine(4) = 7.82                  For champagne
        wine(5) = 1.94          For hock
        wine(6) = 2.33
        wine(7) = 4.76                  For sauterne
                                For chianti

              The array index showing which item is being referred to.
```

There are various ways in which you can now manipulate the information. Suppose, for example, you want to print out the price of the Moselle. You could do it with the following two lines of program:

```
150 n=3
160 PRINT wine(n)
```

or

```
150 Moselle=3
160 PRINT wine(Moselle)
```

You could print out the whole list of prices with either of the following:

```
170 FOR n=1 TO 7
180    PRINT wine(n)
190 END FOR n
```

or

```
170 FOR n=1 TO 7 :PRINT wine(n)
```

11.3 Introducing an array variable into a program

It is essential to tell the QL that the program is going to use tabular information in the form of an array. This requires a line of the form:

```
100 DIM wine(7)
```

This statement informs the QL of several things: that the program is going to make use of an array variable; that its name is to be 'wine'; and that there will be seven items in the list. (See the Points to Ponder in Section 11.9).

If the array is to hold strings rather than numbers, the array name must end with a dollar symbol $. For example an array to hold the names of the wines might be called 'wine$'. It is also important to give the QL advance warning of the maximum length of string that it is going to have to store. There are 7 wines in the list with a maximum of 9 letters in the longest name which is 'Champagne'. A line like the following informs the QL of the size of this array:

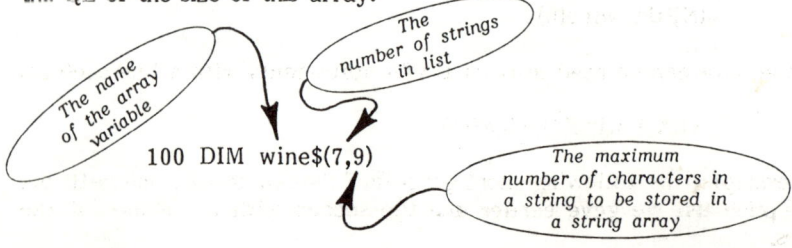

```
100 DIM wine$(7,9)
```

- The name of the array variable
- The number of strings in list
- The maximum number of characters in a string to be stored in a string array

11 Handling Tables

This operation of informing the QL of the size and name of an array is called 'dimensioning' the array. If several arrays are to be used in the same program, they can all be dimensioned with a single program line such as the following:

        100 DIM salary(60),wine(7),wine$(7,9)

This dimensions the arrays

It is just as simple to use an array which holds strings as it is to use one which holds numbers. For example, you can list the names of the wines using a simple loop, such as the following:

        100 FOR n=1 TO 7
        110   PRINT wine$(n)
        120 END FOR n

This could be extended to give a list of wines and their prices in the following way:

        100 PRINT" Price   Wine"\\
        110 FOR n=1 TO 7
        120   PRINT wine(n),wine$(n)
        130 END FOR n

11.4 Putting data into an array

You can put the data into an array in just the same way as you would give an ordinary variable a value in a program, i.e. by using a LET statement of the following form:

    wine$(5)="Hock"

Alternatively you can use an INPUT statement such as:

    INPUT wine(n)

Or the data can be read in from DATA statements with a line such as:

    READ wine(4),wine$(4)

For example, the following short program fills two arrays, one with the wine price list we gave earlier and the second with the names of the wines.

```
100 DIM  wine(7),wine$(7,9)
110 RESTORE 1000
120 FOR n = 1 TO 7
130    READ wine$(n),wine(n)
140 END FOR n
150 :
1000 DATA  "Reisling",2.65,"Sekt",3.83,"Moselle",3.86
1010 DATA  "Champagne",7.82,"Hock",1.94,"Sauterne",2.33
1020 DATA  "Chianti",4.76
```

As you will remember, RESTORE (as in line 110) sets where the next READ statement should obtain its data.

11.5 Manipulations using arrays

Once the program has read the data into the array, you can easily get the QL to manipulate it. For example, you could print it out in reverse order using the following three lines:

```
100 FOR i=7 TO 1 STEP -1
110    PRINT wine$(i)
120 END FOR i
```

Another possible manipulation would be to swop round the order of two items. For example, the following lines of program swop item 1 for item 4, i.e. Reisling for Champagne in the list of names:

```
300 r$ = wine$(1)
310 wine$(1) = wine$(4)
320 wine$(4) = r$
```

Actually this operation would be best done in a procedure if it needs to be done often. Then the main program would be easier to understand. The procedure definition could be:

```
100 DEFine PROCedure swop(a$,b$)
110    LOCal  r$
120    r$=a$ :a$=b$ :b$=r$
130 END DEFine swop
```

The LOCal of line 110 reserves the variable r$ specially for this procedure. Consequently if r$ is used elsewhere in the program, its value will not be altered by the procedure. The procedure will save the previous value of r$ and return it when it has finished using the variable.

The following additional line would swop the second name in the list with the third:

11 Handling Tables

120 swop wine$(2),wine$(3)

We shall now illustrate how you may sort an array into alphabetical order, using the wine array as an example. As you saw in Section 6.2, the following comparison will be true if a$ comes earlier in the alphabet than b$:

IF a$<b$ THEN ...

You can make similar comparisons between two items in the array. If they are in alphabetical order and the value of item j is less than that of item k, the following comparison is never true and no swopping will occur:

400 IF wine$(j) > wine$(k) THEN swop wine$(j),wine$(k)

If an alphabetically-earlier item is found later in the list, there has to be a swop of the two items. A sort called the 'selection sort' uses just this idea. In the selection sort the QL is programmed systematically to compare the first item in the array with every other one. Where it finds one earlier in the alphabet than the first, it swops them. When it has been through the list just once, the first item must be the first in the alphabet for the entire list. The process is then repeated starting at the second item in the list. This done, the first two items are in alphabetical order. With sufficient repetitions of the process, the alphabetical sorting is complete. Although this may seem a very tedious way of operating, a computer is ideally suited to it.

The following program lines achieve the systematic comparison of a selection sort for the array containing the names of the wines:

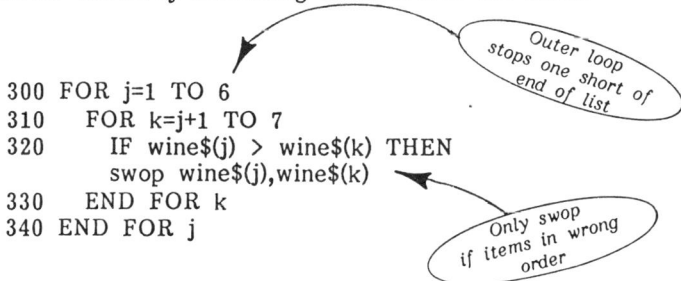

```
300 FOR j=1 TO 6
310    FOR k=j+1 TO 7
320       IF wine$(j) > wine$(k) THEN
              swop wine$(j),wine$(k)
330    END FOR k
340 END FOR j
```

Outer loop stops one short of end of list

Only swop if items in wrong order

In you wanted to keep the prices of the wines in one array and the names in another, both with the same order, it would be necessary to alter the procedure 'swop' to make it swop corresponding items in both arrays.

Although we have shown just three examples of how data within an array can be manipulated, there are many more ways. Items can be added to, or deleted from the list, under control of the program. Also a list can be sorted into numerical or any other order.

```
This program sorts and prints your
numbers in ascending order.

How many numbers are to be sorted?
(There must be more than two.) 4

    What is your first number? 1
    What is your next number? 99
    What is your next number? 33
    What is your next number? 4

    These are your numbers in order:
1
4
33
99
```

Screen Display 11.1

11.6 Activities

i. The program of Listing 11.1 asks a person to type in a list of numbers. It then sorts them with a selection sort and prints them as a list in ascending order, as shown in Screen Display 11.1. Run the program and see that it operates as you would expect. Then modify it to do the same operation with strings.

ii. Can you think of a method using two arrays, one numerical and the other string, for sorting a connected double list such as the following, first into alphabetical order and then into numerical order?

          3.52 Reisling
          2.85 Sekt
          3.25 Moselle
          8.95 Champagne
          4.25 Hock
          2.95 Sauterne
          3.99 Chianti

Listing 11.1

```
100 MODE 8 :CLS
110 get_how_many_numbers
120 DIM n(num)
130 get_list_of_numbers
140 sort_into_order
150 display_sorted_list
160 STOP
170 :
180 DEFine PROCedure get_how_many_numbers
190   AT 5,2:PRINT "This program sorts and prints your"
200   AT 7,2:PRINT "numbers in ascending order."
210   AT 11,2:PRINT "How many numbers are to be sorted?"
220   REPeat ask:AT 12,2:INPUT "(There must be more than
      two)";num:IF num>2 THEN EXIT ask
230 END DEFine get_how_many_numbers
240 :
250 DEFine PROCedure get_list_of_numbers
260   INPUT \\"   What is your first number? ";n(1)
270   FOR j=2 TO num
280     INPUT"   What is your next number? ";n(j)
290   END FOR j
300 END DEFine get_list_of_numbers
310 :
320 DEFine PROCedure sort_into_order
330   FOR j=1 TO num-1
340     FOR k=j+1 TO num
350       IF n(j) > n(k) THEN swop j,k
360     END FOR k
370   END FOR j
380 END DEFine sort_into_order
390 :
400 DEFine PROCedure display_sorted_list
410   PRINT \"   These are your numbers in order:"\
420   FOR j=1 TO num:PRINT n(j)
430 END DEFine display_sorted_list
440 :
450 DEFine PROCedure swop(j,k)
460   LOCal r
470   r=n(j) :n(j)=n(k) :n(k)=r
480 END DEFine swop
```

iii. Try writing such a program and get it to ask whether the sort should be numerical or alphabetical. Get it to print out the list when the sort is complete, as illustrated in Screen Display 11.2 (towards the end of this chapter). We give a suitable program in Listing 11.2, which we discuss in Section 11.11 - although we hope you will develop one of your own.)

11.7 Arrays of two dimensions

We shall now think about using arrays to process a table of more than one column, taking Table 11.1 of Section 11.1 as an example. It is a monthly record of some household accounts. If you wanted to write a program to process its information, one way would be by storing the accounts in a number of arrays, one for each column of figures. Each would be an example of a 'one dimensional array' because it would be characterized by requiring only one variable to reference any item in the column.

You can, however, store all the table in a single array, and, by so doing, gain a great deal of freedom in ease of manipulation. The principle relies on the fact that any item in the table is uniquely specified in terms of its line and column, i.e. by just two numbers. These two numbers specify the item that you, or the program, want to refer to in the array. For example the number in the third line and second coloumn of Table 11.1 is 80. With the whole table stored in the array variable 'accounts', the following line would print this number:

    140 PRINT accounts(3,2)

In a program, it would more probably be written as:

    140 PRINT accounts(line,column)

Just as with one-dimensional arrays, the array has to be declared so that the QL sets aside sufficient storage space. The following line would be suitable:

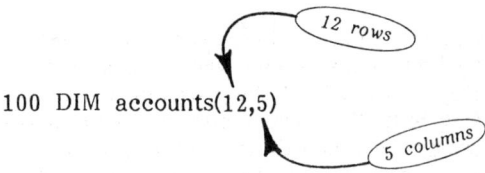

    100 DIM accounts(12,5)   *(12 rows, 5 columns)*

If the array is for strings, the DIM statement is almost identical, except that its name must end with $ and that you must indicate the number of characters in the longest string with the last number inside the brackets. Thus the following DIM statement dimensions a string array 'accounts$' with the same dimensions as the numerical array 'accounts':

11 Handling Tables

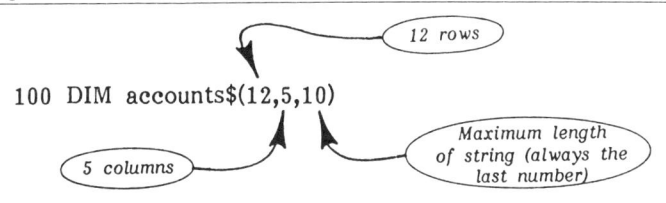

```
              ┌─────── 12 rows ───┐
              ↓
  100 DIM accounts$(12,5,10)
              ↑   ↑
              │   └──── Maximum length
   5 columns ─┘         of string (always the
                        last number)
```

Lines of the following form read the accounts data from a set of DATA statements:

```
120 FOR line=1 TO 12
130   FOR column=1 TO 5
140     READ accounts(line,column)
150   END FOR column
160 END FOR line
```

To make editing and checking easier, the data is best arranged with an order and appearance which corresponds to the original table. So, for our example, we shall arrange the data in the following form:

```
1000 DATA  1, 80, 24,102,  0
1010 DATA  2, 80, 24, 20, 20
1020 DATA  3, 80, 24, 80,  0
1030 DATA  4, 80, 24, 43, 10
     ........
     ........
```

It would be just as simple to read the data a whole column at a time. Then references to line and column would have to be swopped round in the program and the data would have to be rearranged accordingly.

11.8 Activities

i. Store the accounts information of the previous section (or your own accounts data) in DATA statements and write a program to read the numbers from them into the array. Get the program to print out a list of the sundry bills starting with the lowest and going on to the highest, together with the corresponding month and savings, as shown in Screen Display 11.3 (towards the end of this chapter). Listing 11.3 is suitable, although we hope you will develop your own. You may like to compare the two. (We discuss our version in Section 11.11. Which is shorter, neater or faster? How important are these differences for you?)

Run the program, either yours or ours.

```
A PROGRAM TO DEMONSTRATE SORTING

There is a list of 7 wines stored in
the computer. This program will print
the list either alphabetically or in
price order.

Enter 'a' for an alphabetical sort or
'p' for a sort by price a

Champagne  £8.95
Chianti    £3.99
Hock       £4.25
Moselle    £3.25
Reisling   £3.52
Sauterne   £2.95
Sekt       £2.85
```

Screen Display 11.2

11 Handling Tables

Listing 11.2

```
100 MODE 8
110 CLS
120 PRINT \\\" A PROGRAM TO DEMONSTRATE SORTING"
130 read_wine_details
140 PRINT \\"There is a list of ";number;
    " wines stored in"
150 PRINT "the computer. This program will print"
160 PRINT "the list either alphabetically or in"
170 PRINT "price order."
180 REPeat get_sort
190   PRINT \"Enter 'a' for an alphabetical sort or"
200   INPUT"'p' for a sort by price ";ans$
210   IF ans$ INSTR "ap" THEN EXIT get_sort
220 END REPeat get_sort
230 sort_into_order
240 display_sorted_wine_list
250 STOP
260 :
270 DEFine PROCedure read_wine_details
280   RESTORE
290   READ number
300   DIM cost(number),wine$(number,9)
310   FOR j=1 TO number :READ cost(j),wine$(j)
320 END DEFine read_wine_details
330 :
340 DEFine PROCedure sort_into_order
350   FOR j=1 TO number-1
360     FOR k=j+1 TO number
370       IF ans$="p" AND cost(j) > cost(k) THEN
              swop cost(j),cost(k),wine$(j),wine$(k)
380       IF ans$="a" AND wine$(j) > wine$(k) THEN
              swop cost(j),cost(k),wine$(j),wine$(k)
390     END FOR k
400   END FOR j
410 END DEFine sort_into_order
420 :
430 DEFine PROCedure swop(a,b,c$,d$)
440   LOCal r,r$
450   r=a:r$=c$
460   a=b:b=r
470   c$=d$:d$=r$
```
                                                P.T.O.

```
Listing 11.2 continued

480 END DEFine swop
490 :
500 DEFine PROCedure display_sorted_wine_list
510   PRINT \\
520   FOR j=1 TO number
530     PRINT wine$(j);" '";cost(j)
540   END FOR j
550 END DEFine display_sorted_wine_list
560 :
570 DATA 7
580 DATA 3.52,"Reisling  "
590 DATA 2.85,"Sekt      "
600 DATA 3.25,"Moselle   "
610 DATA 8.95,"Champagne"
620 DATA 4.25,"Hock      "
630 DATA 2.95,"Sauterne "
640 DATA 3.99,"Chianti   "
```

ii. Now write a program using graphics mode 8 to display the sundry bills as a histogram with the months horizontally across the screen and the sundry bills as the vertical columns (see Screen Display 11.4 at the end of this chapter). We discuss our version in Section 11.11 (see Listing 11.4).

iii. Once your program is working correctly, add a routine to draw a line, joining points representing the savings for each month. Use different colours for the sundry bills and savings. (We give a version in Section 11.11. It is Listing 11.5.)

11.9 Points to ponder

a. When computers count, they start from zero, i.e. 0, 1, 2, 3, etc. So how many items are there in a list when the computer has counted to 7?

b. In Section 11.3 we dimensioned an array for a list of 7 items by means of DIM wine(7). This was so that the number in the list would correspond to the number in the DIM statement. How many items does the array actually hold?

11.10 Discussion on the points to ponder

a. 8.

b. 8. All arrays start at zero. If we had been short of memory, we could have saved space by using DIM wine$(6) - but this might have been confusing.

11.11 Discussion of activities

Activity 11.6iii: We propose the program of Listing 11.2. It reads a list of numbers and names into two arrays and asks whether the printout should be in numerical or alphabetical order. It sorts the arrays accordingly and, as you can see from Screen Display 11.2, prints out the newly ordered list. The numerical sort, which comes first, has been kept entirely separate from the alphabetical one. You will probably be able to think of alternatives.

Activity 11.8i: The program of Listing 11.3 reads in sundry bill amounts stored in DATA statements and sorts into order of increasing size. As you can see from Screen Display 11.3 (overleaf), it then prints the amount together with the month in which it occurred and the savings during that month. Note the use of a special procedure for swopping the contents of the accounts array around if they are found in the wrong order.

Activity 11.8ii: As you can see from Screen Display 11.4, the program of Listing 11.4 (at the end of this chapter) displays the sundry bills as a histogram for each month for the year.

Activity 11.8iii: Listing 11.5 is similar to that of Listing 11.4 and there is an additional routine which draws a black line joining the savings for each month. You can see the effect in Screen Display 11.5 (at the end of this chapter).

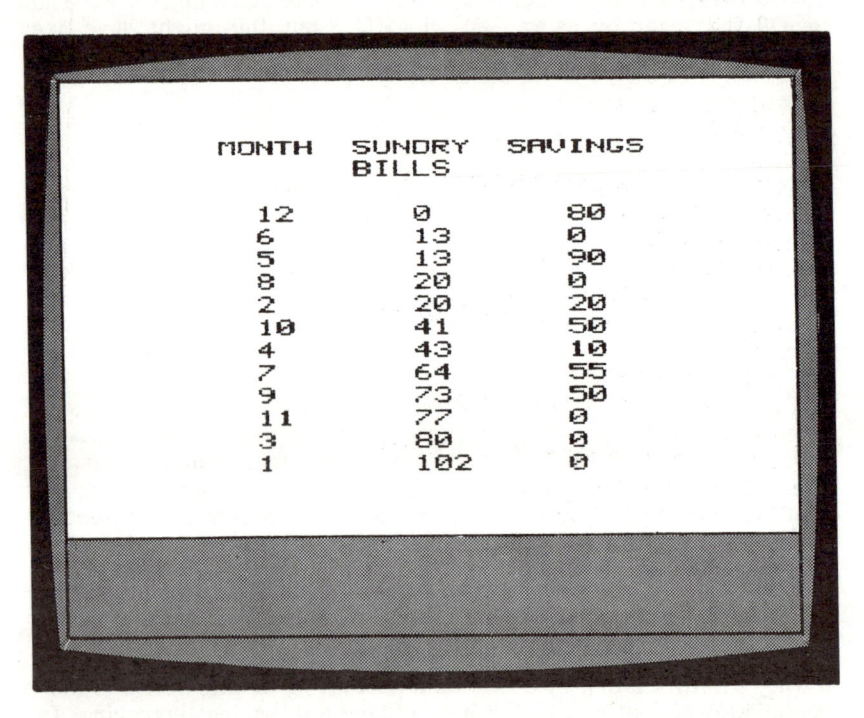

```
MONTH    SUNDRY    SAVINGS
         BILLS
  12       0         80
   6      13          0
   5      13         90
   8      20          0
   2      20         20
  10      41         50
   4      43         10
   7      64         55
   9      73         50
  11      77          0
   3      80          0
   1     102          0
```

Screen Display 11.3

11 Handling Tables 179

Listing 11.3

```
100 MODE 8
110 CLS
120 read_accounts
130 sort_into_order
140 display_accounts
150 STOP
160 :
170 DEFine PROCedure read_accounts
180   DIM accounts(12,5)
190   RESTORE
200   FOR month=1 TO 12
210     FOR column=1 TO 5
220       READ accounts(month,column)
230     END FOR column
240   END FOR month
250 END DEFine read_accounts
260 :
270 DEFine PROCedure sort_into_order
280   sundrybills=4
290   FOR month=1 TO 11
295     PRINT "*";
300     FOR later=month+1 TO 12
310       IF accounts(month,sundrybills)>accounts(later,
              sundrybills) THEN
320         swop month,later
330       END IF
340     END FOR later
350   END FOR month
360 END DEFine sort_into_order
370 :
380 DEFine PROCedure swop(a,b)
390   LOCal r,column
400   FOR column=1 TO 5
410     r=accounts(month,column)
420     accounts(month,column)=accounts(later,column)
430     accounts(later,column)=r
440   END FOR column
450 END DEFine swop
460 :
470 DEFine PROCedure display_accounts
475   CLS                                    P.T.O.
```

Listing 11.3 continued

```
480 AT 3,6:PRINT "MONTH  SUNDRY  SAVINGS"\
490 AT 4,13:PRINT "BILLS"
500 savings=5
510 mth=1
520 FOR month=1 TO 12
530   AT month+5,8:PRINT accounts(month,mth),
      accounts(month,sundrybills),accounts(month,savings)
540 END FOR month
550 END DEFine display_accounts
560 :
570 DATA  1, 80, 24,102,0
580 DATA  2, 80, 24, 20,20
590 DATA  3, 80, 24, 80,0
600 DATA  4, 80, 24, 43,10
610 DATA  5,100, 24, 13,90
620 DATA  6,120, 24, 13,0
630 DATA  7,120, 26, 64,55
640 DATA  8,120, 10, 20,0
650 DATA  9,120, 26, 73,50
660 DATA 10,120, 26, 41,50
670 DATA 11,120, 26, 77,0
680 DATA 12,120, 26,  0,80
```

11 Handling Tables

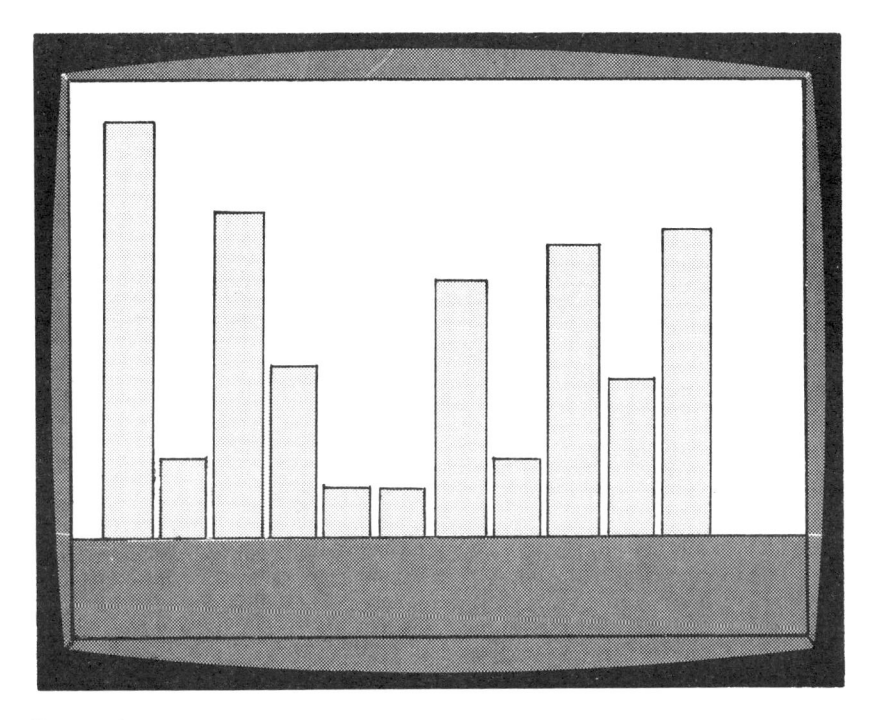

Screen Display 11.4

```
Listing 11.4

100 SCALE 110,0,0
110 REMark A program to draw a histogram
120 REMark showing the sundry bills each month
130 MODE 8 :PAPER 1 :INK 4 :CLS
140 read_accounts
150 sundrybills=4
160 draw_histogram sundrybills
170 STOP
180 :
190 DEFine PROCedure read_accounts
200   DIM accounts(12,5)
210   RESTORE
220   FOR month=1 TO 12
230     FOR column=1 TO 5
240       READ accounts(month,column)
250     END FOR column
260   END FOR month
270 END DEFine read_accounts
280 :
290 DEFine PROCedure draw_histogram(c)
300   FOR month=1 TO 12
310     FILL 1
320     LINE month*14,0 TO  month*14,accounts(month,c)
330     LINE month*14+12,0 TO month*14+12,accounts(month,c)
340   END FOR month
350   FILL 0
360 END DEFine draw_histogram
370 :
380 DATA  1, 80, 24,102,0
390 DATA  2, 80, 24, 20,20
400 DATA  3, 80, 24, 80,0
410 DATA  4, 80, 24, 43,10
420 DATA  5,100, 24, 13,90
430 DATA  6,120, 24, 13,0
440 DATA  7,120, 26, 64,55
450 DATA  8,120, 10, 20,0
460 DATA  9,120, 26, 73,50
470 DATA 10,120, 26, 41,50
480 DATA 11,120, 26, 77,0
490 DATA 12,120, 26,  0,80
```

11 Handling Tables 183

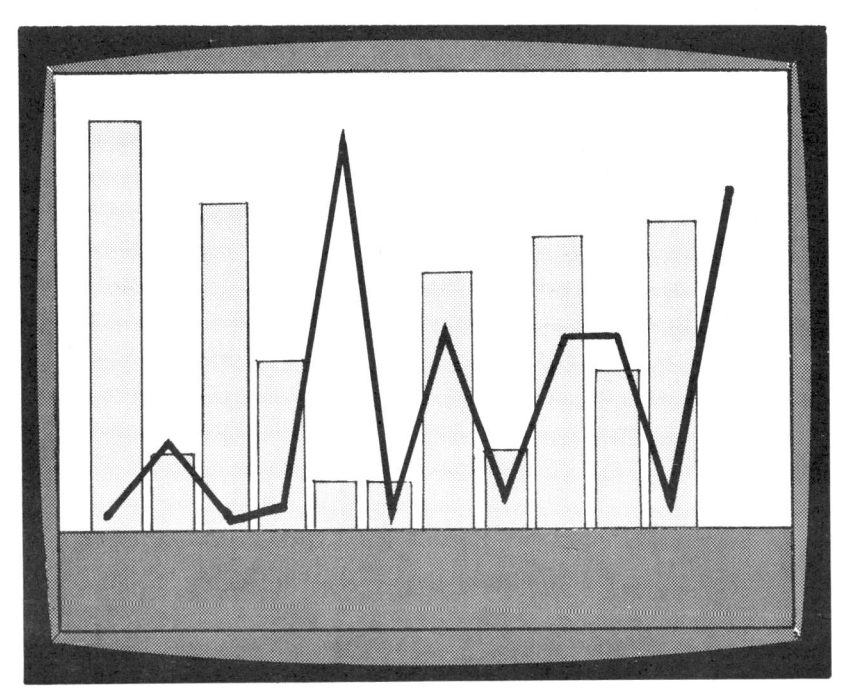

Screen Display 11.5

Listing 11.5

```
100 SCALE 110,0,0
110 REMark A program to draw a histogram
120 REMark showing the sundry bills each month
130 MODE 8 :PAPER 1 :INK 6 :CLS
140 read_accounts
150 sundrybills=4
160 savings=5
170 draw_histogram sundrybills
180 draw_line_savings savings
190 STOP
200 :
210 DEFine PROCedure read_accounts
220   DIM accounts(12,5)
230   RESTORE
240   FOR month=1 TO 12
250     FOR column=1 TO 5
260       READ accounts(month,column)
270     END FOR column
280   END FOR month
290 END DEFine read_accounts
300 :
310 DEFine PROCedure draw_histogram(c)
320   FOR month=1 TO 12
330     FILL 1
340     LINE month*14,0 TO  month*14,accounts(month,c)
350     LINE month*14+12,0 TO month*14+12,accounts(month,c)
360   END FOR month
370   FILL 0
380 END DEFine draw_histogram
390 :
400 DEFine PROCedure draw_line_savings(c)
410   prev_x=0:prev_y=0
420   INK 2
430   FOR month=1 TO 12
440       LINE prev_x,prev_y TO month*14+6,accounts(month,c)
450       prev_x=month*14+6
460       prev_y=accounts(month,c)
470     END FOR month
480 END DEFine draw_line_savings
490 :
500 DATA  1, 80, 24,102,0
```

P.T.O.

Listing 11.5 continued

```
510 DATA  2, 80, 24, 20,20
520 DATA  3, 80, 24, 80,0
530 DATA  4, 80, 24, 43,10
540 DATA  5,100, 24, 13,90
550 DATA  6,120, 24, 13,0
560 DATA  7,120, 26, 64,55
570 DATA  8,120, 10, 20,0
580 DATA  9,120, 26, 73,50
590 DATA 10,120, 26, 41,50
600 DATA 11,120, 26, 77,0
610 DATA 12,120, 26,  0,80
```

12

Functions

- 12.0 Introduction
- 12.1 Built-in functions
- 12.2 Activities
- 12.3 User-defined functions
- 12.4 Recursion
- 12.5 Activities
- 12.6 Points to ponder
- 12.7 Discussion on the points to ponder
- 12.8 Discussion of activities

12.0 Introduction

You are probably familiar with functions from pocket calculators. Some examples are: square root, log, sine, tangent and cosine.

Most of the common functions are incorporated into SuperBASIC. For example, if you want the square root of a number, there is a BASIC term SQRT which the QL recognizes and can respond to immediately. We shall call such functions .built-in. functions. If there is no built-in function for what you want, SuperBASIC allows you to define it for yourself. We shall call these functions .user-defined. functions. This chapter is concerned with both built-in and user-defined functions.

12.1 Built-in functions

With built-in functions BASIC can work out a value for the function in terms of the value which you assign to a variable. For example, the following program line evaluates the SQRT (square root) function: it prints 3 in response to your 9.

        120 PRINT SQRT(9)   *A built-in function to evaluate a square root*

The function is said to have 'returned' the value of 3.

If you look at either the User Guide or the Glossary at the end of this book, you will see that the QL has a commendable number of built-in functions. To begin with, at least, you will probably be mainly concerned with those involving angles. Examples include sine, cosine, and tangent: SIN(R), COS(R) and TAN(R). For example, the following program line returns the value of the sine of 1.23:

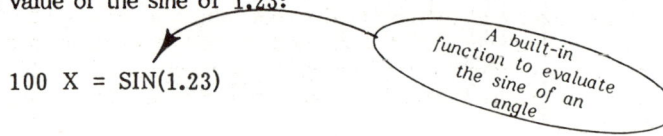

        100 X = SIN(1.23)   *A built-in function to evaluate the sine of an angle*

You may be surprised to see an angle written as 1.23, especially if you have been brought up to think of angles in degrees. SuperBASIC does not recognize degrees, but requires angles to be in a unit called the radian. (A radian is the angle subtended at the centre of a circle by an arc of the same length as the radius.) For conversion purposes, a radian is equal to 57.295 degrees. A full circle of 360 degrees contains 2π radians, written as 2*PI (where PI is the ratio of the circumference of a circle to its diameter). The QL takes the value of PI to six decimal places as 3.141593. Fortunately, it provides a means of converting between degrees and radians. This is another function, the RAD(D) function, where D is in degrees. The following is a line of program to give A the value in radians corresponding to 90 degrees:

110 A = RAD(90)

A built-in function to evaluate the radian equivalent of a number of degrees

The following is a short program to print the values of the sines of all angles between 0 and 90 degrees in steps of 10 degrees:

```
100 FOR a=0 TO 90 STEP 10
110   rd = RAD(a)
120   PRINT SIN(rd)
130 END FOR a
```

It can also be written as:

```
100 FOR a=0 TO 90 STEP 10
110   PRINT SIN(RAD(a))
120 END FOR a
```

However for speed of execution the next version is slightly better, because the RAD function is only evaluated twice, rather than nine times.

```
100 FOR rd=0 TO RAD(90) STEP RAD(90)/10
110   PRINT SIN(rd)
120 END FOR rd
```

The variations of many of the angular mathematical functions are best demonstrated by plotting them on a graph. The program of Listing 12.1 draws a set of axes and then plots the sine function for angles from 0 to 35 radians - which is about five and a half cycles. A scale of 2 conveniently represents the range of y. The x co-ordinate is divided by 12 to keep it in the right range. You can see the result in Screen Display 12.1 (overleaf).

The step size in the FOR loops is such that each new value moves on to the next pixel on the screen. A smaller loop increment would just slow the program down, without giving any difference to the display. The position of the origin and the 'extent' of the axes are all set at the beginning of the program.

There is a function, the ATAN(T) function, for converting from the tangent of an angle back to the angle. T is the tangent of the angle and the result is the angle in radians. A conversion from radians to degrees is provided by DEG(R) which takes R in radians and gives a value in degrees. If, in a program, you have a value for, say, T as the tangent of an angle X, the following lines return X in degrees:

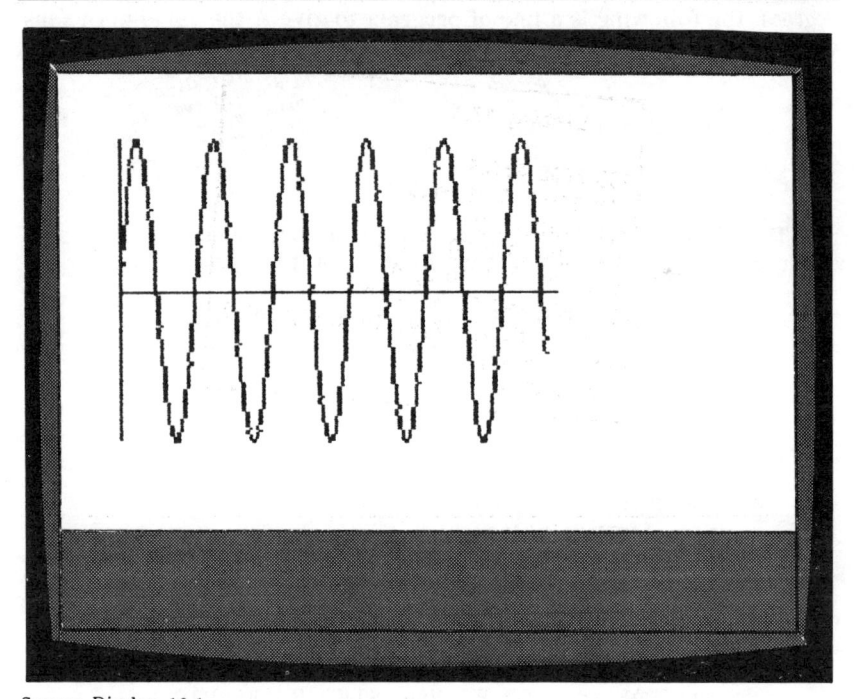

Screen Display 12.1

```
           100 R = ATAN(T)
           110 X = DEG(R)
or
           100 X = DEG(ATAN(T))
```

The QL has an interesting function called date$. It returns the value of the current date held inside the QL as a string. To demonstrate it simply, merely enter:

    PRINT date$

This causes a printout of the form:

    2026 Mar 02 04:09:11

The SDATE instruction sets the date and time, as follows:

```
Listing 12.1

100 MODE 4:CLS
110 SCALE 3,-1,-1.5
120 xp=0:yp=0
130 LINE 0,0 TO 3,0
140 LINE 0,1 TO 0,-1
150 FOR x=0 TO 35 STEP .1
160   LINE xp/12,yp TO x/12,SIN(x)
170   xp=x:yp=SIN(x)
180 NEXT x
```

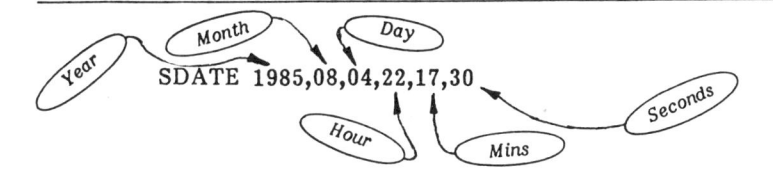

SDATE 1985,08,04,22,17,30

(Year, Month, Day, Hour, Mins, Seconds)

These then advance automatically until the QL is turned off. They are driven by the quartz clock inside the QL. SDATE can be used within a program or as an immediate action. We show an example of its use in the activities section of Section 12.2.

12.2 Activities

i. Write a program to display the current date and time continuously on the centre of the screen. Use large size writing, which can be set by CSIZE 3,1. We provide a suitable program in Section 12.8.

ii. Enter and run the program of Listing 12.1. Note how slowly it draws the sine wave. Time the execution of the program by adding the following two lines:

    105 PRINT DATE$
    190 PRINT DATE$

Table 12.1 (overleaf) gives all the QL's built in functions.

FUNCTION	PURPOSE
ABS(n)	Absolute value of n
ACOS(n)	Arc cosine of n in radians
ASIN(n)	Arc sine of n in radians
ATAN(n)	Arc tangent of n in radians
BEEPING	Test whether the QL is presently emitting a beep
CHR$(n)	Forms a character string for ASCII code n
COS(n)	Cosine of n in radians
COT(n)	Cotangent of n in radians
DATE	Returns the current date as a number
DATE$	Returns the current date as a string
DAY$	Returns the current day as a string last new line
DEG(n)	Degrees equivalent of n in radians
EXP(n)	e(2.7183...) raised to power n
INKEY$(n)	String value of key pressed (waits for n TV frames)
INSTR	("n" INSTR "s") Position of "n" in "s"
INT(n)	Integer part of n
LEN("n")	Length of string "n"
LN(n)	Natural logarithm of n
LOG10(n)	Logarithm of n to base 10
NOT	Reverses condition. i.e. NOT TRUE equals FALSE
PEEK(n)	Returns the contents of memory address n as 8 bit number
PEEK_W(n)	Returns the contents of memory address n as 16 bit number
PEEK_L(n)	Returns the contents of memory address n as 32 bit number
PI	Value of π (3.141593)
RAD(n)	Radians for angle n in degrees
RND(n)	Random number between 1 and n or 0 to 1 if n is 1
SIN(n)	Sine of n in radians
SQRT(n)	Square root of n
TAN(n)	Tangent of n in radians

Table 12.1

ii. Try plotting out the shape for COS(R) and TAN(R). The TAN(R) function has a value of infinity for certain angles. Could this cause an error message?

12.3 User-defined functions

If there is some function that you wish the computer had, and you can think of some program lines for the task, you can put them into your program as your own 'user-defined' function. You can name it whatever you like provided you have not chosen one of the QL's existing keywords. For example if you wanted a function to return the mean of the numbers A,B,C, you might call it 'mean'. You would then use it by entering its name followed by whatever numbers are required. For example:

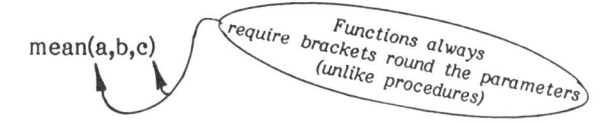

mean(a,b,c) *(require brackets Functions always round the parameters (unlike procedures))*

You would have to define it using 'DEFine FuNction', as in the following line:

    1000 DEFine FuNction mean(a,b,c) :RETurn (a+b+c)/3

(All definitions end with RETURN)

Function definitions may extend to many lines. Then the first line will normally just contain the words 'DEFine FuNction name'. The following lines carry out the calculations to find a value. The value the function is to return must then be placed after the word RETurn. As an illustration, the previous definition could be written, rather wastefully, on three lines as follows:

    1000 DEFine FuNction mean(a,b,c)
    1010   sum = a+b+c
    1020   RETurn sum/3
    1030 END DEFine mean

Many computers only allow functions where the definition extends to only one line. There is no such restriction with the QL.

User-defined functions can appear in PRINT statements, mathematical expressions, comparisons and in most places where there can be a normal variable name. For instance the following are some standard ways of using functions:

    100 PRINT mean(x,y,z)

and

    150 X = 100*N*mean(g,35,cost)

and

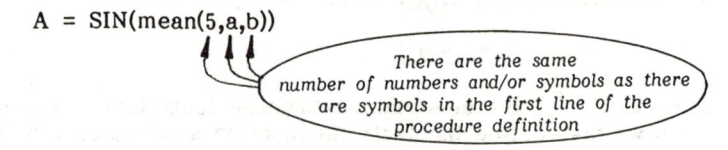

        A = SIN(mean(5,a,b))

There are the same number of numbers and/or symbols as there are symbols in the first line of the procedure definition

Just as with procedures, values passed to a function must be in the order that you, the programmer, assume when writing the function definition.

Lines which define a function are clearly somewhat different from those which define a procedure. Within a function there must be a line showing the word RETurn to return the value of the function. Also, whereas a program calls on a procedure by means of a statement which can appear alone on a program line, a function must appear within a normal program statement. It is normally, but not exclusively, on the right of an equals or other comparison sign.

12.4 Recursion

It is possible for a function to call itself. The process, which is called 'recursion', provides a very powerful means of solving certain problems.

Every time a function or a procedure is called, the computer has to remember the address of the line which called it. As this takes up memory, there is a limit to how may times a function may call itself recursively. This limit is called the depth of recursion. As with procedures, functions can carry on calling themselves until the QL runs out of memory.

A classic problem which is simply solved by recursion is calculating a factorial. Every number has a factorial. You get it by multiplying the number by all the integers below it, down to 1. For example factorial 7, written as 7!, is 7x6x5x4x3x2x1, and factorial 3 is 3x2x1. In BASIC, factorial N (or N!) is written as:

        N! = N*(N-1)*(N-2)* . . . 3*2*1

The following program provides the function factorial(n). We have written it with a FOR loop with the loop variable decreasing to make for an easier comparison with the recursive definition later:

```
200 DEFine FuNction factorial(n)
210   fact=1
220   FOR j=n TO 1 STEP -1
230     fact=fact*j
240   END FOR j
250   RETurn fact
260 END DEFine factorial
```

The definition of factorial N can be re-written as:

N! = N * (N-1)!

Factorial 1 is 1. (Mathematicians also define factorial 0 as 1.) Using these ideas we may define the factorial function as of value 1 if N<=1, but otherwise of value N times the factorial of N-1. Using recursion, the function definition becomes:

```
200 DEFine FuNction factorial(n)
210   IF n<=1 THEN
220          RETurn 1
230      ELSE
240          RETurn n*factorial(n-1)
250      END IF
260 END DEFine factorial
```

With a FOR loop, the loop is executed a fixed number of times. With recursion, there is no such fixed number. So it is vitally important that, as the first step in a recursive routine of any sort, you test to see if the end has been reached. This test is performed in line 210 of the recursive function. If the end value (1 or 0) is reached, then the answer is known (factorial 1 is 1). So it is given as the value following THEN RETurn (value is 1 so RETurn 1). If the end has not been reached, the final value is written in terms of a further factorial in the following way:

final value = (current value of n) * (factorial of n-1)

Line 240 in the recursive definition only performs one step of the calculation, and then hands over to the function factorial to do the rest! It seems rather like putting off the calculation to the last possible moment. The whole process stops when the factorial of 1 is requested. At this moment the recursive function returns the value 1. This is then multiplied by all the numbers up to and including the original number.

12.5 Activities

i. Try writing a function to give the largest of a set of numbers. It could be called by a statement such as max(a,b,c,d). (For further hints and a discussion, see Section 12.8.)

ii. Enter the recursive factorial function definition, together with the following lines:

```
100 MODE 8
110 REPeat forever
120   INPUT \"Type in an integer between 1 and 33 "p
130   PRINT \"The factorial of ";p;" is ";factorial(p)
140 END REPeat forever
```

This program does not check for valid numbers. So try running it to see if it works. Note the long time it takes for large numbers, and see the error message for supplying a number which is too large.

iii. Is the error of ii due to (a) too large a final number or (b) too many recursions of the function? (This is discussed in Section 12.8.)

iv. Write a function to return a Centigrade temperature from a Fahrenheit one. Call it with the statement centigrade(F) where F is the Fahrenheit temperature. (See Section 12.8 for an example.)

v. Try modifying the recursive factorial function to convert it to one which will add all the numbers from 1 to n. (See Section 12.8 for a possible version.)

vi. Try writing a recursive function to add the squares of all numbers from 1 to n. (See Section 12.8 for a possible version.)

12.6   Points to ponder

a. Can you define a function which would return the cube of a number?

b. Can you define a function which would return the volume of a cylinder, given the radius and the height?

12.7   Discussion on the points to ponder

a. The following function would return the cube of x:

```
100 DEFine FuNction cube(x)
110    RETurn x^3
120 END DEFine cube
```

b. The following function would return the volume of a cylinder of radius r and height h:

```
100 DEFine FuNction vol(r,h)
110    RETurn PI*r^2*h
```

120 END DEFine vol

12.8 Discussion of activities

Activity 12.2i: Here is our version of a program to continuously display the current date and time on the centre of the screen in large writing:

```
100 CLS
110 INPUT "Please give me the year ";year;
    ", month ";month;", day ";day;", hour ";
    hour;", min ";min;", secs ";secs
120 SDATE year,month,day,hour,min,secs
130 CLS
140 CSIZE 3,1
150 REPeat time
160    AT 4,4 :PRINT DATE$
170 END REPeat time
```

Activity 12.5i: Sorting out the maximum of four values is probably best done with simple comparisons of the following form:

```
1000 DEFine FuNction max(a,b,c,d)
1010 LOCal mx
1020 mx=a
1030 IF b>mx THEN mx=b
1040 IF c>mx THEN mx=c
1050 IF d>mx THEN mx=d
1060 RETurn mx
1070 END DEFine max
```

The LOCal statement of line 1010 declares the variable mx to be local to the procedure. This means that if mx is used elsewhere in the program, its value is stored and then returned to mx at the end of the procedure. A wise precaution is to make all variables in a procedure local to that procedure.

Activity 12.5iii: The error will be for a number that is too large. The number of recursions allowable for a function or procedure depends on the amount of memory available, which is very large in the QL. When the error occurs you may like to print out the value of n. You should find that it is 301. Print the factorial of 300 and then try multiplying it by 301. This will cause the same error message 'overflow' that you got when calling the function with any number greater than 300.

Activity 12.5iv: The function could be as follows:

```
10 DEFine FuNction centigrade(F)
20  RETurn (F - 32)*5/9
30 END DEFine centigrade
```

Activity 12.5v: The following is one version of how you could modify the recursive factorial function to one which adds all the numbers from 1 to n:

```
100 DEFine FuNction sumto(n)
110  IF n=1 THEN RETurn 1
120  RETurn n+sumto(n-1)
130 END DEFine sumto
```

Activity 12.5vi: The following is one version of how you could write a recursive function to add the squares of all numbers from 1 to n.

```
100 DEF FuNction sumsquares(n)
110  IF n=1 THEN RETurn 1
120  RETurn n*n+sumsquares(n-1)
130 END DEFine sumsquares
```

13

Handling strings

13.0 Introduction
13.1 Inputting a complex string
13.2 Inputting a single character
13.3 Manipulating portions of strings
13.4 Searching within a string
13.5 Activities
13.6 Repetition within strings
13.7 Activities
13.8 Conversion between a character and its code
13.9 Activities
13.10 Discussion of activities

13.0 Introduction

You will remember that strings can be made up of any text, including punctuation and numbers, and can be of almost any length. In programs they are represented by string variables which are distinguished from numerical variables by having dollar signs at the end of their names. This chapter is concerned with how to manipulate strings, i.e. extract parts, search for parts, etc. The techniques are widely applicable.

13.1 Inputting a complex string

A normal INPUT statement, such as the following, can read in a string from the keyboard and give it to the variable a$:

        50 INPUT a$

There are no limitations on the characters that you can put into a string because, unlike most BASICs, SuperBASIC accepts all punctuation marks right up until ENTER is pressed. There is however, a limitation on length. The string can only be as long as the type-ahead buffer which allows 127 characters.

13.2 Inputting a single character

In games programming particularly, you may want a program to accept just one character from the keyboard - often without the user even having to press the ENTER key. For example you might want the program to accept 'Y' for 'yes'. This may be done with the INKEY$ statement. It makes the program pause while looking for a key, and you can program the duration of the pause. If a key is pressed during this pause, the string value of the key is returned. Otherwise a null string (one of zero length) is returned. INKEY is used in the form:

        50 G$=INKEY$(10)   *(Duration of pause in 50th of a second)*

The number in brackets after the INKEY$ statement is the time for which the program should pause, measured in the time it takes for each frame of the picture on the TV to be formed. (1/50 of a second). This means that INKEY$(50) will wait for up to one second.

In the normal way, INKEY will cause the QL to wait a specified time until a key - any key - is pressed. It is possible, however, to use it in such a way that it will cause the QL to pause only momentarily to see if a specific key is pressed. For this you use INKEY$ with no number, like this:

50 G$=INKEY$ ← *Gives only a quick glance at the keyboard*

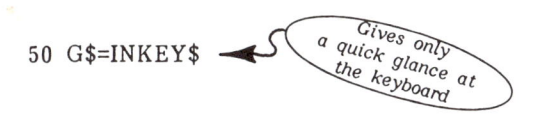

It is also possible to cause the QL to stop and wait for whatever time is necessary until a key is pressed. This form of the INKEY$ function is INKEY$(-1) as in:

150 k$=INKEY$(-1) ← *Causes the QL to wait indefinitely until a key is pressed*

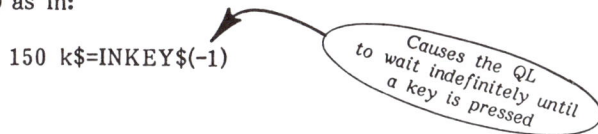

13.3 Manipulating portions of strings

SuperBASIC has a powerful built-in function for specifying a portion of a string, in readiness for manipulating it in some way. For example, assuming that the string a$ has previously been defined, the following specifies the third to the fifth character:

a$(3 TO 5) ← *This specifies characters 3 to 5 inclusive in the string a$*

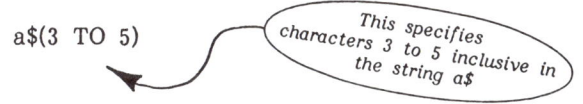

Once identified, the portion can be extracted. For example, the following extracts and prints the word 'hat' from a longer string:

```
100 a$="mad hatter's tea party"
110 PRINT a$(5 TO 7)
```

The identified portion can also be replaced. For example the following replaces the last four characters of a string (i.e. one name with another):

```
100 a$="Hello there John"
110 a$(13 TO 16)="Jane"      ← Replaces the last 4 letters in a$ with Jane
120 PRINT a$
```

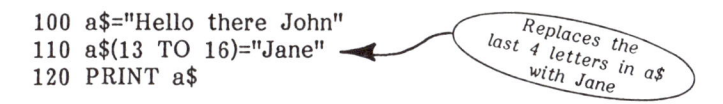

So this program prints the message:

Hello there Jane

If the numbers in brackets go beyond the actual length of string, the extra will be ignored.

Some other string manipulations require a means of determining how long a string is. This is what the built-in function LEN does. For example, the following line gives x a value equal to the number of characters in the string a$:

```
155 x = LEN(a$)
```

An example of its use could be:

```
160 IF LEN(ans$) > 3 THEN PRINT "Please
    answer with YES or NO"
```

Knowing the length of a string, portions from the end can be extracted. The following program will print the last 5 characters of the string a$:

```
100 a$="mad hatter's tea party"
110 PRINT a$(LEN(a$)-4 TO LEN(a$))
```

Many other BASICs provide a function called 'right$' which extracts the right-most n characters in a string. Although this doesn't exist in SuperBASIC, we can define it for ourselves. It will be used in the following form, where it returns the right-most n characters of a$:

```
right$(a$,n)
```

This user-defined function relies on LEN, and is:

```
100 DEFine FuNction right$(a$,n)
110   RETurn a$(LEN(a$)+1-n TO LEN(a$))
120 END DEFine right$
```

This is a good example of capitalizing on the powerful aspects of the SuperBASIC, namely by using it to program additional facilities, as required.

13.4 Searching within a string

INSTR is a built-in function for performing a search for one string within another. It can be used in a wide variety of ways.

Suppose you want to search for the string 'short$' within the string 'long$'. The INSTR function is used in the following way, where P becomes the character position in the long string where a match is found with the short string:

```
190 P = short$ INSTR long$
```
Searches for one string within another

INSTR returns the value 0 if it does not find the string. This is particularly valuable for the following reason. With a comparison, such as IF x<y THEN ... the QL works out a 'value' for x<y. This 'value' is either 0 or 1. The 0 corresponds to the condition not being true, i.e. false; and the 1 to the condition of it being true. Thus if you were to run the following program the message 'goodbye' would be printed:

```
100 IF 0 THEN
110     PRINT "hello"
120 ELSE
130     PRINT "goodbye"
140 END IF
```

This is because the condition has been replaced by 0, which is taken as false.

It is worth noting that any non-zero value is treated by the QL as true. Thus, if any condition is replaced by INSTR, then statements such as the following become possible:

230 IF short$ INSTR long$ THEN PRINT "found"

This one prints the message 'found', if the short string appears in the long one.

You can arrange for the computer to wait for one of the keys Y, y, N or n to be pressed with a set of lines, such as:

```
100 REPeat YyNn
110    k$=INKEY$
120    IF k$<>"" AND k$ INSTR "YyNn" THEN EXIT YyNn
130 END REPeat YyNn
```

Line 120 is necessarily rather complex because the null string (returned by INKEY$ when no key is pressed) will always be found in any other string. If you want to wait for an input YES, yes, NO or no, the technique is the same, irrespective of the actual string. You merely use the INPUT statement and a line such as:

IF reply$<>"" AND reply$ INSTR "YESyesNOno" THEN ...

With INSTR it is also simple to get a series of keys to produce a predetermined set of notes. For example suppose you want each of the keys 123456789 to produce a note, each one a semitone higher than the one before. You could use the following, which would have a value of 1 to 9, if a number key were pressed. Otherwise it would have a value of zero.

(INKEY$(-1) INSTR "123456789")

13 Handling Strings

```
This program demonstrates printing
text to whatever line-length you
request. It ensures that the text is
written with no lines split between
the end of one line and the beginning
of the next.
 What number of characters per line
would you like to see demonstrated?
20
```

```
This program
demonstrates
printing text to
whatever
line-length you
request. It ensures
that the text is
written with no
lines split between
the end of one line
and the beginning
of the next.
 What number of
characters per line
would you like to
see demonstrated?
38
```

Screen Displays 13.1

13 Handling Strings

Listing 13.1

```
100 DIM colr(3,7)
110 MODE 8 :PAPER 1 :INK 0 :CLS
120 line_length=38
130 REPeat word_process
140   CLS :AT 5,0
150   print_whole "This program demonstrates printing text to whatever line-length you request. It ensures that the text is written with no lines split between the end of one line and the beginning of the next.",line'length
160   print_whole " What number of characters per line would you like to see demonstrated?",line'length
170   INPUT line_length
180 END REPeat word_process
190 :
200 DEFine PROCedure print_whole(a$,length)
210   REPeat print_lines
220     maxline=length
230     IF LEN(a$)<maxline THEN maxline=LEN(a$)+1:a$=a$&" "
240     FOR i=maxline TO 1 STEP -1
250       IF a$(i)=" " THEN EXIT i
260     END FOR i
270     PRINT a$(1 TO i-1)
280     IF LEN(a$)<=length THEN EXIT print_lines
290     IF i< LEN(a$) THEN a$=a$(i+1 TO LEN(a$))
300   END REPeat print_lines
310 END DEFine print_whole
```

As our 'tone' procedure of Chapter 7 takes the pitch as a number of semitones, you merely have to use an expression such as the following to convert the number keys so that each gives a note one semitone higher than the next:

```
300  tone 10000,INKEY$(-1) INSTR "123456789"
```

13.5 Activities

The program of Listing 13.1 is a demonstration of part of a word processing package. As you can see from the Screen Displays, it demonstrates a procedure to print long messages on the screen without splitting any of the words between the end of one line and the start of the next. Can you see how it works? When you come to enter and run it, note that spaces are essential between the inputted words.

13.6 Repetition within strings

FILL$ is yet another function available in the SuperBASIC but not many other BASICs. It provides a compact way of writing any string which is a repetition of groups of characters. For instance the following line gives a string of 20 'a's:

320 a$ = FILL$("a",20)   *Makes a string of 20 a's*

It is equivalent to:

320 a$ = "aaaaaaaaaaaaaaaaaaaa"

The general form of the function is as follows, where n is the number of times the string a$ is to be joined to itself to produce the final string:

FILL$(a$,n)

13.7 Activities

i. The following two procedures are very simple and as they stand rely only on the LEN function. As an exercise in string handling, examine them and see if you can modify them both to produce a function instead. These should both give a string of length 36 characters: the first with the string a$ embedded in the centre and the second with the string as far to the right as possible. See Section 13.10 for a solution to these problems.

1. A procedure to print the string a$ centred on the line with spaces either side.

```
1000 DEFine PROCedure centre(a$)
1010    a$=FILL$(" ",(36-LEN(a$)/2))&a$
1020    PRINT a$
1030 END DEFine centre
```

2. A procedure to print the string a$ on the right of the screen when in a mode giving 36 characters per line.

13 Handling Strings

```
1000 DEFine PROCedure right(a$)
1010   a$=FILL$(" ",36-LEN(a$))&a$
1020   PRINT a$
1020 END DEFine right
```

13.8 Conversion between a character and its code

The QL holds all numbers, letters, symbols and punctuation marks as codes which are listed in the User Guide. There are two string functions which allow conversion between a character and its code:

One is CHR$(v) which converts from the code number held in the numerical variable v to the character it represents which is a single character string. For example, the code for H is 72. This means that CHR$(72) is H. So the following instruction will print the single character H:

PRINT CHR$(72) ← *Prints H - the character whose code is 72*

The code extends between 0 and 255.

The following short program will print out most of the characters available on the QL by using a FOR loop to go through the codes and a PRINT statement to print out the corresponding characters:

```
100 MODE 8 :count=0
110 FOR i = 32 TO 255
120    PRINT CHR$(i);
130    count = count + 1
140    IF count = 36 THEN PRINT : count = 0
150 END FOR i
```

CODE(a$) is the reverse of CHR$ in that it converts the first letter of the string a$ to the corresponding code. Thus if the string a$ = "HELP", then CODE(a$) is equivalent to CODE("HELP") which gives 72 because the code for H is 72.

13.9 Activities

To see the QL character set, run the program of the previous section.

13.10 Discussion of activities

Activity 13.7i: The following is a function which returns a string 36 characters long with a$ embedded as near the centre as possible.

```
1000 DEFine FuNction centre$(a$)
1010   LOCal s$
1020   s$=FILL$(" ",36)
1030   s$(18-LEN(a$)/2 TO 18+LEN(a$)/2)=a$
1040   RETurn s$
1050 END DEFine centre
```

The following is a function which returns a string of 36 characters with a$ embedded as near to the right as possible.

```
1000 DEFine FuNction right(a$)
1010   RETurn FILL$(" ",36-LEN(A$))&a$
1020 END DEFine right
```

Neither of these functions have any check on the length of the string a$. If a$ is likely to be equal or greater in length than 36 characters, a check such as the following should be built in:

```
1005 IF LEN(a$)>=36 THEN RETurn a$
```

14

Handling files

14.0 Introduction
14.1 Microdrive cartridges as storage media for files
14.2 Creating and writing to a new file
14.3 Reading from a file
14.4 Activities
14.5 Writing to an existing file
14.6 Copying a file
14.7 Activities
14.8 Points to ponder
14.9 Discussion on the points to ponder
14.10 Discussion of activities

14.0 Introduction

A 'file' is a block of stored information. The information may be a program, an account of yearly earnings, a letter composed on a word processor, or almost anything else you can think of. It becomes a file when it has an identifying name, by which it can be saved and retrieved. So you have already created and used files when you saved and loaded programs to and from microdrive cartridges. However, the real fascination and value of file-handling comes from being able to manipulate files from within programs - and this is what we explain in this chapter.

14.1 Microdrive cartridges as storage media for files

With the QL you have to hold your files on microdrive cartridges - a storage medium which offers considerable advantages over the cassette tape which most micros use. The recording medium is still high quality tape but it is in the form of a continuous loop which moves very fast.

We shall now briefly look at some of the similarities and differences between the various media for storage: microdrive cartridge, cassette tape and disc. A disc is made of a magnetic medium which revolves many times a second in use. The information is written in lots of small sub-packages at various places over the disc, and while the disc revolves, the computer keeps track of them and can almost instantaneously put them together into a unified whole. Alternatively, the computer can merely pick out and use various parts of the information from anywhere in the file. This type of access is termed 'random access' and makes for very fast file-handling. With a cassette tape, reading normally has to start at the beginning and proceed in order to the end - which is termed 'serial access' and which is rather slow. Microdrive cartridges also use serial access but they are quicker to use. This is for two reasons. One is the speed of the tape inside the microdrive cartridge and the other is that you don't have to wait for a microdrive to stop before you carrying on working on the QL.

With a disc system, once you have asked for a particular file, the reading typically starts in less than a second from pressing the ENTER key and is complete in a matter of seconds - quite a bit faster than with microdrive cartridges and very much faster than with cassette tapes. Also with a disc system you can read from more than one file at a time and need not start from the beginning. You can also do this with the QL microdrive system, but it is very much slower. You can't do it with cassette tape. Both a disc system and a microdrive system keep records of all the files.

14.2 Creating and writing to a new file

If you want to create a new file, you must provide a channel number, stipulate the microdrive and provide a name for the file. The OPEN_NEW statement does just this. You use it in the following form:

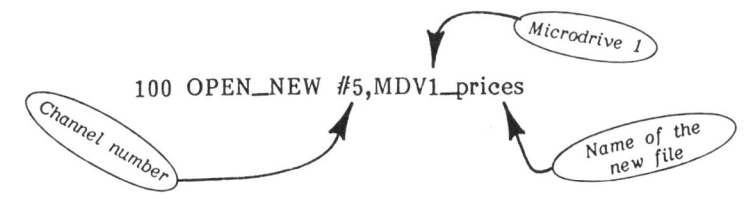

100 OPEN_NEW #5,MDV1_prices

(Channel number, Microdrive 1, Name of the new file)

If a file with the same name already exists, there will be the following error message:

   already exists

Putting information into a file is called 'writing to' that file. You do it with a PRINT statement, just as you would with any other channel. The data may be numbers or strings and can be mixed in any fashion. By way of illustration, the following is an instruction to write data to channel 7, where the data consists of a numerical value from an array, the number 567 and the strings "hello" and stock$:

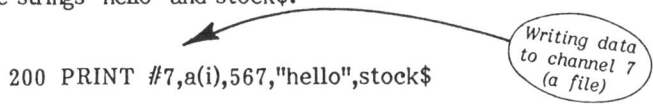

200 PRINT #7,a(i),567,"hello",stock$

(Writing data to channel 7 (a file))

You can carry on putting data into the file for as long you wish. Although the amount is eventually limited by the storage capacity of the microdrive cartridge, this is rarely a serious limitation.

The file is only saved completely on the microdrive cartridge when you 'close' it with a CLOSE instruction. For example:

540 CLOSE #7

(Closes channel 7)

The following program shows how you can create, write to and close a file within a program. It reads some data from DATA statements and then writes them out to a file named 'trial1'. The first number in the data is the number of following pairs of items to be read in:

```
100 OPEN_NEW #7,MDV1_trial1
110 READ n
120 PRINT #7,n
130 FOR j = 1 TO n
```

```
140    READ d,d$
150    PRINT #7,d,d$
160 END FOR j
170 CLOSE #7
180 PRINT "File writing complete"
1000 DATA 4
1010 DATA 345,"squirrel",4,"rabbit"
1020 DATA 28,"cat",38,"canary"
```

14.3 Reading from a file

To get information out of a file, you first inform the QL which file you wish to read. You do this by stipulating the microdrive, opening the file by name, and attaching it to a channel with a statement such as the following:

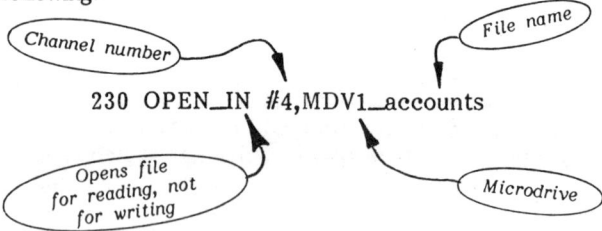

```
230 OPEN_IN #4,MDV1_accounts
```

- Channel number
- File name
- Opens file for reading, not for writing
- Microdrive

With the QL you can now retrieve information from a file, either a line at a time or a character at the time. In the following example, the INPUT statement reads a line from the open file, from channel 5 into the string variable name$:

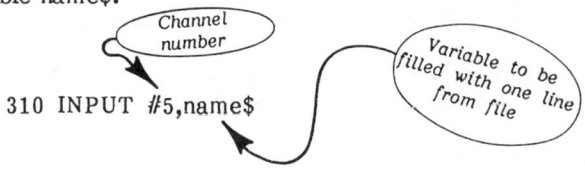

```
310 INPUT #5,name$
```

- Channel number
- Variable to be filled with one line from file

The following uses the INKEY$ statement to read a character from the open file, from channel 7 into the string variable d$:

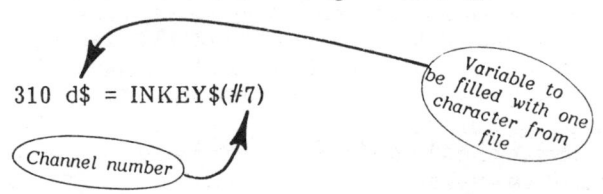

```
310 d$ = INKEY$(#7)
```

- Channel number
- Variable to be filled with one character from file

We can illustrate the effects of these two statements by considering a file of names and telephone numbers like this:

```
Neil Norman    01-001-1234
Pat Wiseman    02-111-4321
Jean Wyman     03-222-6848
...........    ............
...........    ............
    etc.
```

With INPUT #3,a$, the first two successive values of a$ will each be a complete line, like this:

```
a$ = "Neil Norman 01-001-1234"
a$ = "Pat Wiseman 02-111-4321"
```

With a$=INKEY$(#3) the first two successive values of a$ will each be a single character, like this:

```
a$ = "N"
a$ = "e"
```

The file appears like lines of typing, with the equivalent of the ENTER key pressed at the end of each line. The net result is that a string variable will be given the value of the whole line while a numerical variable will be given the value of the first item in the line. Reading always starts at the beginning and works through in strict order.

By means of the following program, you could read back the data from the file-writing program of the previous section:

```
100 OPEN_IN #3,MDV1_trial1
110 INPUT #3,n
120 FOR j = 1 TO n
130   INPUT #3,m$ :PRINT m$
140 END FOR j
150 CLOSE #3
```

When line 100 is executed, the QL searches microdrive 1 for a file with the name 'trial1'. If it is found, it opens it at the beginning for reading. Line 130 both reads in the data and prints it out on the screen. Line 150 closes channel 3. All file-handling programs must close the associated channel when they have finished with the file. The CLOSE statement is the same irrespective of whether a file is opened for writing or for reading. If you forget to close a file which was opened for reading, it is not as serious as if you forget to close it when it was opened for writing. You will, however, get an error message if you try to open the same channel with a different file. So it is good programming practice to close all files when you have finished using them.

14.4 Activities

i. Enter and run the program of Section 14.2 which creates and writes a file with the name 'trial1'.

ii. Enter and run the program of Section 14.3 for reading from the file 'trial1'. Is the correct data written on the screen?

iii. Why is there a delay before the data is written to the screen? (Section 14.10 deals with this point.)

14.5 Writing to an existing file

There are different instructions for opening a new file and for opening an existing file. As you know, you open a new file with the OPEN_NEW statement. If, however, you want to open an existing file to add new material to it, you have to open with the OPEN statement. Here is an example, which opens the file called 'accounts', on microdrive 2, as channel 3:

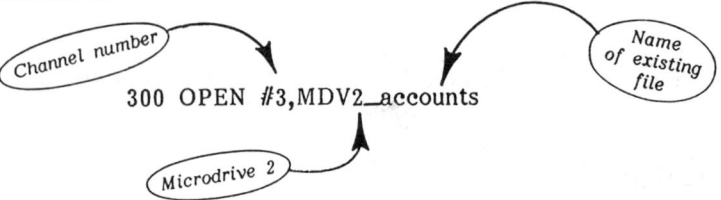

```
300 OPEN #3,MDV2_accounts
```

Channel number → 3
Microdrive 2 → MDV2
Name of existing file → accounts

Any writing will now take place at the beginning of the file. To move the writing position to anywhere else, you move through the file by reading, using the INKEY$ or INPUT statements. You can then write to the file, as described in Section 14.2 and close it with a CLOSE statement.

While you read, you can check whether you have reached the end of the file with EOF, which is used in the following way:

```
270 IF EOF(#3) THEN ....
```

Action to take place if end of file on channel 3 is reached

You will get an error message if you try to read from a file, after reaching the end.

When writing to an existing file, the problem is that new writing

14 Handling Files

overwrites old, rather than displacing it - which you will probably find unacceptable. The solution is to open a new file, copy across the first part from the old file, then do the insertion and then continue copying. So you essentially read from one file and write to another. The following program illustrates this idea by effectively inserting 4 new lines of text 5 lines into an existing file.

```
100 MODE 4 :INK 7
110 INPUT"Name of file to extend ";from$
120 from$="MDV1_"&from$
130 OPEN_IN #3,from$
140 out$=from$&"_new"
150 OPEN_NEW #4,out$
160 :
170 FOR skip=1 TO 4:INPUT #3,a$:PRINT #4,a$
180 :
190 PRINT \\"Please enter the 4 new lines"
200 FOR newline=1 TO 4
210    PRINT "line ";newline;
220    INPUT a$
230    PRINT #4,a$
240 END FOR newline
250 :
260 REPeat copy_rest
270    IF EOF(#3) THEN EXIT copy_rest
280    INPUT #3,a$
290    PRINT #4,a$
300 END REPeat copy_rest
310 CLOSE #3 :CLOSE #4
```

14.6 Copying a file

There is a COPY command which allows you to transfer a file from one 'device' to another. The following are examples of devices in this context:

- a file on a cartridge
- a serial port
- a television screen
- a network port

The following examples show how you could copy from one device to another:

COPY mdv1_file_original TO mdv2_file_new

and

Copies a file from one microdrive file to another

```
            COPY ser2 TO mdv1_file_new
and
            COPY mdv1_file1 TO ser2

and
            COPY mdv1_file1 TO scr
```

Copies any information from the serial port to a file

Copies the file to serial port 2

Presents a copy of the file on the screen

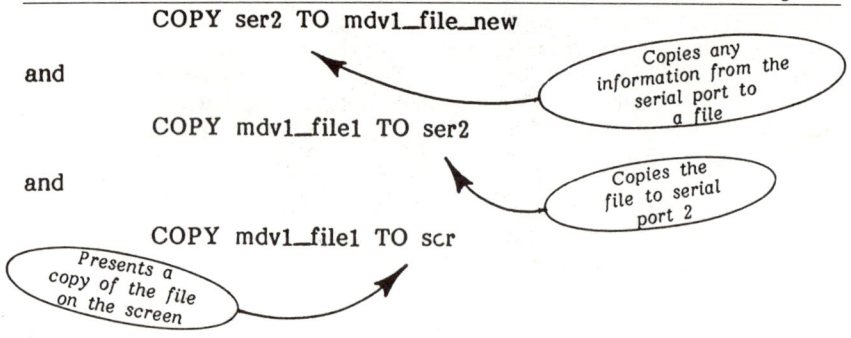

14.7 Activities

i. Create a test file of any sort and then add some lines to it using the technique of the program in Section 14.5.

ii. Use the COPY command to put a copy of the old test file on the screen. Verify that the new lines are successfully inserted by repeating the operation with the newly created file.

14.8 Points to ponder

a. Why is it necessary to open files for writing as nothing seems to need doing before writing starts?

b. Even if the OPEN statement is necessary before starting to write to a file, no CLOSE might seem to be, if no more writing is to take place. Why will you have trouble if you leave off the CLOSE statement?

14.9 Discussion on the points to ponder

a. The QL needs to know whether it is to open a new file or add to an old one. The only way it can know the difference is if you declare the file for opening first. It can then search to see if this file exists or not.

b. Each file is written in blocks of a fixed length. Thus while a program is writing characters to a file, the operating system will hold these in a buffer until sufficient have accumulated to make up the standard number it writes out. The whole block is then written in one go. The CLOSE statement is an instruction to the operating system to write out the rest of its buffer without waiting for it to be filled up. It does this by filling the remaining spaces in the buffer with nulls (0). So the omission of CLOSE prevents the last block from being written out.

14.10 Discussion of activities

Activity 14.4 iii: The program searches the cartridge for a file called 'trial1'. So there is a delay until it is found.

15

Structured programming

15.0 Introduction
15.1 Subroutines and procedures
15.2 Jumping versus branching
15.3 Designing structured programs
15.4 Flowcharting
15.5 Preparing flowcharts
15.6 Activities
15.7 Discussion of activities

15.0 Introduction

As we have mentioned several times in this book, a special feature of SuperBASIC is that it helps what is called 'structured programming'. For a program to be structured, it has to be built up of clearly identifiable separate blocks of program lines, each with its own purpose. The advantage of a structured program is that it is particularly easy to read and write and hence also easier to check and debug.

In this chapter we gather together those features of SuperBASIC that especially facilitate structured programming. Then, by way of comparison, we illustrate certain programming practices that detract from structuring. Finally we give guidance on how to design programs so that they are well structured.

15.1 Subroutines and procedures

There can be little doubt that the feature of SuperBASIC which most helps with structuring programs is the procedure - which was virtually unknown in early BASICs. As you know, a procedure is a group of program lines which are isolated and named. The name can be chosen to show clearly the purpose of the lines. Both the start of the procedure and where it ends are clearly identified.

The grossly inferior alternative to a procedure is a 'subroutine' which is available in most BASICs. It is even available within SuperBASIC, but we have not bothered to mentioned this before because a subroutine offers nothing that a procedure cannot do much better. A subroutine could be the same group of program lines which you would normally place in a procedure - but the beginning of a subroutine has nothing to identify it as different from all the surrounding program lines. The end of the subroutine is marked with the statement RETURN. A subroutine has to be called with a statement such as GOSUB 592 which causes the execution of the program to temporarily jump to line number 592. Such an anonymous call hides the purpose of the call and, even, line 592 has no indication on it to show that it is really the start of a subroutine!

Just in case you are not already put off subroutines, there are further advantages that procedures have which subroutines do not. As you know, when a procedure is called, numbers and strings can be passed for it to work on. There is no similar mechanism with subroutines. Furthermore any other variables which the procedure uses can be declared local to that procedure. So, if the procedure uses the variable X and it is declared local, then on entry to the procedure the value previously held in X is stored away in memory and then restored to the variable upon exit from the procedure. In consequence you don't have to check whether the variables used in a procedure are the same as those used elsewhere. For subroutines you have to be very careful to make sure that all variables have names which are unique. Many a program crashes because of lack of

15 Structured Programming

attention to this point.

As an example of the superiority of procedures, consider two programs to achieve the same thing, namely to print any message, centred in a line of 36 characters.

The first of the two programs uses a subroutine, which is called by the statement GOSUB 130 in line 110. It is as follows:

```
100 INPUT "Enter a message for display ";message$
110 GOSUB 130
120 STOP
130 PRINT FILL$(" ",18-LEN(m$)/2);message$
140 RETurn
```

Execution of this program follows the line number sequence 100, 110, 130 140, 120. The end of the subroutine is marked with RETurn, which causes the program execution to return to the statement following the GOSUB, in this case to line 120.

The second program achieves the same thing, this time with a procedure:

```
100 INPUT "Enter a message for display ";message$
110 printcentred message$
120 STOP
130 DEFine PROCedure printcentred(m$)
140   PRINT FILL$(" ",18-LEN(m$)/2);m$
150 END DEFine printcentred
```

In contrast to the GOSUB 130 of the first program, line 110 of the second program gives some indication of what is to be achieved. The whole program is easier to read and to check. For anyone used to thinking in structured terms, it is also easier to write.

15.2 Jumping versus branching

Another feature of SuperBASIC is that its excellent REPeat loop construction, combined with the use of procedures and functions, almost completely eliminate the need for a statement which is widely used on other BASICs: the GOTO. Actually this statement is still accepted by SuperBASIC, although it is unlikely that anyone who is concerned with structured programming would want to use it.

The GOTO statement is a simple way of forcing the QL to execute a program in an order other than the line numbers dictate. It is an instruction to jump or branch to a new line somewhere else. For example the following line causes the QL to continue execution at line 200:

```
100 GOTO 200
```

The statement also allows jumping to, say, line X, where X is calculated by the QL from the information that you feed into it. The following would be an appropriate instruction, provided that the previous part of the program calculated X:

    110 GOTO X

This form of the GOTO statement is probably more disastrously anti-structuring than anything else and should never be used.

GOTO statements are bad for two main reasons. The first is related to the line with the GOTO in it. This might be:

    50 IF 'condition' THEN GOTO 95

Such a line does not give any indication of what is going to happen as a result of the jump. In contrast, a line such as the following is precise and unambiguous:

    150 IF cold THEN turn_heater_on

The second and perhaps more important objection to the GOTO statement is that the line 95, mentioned in the above line 50, would have nothing on it to show anyone reading the listing that the program execution could be branching to that point. Consequently it is very difficult to keep track of what is happening.

The ON ... GOTO statement is an extension of the GOTO statement. It allows jumping to one of a number of lines, according to the value of a variable. An example might be:

    100 ON X GOTO 100,200,300,105,500

This causes a branch to:

    line 100 if X=1
    line 200 if X=2
    line 300 if X=3
    line 105 if X=4
    line 500 if X=5.

It causes an error message if X<1 or X>5.

Similar branches and error messages are possible with a statement called ON ... GOSUB, for example with:

    100 ON X GOSUB 100,200,300,105,500

It would be difficult to stress too strongly how much SuperBASIC has contributed to good programming practice. With SuperBASIC there is really no excuse for unstructured programs. Nevertheless, the message seems slow to come home to many people who learnt their programming before the QL came onto the scene. For example, in a recent software magazine one program had 31 GOTOs/GOSUBs in 31 consecutive lines. The program was quite unreadable!

15.3 Designing structured programs

With programs of even the slightest complexity, it is not advisable just to sit down and type in a program as you develop it. This is true even if you are experienced! You might get away with it sometimes, but the programs would be difficult to follow – both for other people and for you when you try to find the inevitable bugs. Before beginning the actual program, it is best to:

(1) Decide what the program is for (or is to do) – in specific terms, not just general ones!

(2) Decide what the screen is to show and where on the screen the various parts of the display are to appear. This tends to be tied up with (1).

(3) Divide your program into manageable sized tasks. Once you have made each task small enough, you should be able to think of the lines of BASIC which will achieve it. Consider whether these should be within a procedure.

(4) Make your main program as short and clear as possible by reference to procedures which are aptly named. Test each one to make sure it does what it is supposed to. It is generally easier to test a small procedure than a whole program.

(5) When writing the program, try to think what the extreme conditions are going to be. Then test the program using them. In this way you can trap any errors due to a user feeding in incorrect data.

15.4 Flowcharting

In order to set about your programming in a carefully structured way, you may find it useful to draw what are called 'flowcharts'. They are not always necessary and not all programmers use them, but they are sufficiently widely accepted as important to be worthy of attention.

A flowchart is a diagram on paper, showing the sequence of events and the steps which need to be made in the solution of a problem. Figure

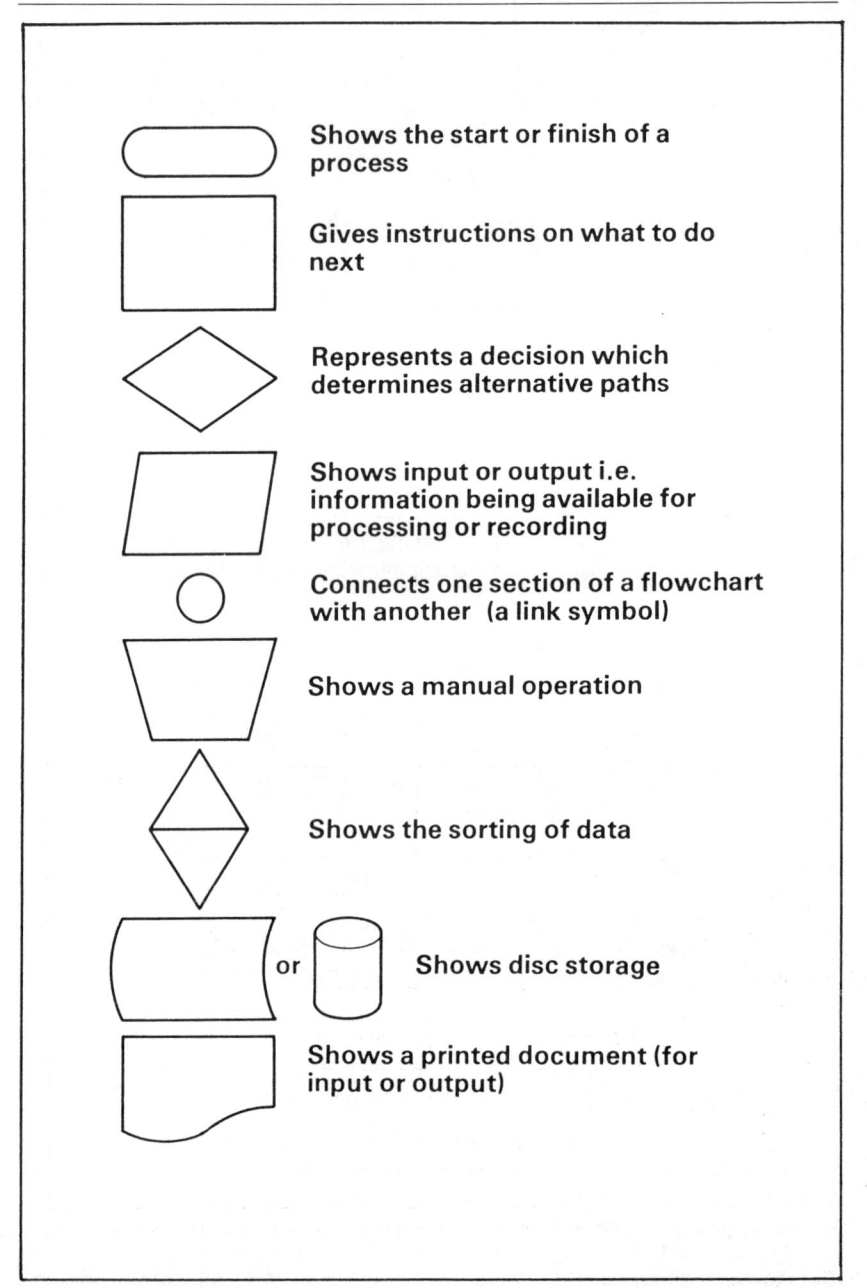

Figure 15.1. The most common symbols for flowcharts.

15 Structured Programming

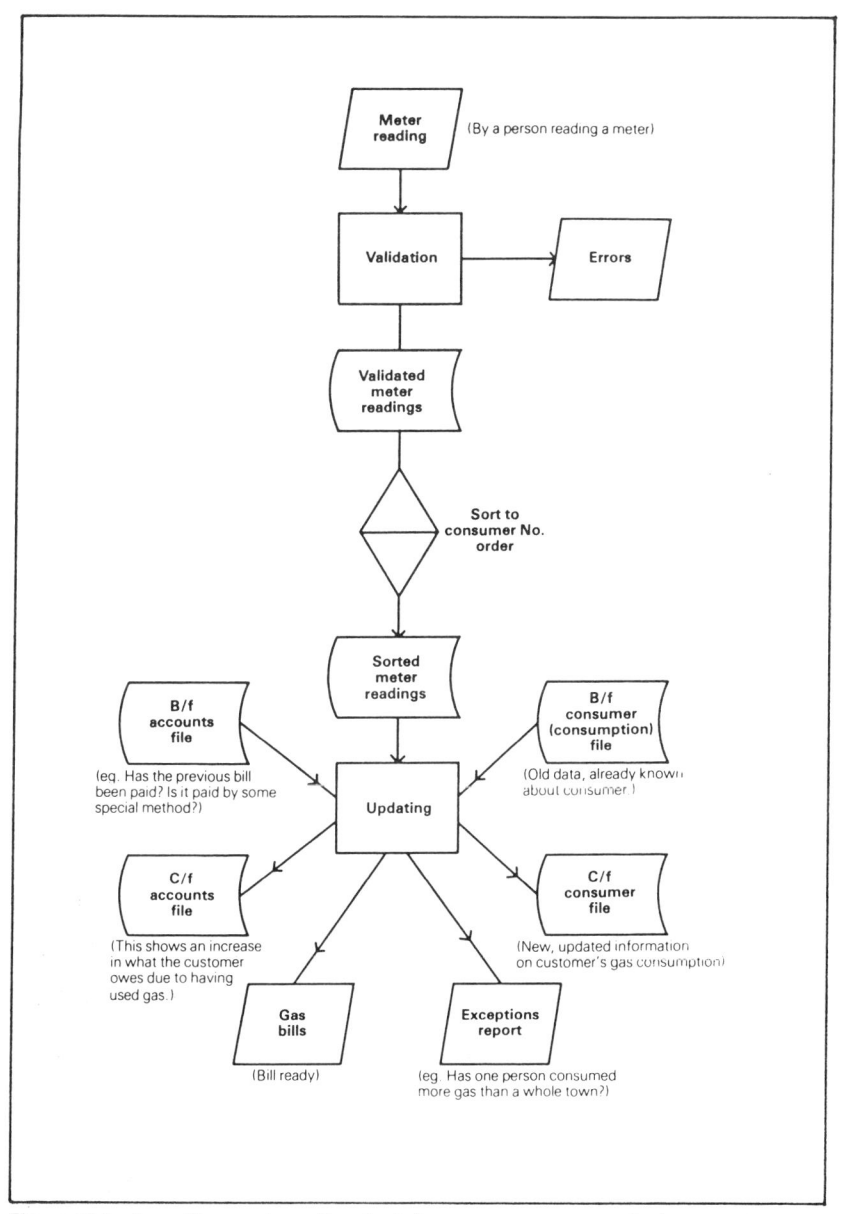

Figure 15.2. An outline systems flowchart for a gas company producing gas bills.

15.1 shows the most common flowcharting symbols - although there are many more. For complex operations it is usual to draw several flowcharts, each one showing increasing detail. The first (the least detailed) is called an 'outline flowchart'. Each box of the outline flowchart may be further broken down into a separate, more detailed, flowchart. If necessary this breaking-down process may continue over many stages and many flowcharts.

Sometimes a flowchart cannot fit onto a single sheet of paper. Then corresponding parts on the separate diagrams are indicated with link symbols (see Figure 15.1). It may often happen that two people's flowcharts for an operation are not identical, even though neither is wrong.

There are several types of flowchart, of which a 'systems' flowchart and a 'program' flowchart are by far the most common.

A systems flowchart indicates all the various processes involved in the task or problem. It is concerned with the complete system and not just the part that the computer plays in it. For example, suppose a clerk is involved in opening letters in an otherwise completely computer-controlled organization of mail. The part played by the clerk has to be included in a systems flowchart, along with the parts played by the computer. So a systems flowchart is essentially a flowchart showing the flow of data. It provides an overall picture of the processing operations in a system. Such a flowchart is useful for professional programmers in industry, commerce or other large organizations. You are unlikely to need it for simple programming - although you will probably want to understand what it is. Figure 15.2 shows an example of an outline systems flowchart for a gas company preparing gas bills. The operations of meter reading and verification are performed manually. The computer copes with the others.

A program flowchart represents operations to be carried out by the computer - and is essentially the computer-related part of a systems flowchart. This is the sort of flowchart that you will probably find most useful in your own programming. In order to make it easy to turn the flowchart into a program, each box should have only one entry point and one exit point.

15.5 Preparing flowcharts

When you come to prepare a flowchart, the first thing to decide is whether you want a systems flowchart or a program flowchart. You need to decide what operation the chart is for, i.e. exactly what it is to achieve. Next decide what the first activity is, i.e. where the operation starts. Jot down the activities in a logical sequence. Trace the steps through one alternative; then tackle the other alternatives. Connect the symbols with flow lines and indicate the direction of the flow with arrows.

15 Structured Programming

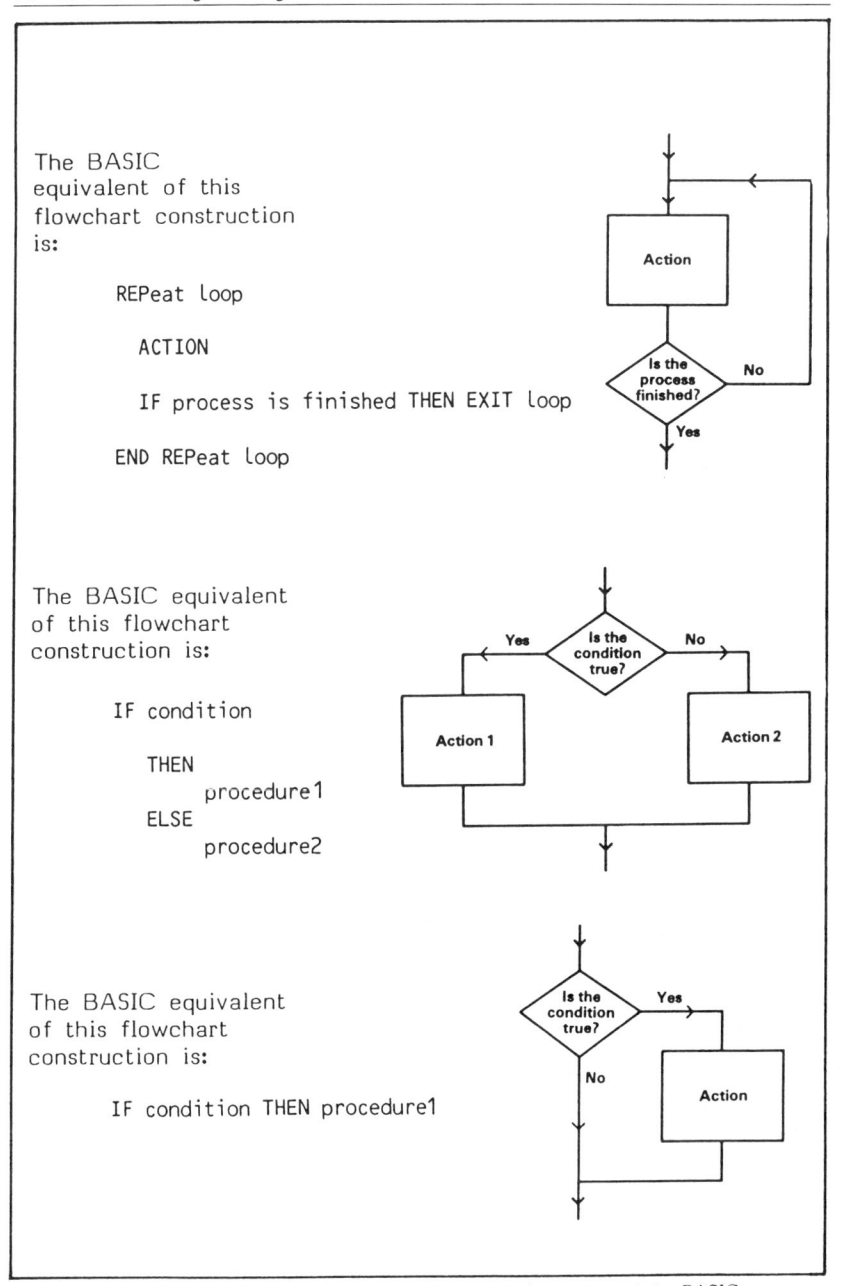

The BASIC
equivalent of this
flowchart construction
is:

    REPeat loop

      ACTION

      IF process is finished THEN EXIT loop

    END REPeat loop

The BASIC equivalent
of this flowchart
construction is:

    IF condition

      THEN
          procedure1
      ELSE
          procedure2

The BASIC equivalent
of this flowchart
construction is:

    IF condition THEN procedure1

Figure 15.3. How some common flowcharting constructions convert to BASIC.

228 *15 Structured Programming*

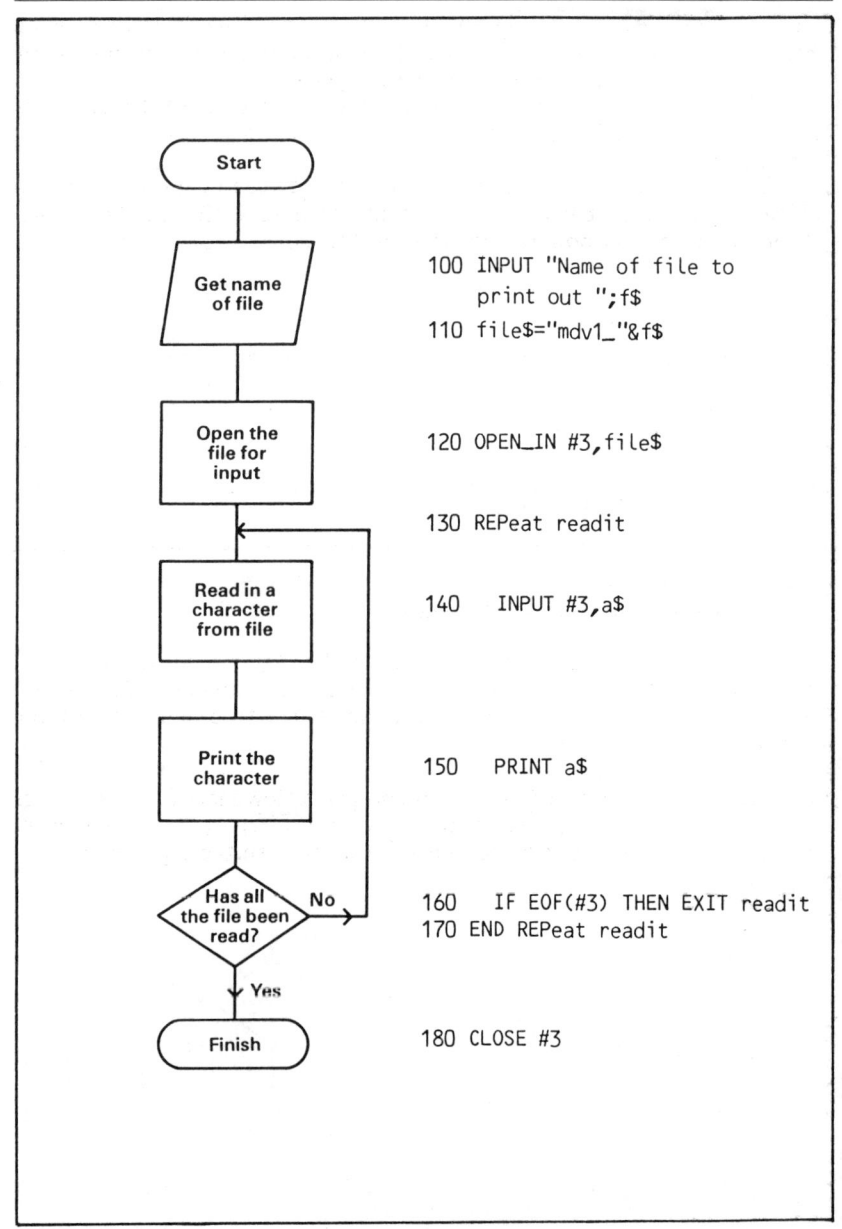

```
100 INPUT "Name of file to
        print out ";f$
110 file$="mdv1_"&f$

120 OPEN_IN #3,file$

130 REPeat readit

140     INPUT #3,a$

150     PRINT a$

160     IF EOF(#3) THEN EXIT readit
170 END REPeat readit

180 CLOSE #3
```

Figure 15.4a. A program flowchart for reading a character from a file.

Figure 15.4b The flowchart of Figure 15.3a translated into BASIC.

15 Structured Programming

Describe the activity within the symbol by labelling it with a name. Finally put in connector symbols to link together the parts of the flowchart which have to be on separate pages.

With a little practice, it is quite easy to convert flowcharting constructions into BASIC programs. Figure 15.3 shows some of the common conversions.

Figure 15.4a is a flowchart which is well-suited to the REPeat type of interpretation. It prints the contents of a text file on the screen. Figure 15.4b shows how it converts to BASIC.

15.6 Activities

i. Design a program flowchart for a computer alarm clock. (We give one possibility in Section 15.7.)

ii. Design a program flowchart for a computer to do an addition sum. (We give a simple version in Section 15.7.)

15.7 Discussion of activities

Activity 15.6i: Figure 15.5 shows one possibility for a program flowchart for a computer to work an alarm clock. Yours is probably different, but this doesn't matter at all as long as it helps you to produce a suitable program.

Activity 15.6ii: Figure 15.6 is a simple program flowchart for a computer to do an addition sum. Again yours may be different, but this doesn't matter at all as long as it helps you to produce a suitable program.

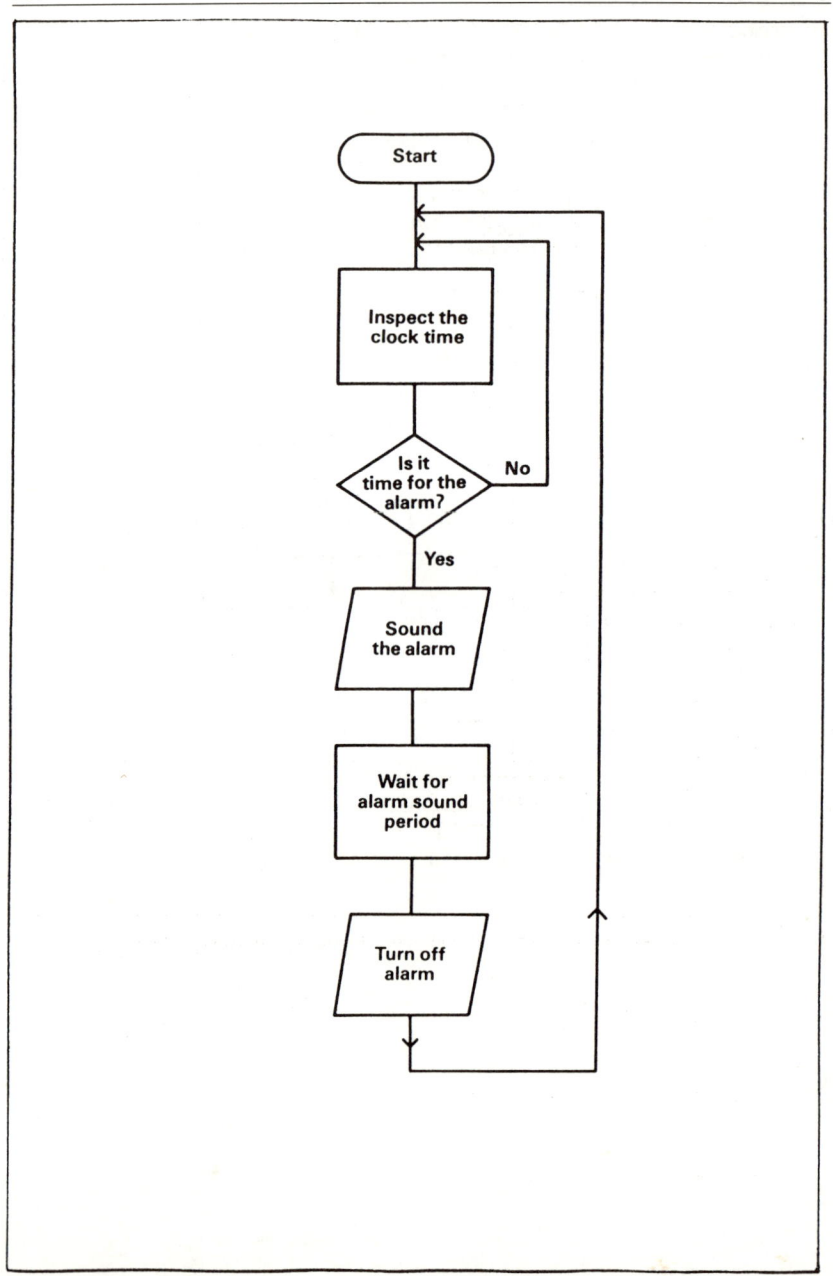

Figure 15.5. A program flowchart for a computer to work an alarm clock.

15 *Structured Programming* 231

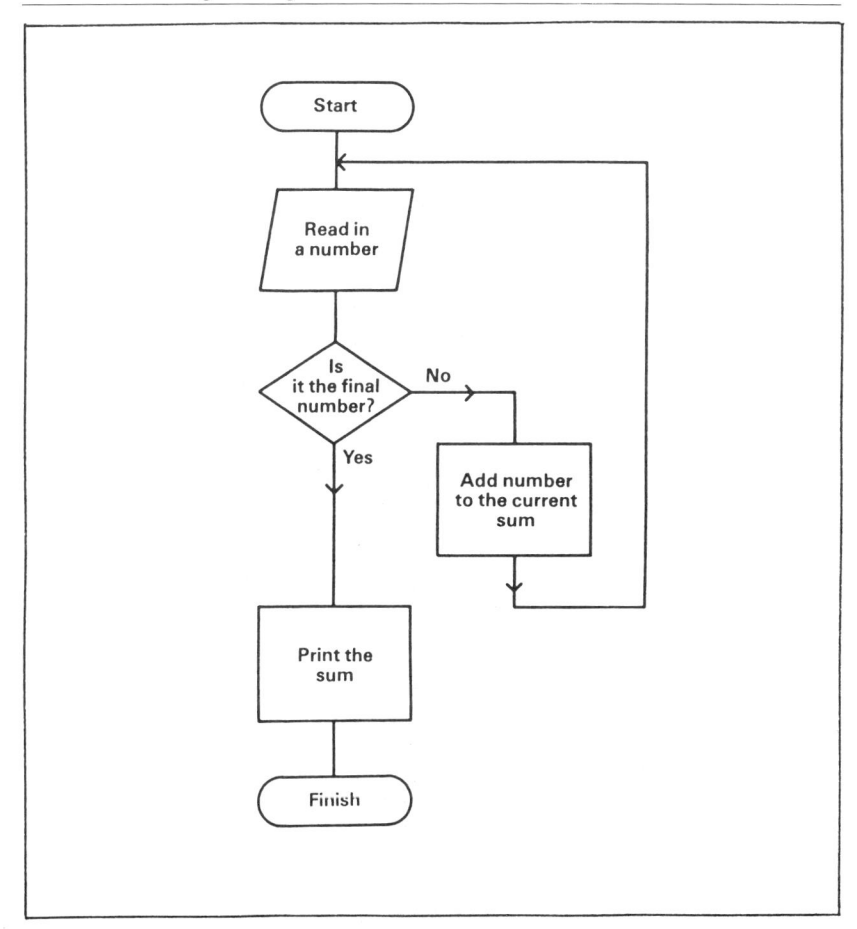

Figure 15.6. A program flowchart for computer to do an additional sum.

16

A games program for the QL

```
16.0  Introduction
16.1  The game
16.2  Programming the display
16.3  The core of the program
16.4  The strategy of the program
16.5  Checking for moves that
      are valid
```

16.0 Introduction

As a conclusion to this book we would like to present a program of some substance. We preferred not to do this earlier because we wanted to illustrate specific points. So we developed short programs accordingly. We wondered which type of program to give. As we realized that the QL does come with business packages of various sorts, we thought you might like a games program. When selecting one, we had to bear in mind that displays on the QL screen cannot change very rapidly. We also wanted a game of intellectual, rather than manipulative skill. Andrew Cryer agreed to program one for us, and we present it now.

In the next section we explain how to play the game. The following sections discuss its program, which is given at the end of the chapter in Listing 16.1.

16.1 The game

The game is played on a rectangular board eight squares across by eight squares down. The QL plays with black pieces and you with white.

The screen starts out with each player having two counters. Then each player takes it in turns to place a piece of his own colour on the board in such a way that he takes his opponent's pieces. Screen Display 16.1 shows a random stage of the game. The the object is to end up with as many pieces as possible.

The rules for placing pieces on the board are:

1. You must place your piece against an opponent's piece.

2. There must be at least one direction in which there is a line of 1 or more of your opponent's pieces ending with one of yours.

3. The QL 'captures' your opponent's pieces for you by reversing their colours, thus making them yours.

We illustrate the first few moves of a game, in Figure 16.1 to clarify the rules.

16.2 Programming the display

The program needed to display both the board and the players' moves. There was room on the TV screen to have the board on the left and the players' moves on the right, as shown in Screen Display 16.1.

The main area of the screen corresponded to channel 2 by default. PAPER was set to give a red background and INK was set to blue, green, white or black, according to what was to be drawn on the screen at the time.

16 A Games Program for the QL

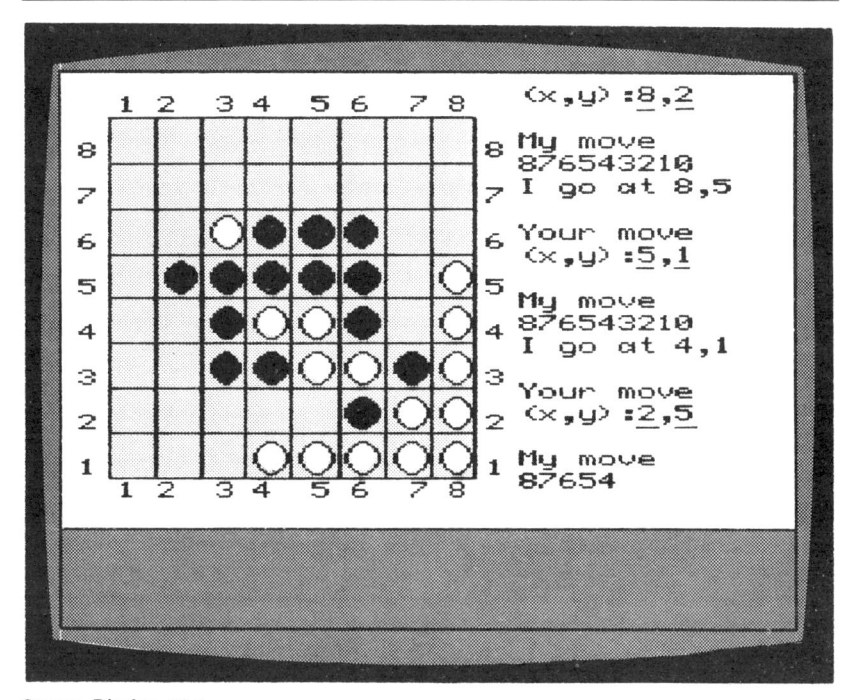

Screen Display 16.1.

A record of the moves was displayed in a window attached to channel 1, the default program output channel. This window was redefined to be just the rectangular area on the right of the screen. The display seemed more dramatic with the black background and with white letters to record the moves. This choice highlighted the other colours. The design of the screen was partially a pen and paper exercise and partially trial and error. The resulting program lines were then made into a procedure called 'set⎵up⎵screen'.

236   *16   A Games Progam for the QL*

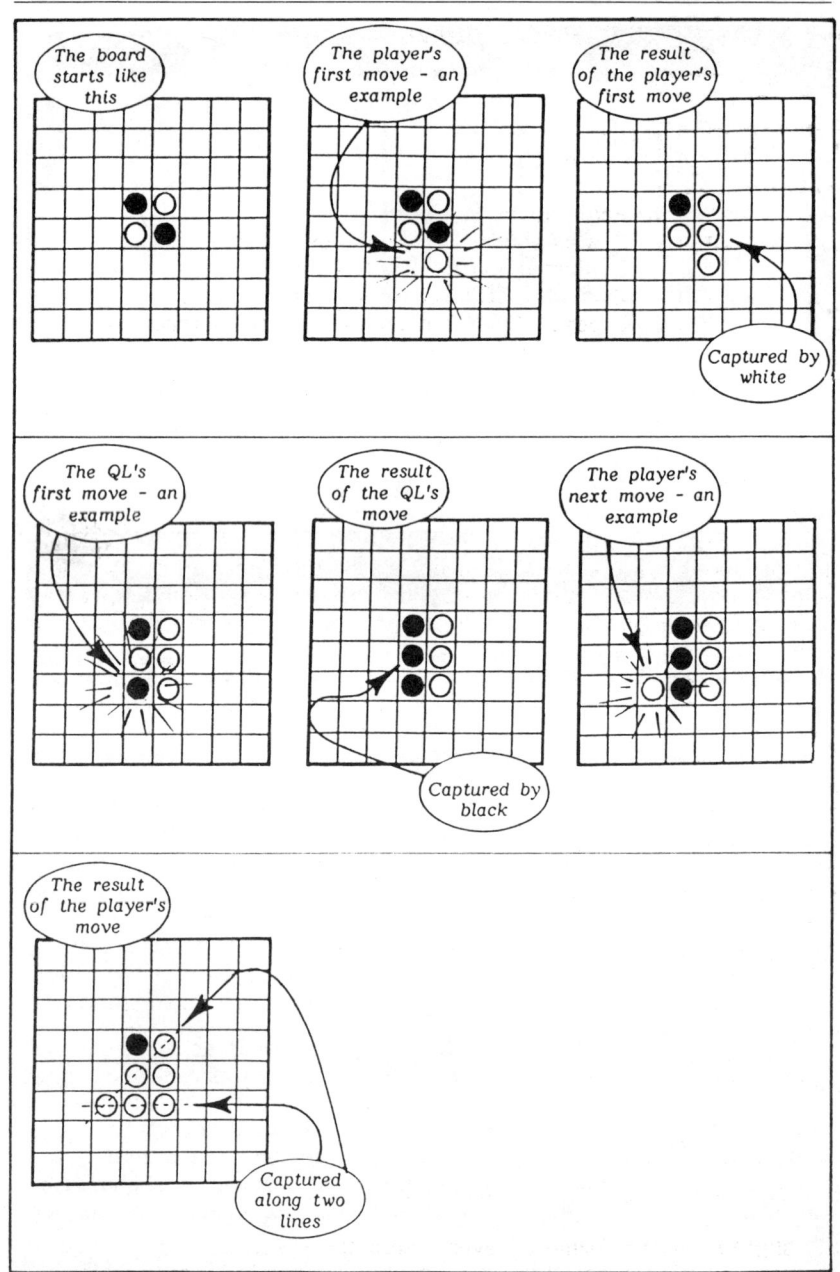

Figure 16.1. The first few moves of a game.

16 A Games Program for the QL   237

16.3 The core of the program

As with many programs the core is deceptively simple. It is:

```
110 set_up_screen
120 set_variables
130 :
140 REPeat moves
150   IF who=player THEN players_go
160   IF who=computer THEN computers_go
170   who=-who :REMark other person's move
180   IF pc=64 OR (com=nomove AND user=nomove)
      THEN EXIT moves
190 END REPeat moves
200 game_over
```

16.4 The strategy of the program

The next step is to devise a strategy for playing the game and a means of implementing it on the QL. Clearly the state of the board at any time must be stored. As the board is a matrix of positions, an array would seem the most appropriate means of doing this. Each position in the array would represent a position on the board and hold a number which has one of three values namely: -1 for the player's piece, 0 for empty and +1 for the QL's piece.

Of all the positions on the board where it is possible to move there must be some which are strategically more desirable than others. The question is how can the computer be programmed to decide which is the best. A minimum method is for the computer to think out all possible current moves and work out which gives the best score. The program does this. An improvement is for the computer to think of all the possible opponent's moves that correspond to all its own moves! The best move is then the one that gives a combination of a good score for the computer and a low score for the opponent. This strategy would have been implemented, but the processing speed of the SuperBASIC was too slow. This process of thinking out not only the best move at the time but which resulting move the opponent is likely to take is called 'looking ahead'. Many games-playing programs are categorized in terms of how many moves ahead they can look. The problem is that much looking ahead takes a lot of computing time and the QL is not fast enough to do this in a reasonable time using BASIC.

An alternative strategy is to try to build into the program some intuitive approach to the problem. This is called a 'heuristic approach'. Most game-solving algorithms are a combination of some looking ahead and some heuristics. This program had to rely rather heavily on the latter and only slightly on the former. Nevertheless the program does provide a reasonable challenge and there is scope for you to play around with the heuristics on which our algorithm is based. Figure 16.2 shows the strategic values assigned to each of the squares on the board. You may like to change them.

96	2	16	20	20	16	2	96
2	1	6	8	8	6	1	2
16	6	20	16	16	20	6	16
20	8	16	8	8	16	8	20
20	8	16	8	8	16	8	20
16	6	20	16	16	20	6	16
2	1	6	8	8	6	1	2
96	2	16	20	20	16	2	96

Figure 16.2. The strategic values applied to each square on the board.

The heuristics are built into a second array as a set of strategic values for the positions on the board. Each square is given a value, such as 96 for a corner position and 2 for the positions either side of the corners. This makes the corner positions very important while one square away from the corner is of low value. When the program works out its own move, it takes into account the strategic values of all the possible positions it could capture. It then decides which is the 'best' move. If it finds two moves of equal value, it will choose between them at random so as to provide a different game each time it plays.

The initial strategic value of each position in the board is set up, together with all the other starting values, in the procedure 'set_up_variables'. A procedure called 'corner' alters the strategic values of some of the positions as the game proceeds, and a function called 'special' looks out for special conditions such as a move between two of the opponent's pieces on the side of the board.

16.5 Checking for moves that are valid

Positions on the board are specified in terms of x and y co-ordinates. These are then be used to refer to the record of the board held in an array; the position of a piece on the screen; and also the strategic values

16 A Games Program for the QL

for each position. A check for an opponent's piece in a neighbouring square is merely a matter of looking at each of the surrounding eight squares and seeing if at least one of his pieces is there. Neighbouring positions are all those represented by moving either one up, one down, one left or one right etc. This is done by adding or subtracting 1 to or from the co-ordinates as shown in Figure 16.2.

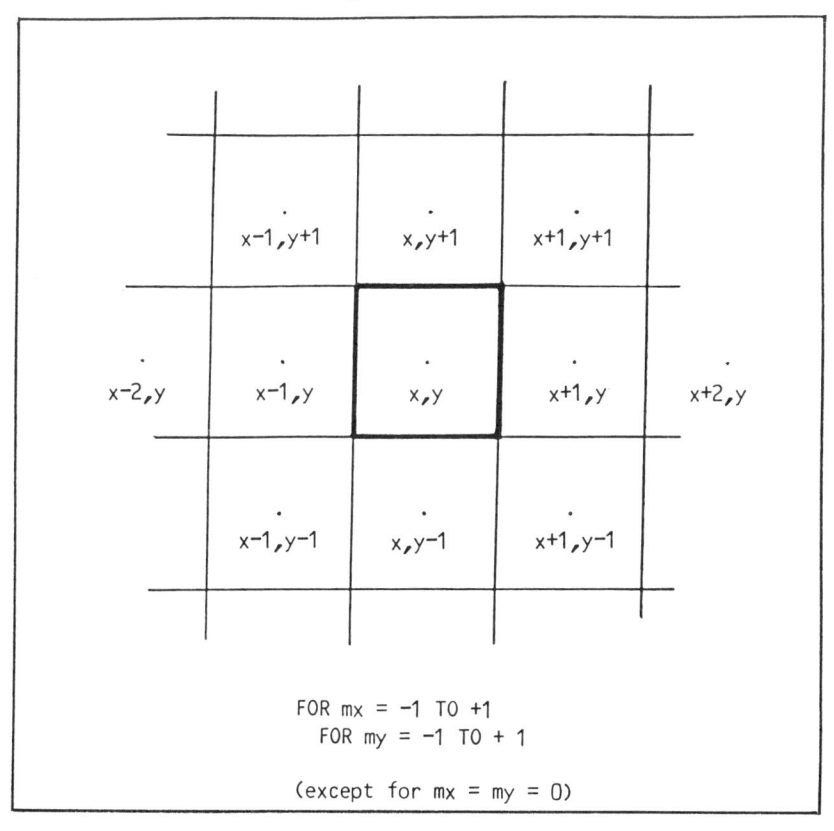

```
                x-1,y+1    x,y+1    x+1,y+1

     x-2,y      x-1,y      x,y      x+1,y     x+2,y

                x-1,y-1    x,y-1    x+1,y-1


              FOR mx = -1 TO +1
              FOR my = -1 TO + 1

              (except for mx = my = 0)
```

Figure 16.3. The board co-ordinates and the moves required to examine the neighbouring squares.

A check for a valid move requires a check that:

- at least one of the surrounding squares must hold an opponent's piece

- a route along a line of opponent's pieces away from the current move position must end in a piece belonging to the current player.

To move repeatedly in any direction requires repeated additions or subtractions to and from x and y of the same amount as is achieved by lines of the form:

    x=x+incx
    y=y+incy

The complete program for the game is in Listing 16.1.

16 A Games Program for the QL

Listing 16.1

```
100 REMark (c) Andrew Cryer 1984
110 set_up_screen
120 set_variables
130 :
140 REPeat moves
150   IF who=player THEN players_go
160   IF who=computer THEN computers_go
170   who=-who :REMark other person's move
180   IF pc=64 OR (com=nomove AND user=nomove) THEN
      EXIT moves
190 END REPeat moves
200   game_over
210 STOP
220 :
230 :
240 DEFine FuNction score(xpos,ypos,f)
250   LOCal k,i,j
260   IF b(xpos,ypos)<>0 OR s(xpos,ypos)<0 THEN RETurn 0
270   k=0
280   FOR i=-1 TO 1
290     FOR j=-1 TO 1
300       IF (i<>0 OR j<>0) AND b(xpos+i,ypos+j)=-who THEN
          k=k+mov(xpos,ypos,i,j,f)
310     NEXT j
320   NEXT i
330   IF k>0 AND f=-1 THEN piece xpos,ypos,who
340   IF k>0 THEN k=special(xpos,ypos,k)
350   RETurn k
360 END DEFine
370 :
380 :
390 DEFine FuNction mov(lx,ly,mx,my,f)
400   LOCal k,x,y
410   x=lx:y=ly
420   k=0
430   REPeat search
440     x=x+mx:y=y+my
450     IF b(x,y)=-who THEN k=k+s(x,y)
460     IF b(x,y)<>-who THEN EXIT search
470   END REPeat search
480   IF b(x,y)<>who THEN k=0
                                                P.T.O.
```

Listing 16.1 continued

```
490  IF k>0 AND f=-1 THEN plot lx,ly,mx,my
500  RETurn k
510 END DEFine
520 :
530 :
540 DEFine FuNction special(x,y,scr)
550  LOCal k
560  k=0
570  IF s(x,y)<3 THEN scr=scr/20
580  IF x=1 OR x=8 THEN IF b(x,y-1)=-who AND
     b(x,y+1)=-who THEN k=128
590  IF y=1 OR y=8 THEN IF b(x,y-1)=-who AND
     b(x,y+1)=-who THEN k=128
600  IF pc<20 THEN IF x<7 AND x>2 AND y>2 AND
     y<7 THEN k=128
610 REMark corner spread!
620  RETurn scr+k+5*s(x,y)
630 END DEFine
640 :
650 :
660 DEFine FuNction onbd(xpos,ypos)
670  IF xpos<1 OR xpos>8 OR ypos<1 OR ypos>8 THEN
     RETurn 0
680 RETurn 1
690 END DEFine onbd
700 :
710 :
720 DEFine PROCedure plot(start_x,start_y,mx,my)
730  LOCal xpos,ypos
740  xpos=start_x:ypos=start_y
750  REPeat plt
760     xpos=xpos+mx:ypos=ypos+my
770     IF b(xpos,ypos)=who THEN EXIT plt
780     IF b(xpos,ypos)=-who THEN change xpos,ypos,who
790  END REPeat plt
800 END DEFine
810 :
820 :
830 DEFine PROCedure players_go
840  LOCal f
850  REPeat your_move
```
P.T.O.

16 A Games Program for the QL

Listing 16.1 continued

```
860    PRINT "Your move    (x,y):";
870    xpos=CODE(INKEY$(-1))-CODE("0") :PRINT xpos;",";
880    ypos=CODE(INKEY$(-1))-CODE("0") :PRINT ypos
890    IF want_move(xpos,ypos)>0 THEN
       user=1:EXIT your_move
900    REMark check that user can make a move
910    IF xpos=0 AND ypos=0 THEN IF no_move=0 THEN
       user=0:EXIT your_move
920   END REPeat your_move
930 END DEFine players_move
940 :
950 :
960 DEFine PROCedure computers_go
970   LOCal c,d,k,e
980   c=0:d=0:k=0:e=0
990   PRINT\"My move"
1000  FOR x=8 TO 1 STEP -1
1010    PRINT x;
1020    FOR y=1 TO 8
1030      k=score(x,y,0)
1040      IF k>e OR (k=e AND RND(3)=1) THEN c=x:d=y:e=k
1050    NEXT y
1060  NEXT x
1070 PRINT "0"
1080  IF e>0 THEN PRINT"I go at ";c;",";d
1090  IF e>0 THEN e=want_move(c,d) : modify c,d :com=1
1100  IF e=0 THEN PRINT"I cannot go." :com=0
1110 END DEFine
1120 :
1130 :
1140 DEFine PROCedure modify(x,y)
1150  IF (x<>1 AND x<>8) OR (y<>1 AND y<>8) THEN RETurn
1160  REMark I've gone in a corner
1170  FOR j=1 TO 2
1180  FOR i=-j TO j
1190    IF onbd(x+i,y+j-ABS(i)) THEN s(x+i,y+j-ABS(i))=96
1200    IF onbd(x+i,y-j+ABS(i)) THEN s(x+i,y-j+ABS(i))=96
1210  NEXT i
1220 NEXT j
1230 END DEFine
1240 :
                                              P.T.O.
```

Listing 16.1 continued

```
1250 :
1260 DEFine PROCedure piece(x,y,c)
1270   LOCal i,j
1280   change x,y,c
1290   FOR i=-1 TO 1
1300     FOR j=-1 TO 1
1310       s(x+i,y+j)=ABS(s(x+i,y+j))
1320     NEXT j
1330   NEXT i
1340   pc=pc+1
1350 END DEFine
1360 :
1370 :
1380 DEFine PROCedure set_up_screen
1390   LOCal i,j
1400   PAPER #2,2
1410   PAPER #1,0
1420   MODE 8
1430   SCALE #2,200,-15,-20
1440   INK #2,4
1450   FILL #2,1
1460   LINE #2,0,0 TO 0,160
1470   LINE #2,168,160 TO 168,0
1480   FILL #2,0
1490   INK #2,1
1500   FOR i=0 TO 8
1510     LINE #2,i*21,0 TO i*21,160
1520     LINE #2,0,i*20 TO 168,i*20
1530     IF i>0 THEN AT #2,19-i*2,21,:PRINT #2,i
1540     IF i>0 THEN AT #2,19-i*2,0:PRINT #2,i
1550     IF i>0 THEN AT #2,1,i*2.5-1:PRINT #2,i
1560     IF i>0 THEN AT #2,18,i*2.5-1:PRINT #2,i
1570   NEXT i
1580   SCALE #2,200,-5.5,-9.5
1590   INK #1,7
1600   WINDOW #1,170,188,304,22
1610   CLS
1620 END DEFine
1630 :
1640 :
1650 DEFine PROCedure change(x,y,c)
```

P.T.O.

16 A Games Program for the QL

Listing 16.1 continued

```
1660  b(x,y)=c
1670  draw x,y,colour(c)
1680 END DEFine
1690 :
1700 :
1710 DEFine FuNction colour(pce)
1720  IF pce=+1 THEN RETurn 0
1730  IF pce=-1 THEN RETurn 7
1740  RETurn 4
1750 END DEFine
1760 :
1770 :
1780 DEFine PROCedure draw(x,y,c)
1790  LOCal loop,delay
1800  FILL #2,1
1810  FOR loop=0 TO 3
1820    INK #2,c
1830    IF loop MOD 2 = 0 THEN INK #2,3
1840    CIRCLE #2,x*21,y*20,7
1850    PAUSE 5:REMark wait for effect
1860  NEXT loop
1870  FILL #2,0
1880 END DEFine
1890 :
1900 :
1910 DEFine PROCedure set_variables
1920  REMark set up board
1930  DIM b(9,9),s(9,9)
1940  DATA -96, -2, -16,-20
1950  DATA  -2, -1,  -6, -8
1960  DATA -16, -6, -20,-16
1970  DATA -20, -8, -16, -8
1980  RESTORE 1940
1990  FOR y=1 TO 4
2000    FOR x=1 TO 4
2010      READ s(x,y)
2020      s(9-x,y)=s(x,y)
2030      s(x,9-y)=s(x,y)
2040      s(9-x,9-y)=s(x,y)
2050    NEXT x
2060  NEXT y
```

P.T.O.

Listing 16.1 continued

```
2070   pc=0
2080   piece 4,4,-1 :piece 5,5,-1
2090   piece 4,5,1 :piece 5,4,1
2100   user=1:com=1
2110 player=-1:computer=1:nomove=0
2120   PRINT"Do you want to go first?";
2130 REPeat question
2140 a$=INKEY$(-1)
2150 IF a$ INSTR "yy" THEN PRINT "Yes":who=-1:
     EXIT question
2160 IF a$ INSTR "nn" THEN PRINT "No":who=+1:
     EXIT question
2170 END REPeat question
2180   RANDOMISE
2190 END DEFine
2200 :
2210 :
2220 DEFine FuNction want_move(xpos,ypos)
2230   LOCal f
2240   REMark check for off board
2250   IF NOT onbd(xpos,ypos) THEN RETurn 0
2260   REMark provisionally put down piece
2270   draw xpos,ypos,2
2280   f=score(xpos,ypos,-1)
2290   REMark if required erase piece
2300   IF f=0 THEN draw xpos,ypos,colour(b(xpos,ypos))
2310 IF f>0 THEN change_waiting xpos,ypos
2320   RETurn f
2330 END DEFine
2340 :
2350 :
2360 DEFine PROCedure change_waiting(xpos,ypos)
2370 IF xpos=8 AND ypos<7 AND ypos>2 THEN s(7,ypos)=12
2380 IF xpos=1 AND ypos<7 AND ypos>2 THEN s(2,ypos)=12
2390 IF ypos=8 AND xpos<7 AND xpos>2 THEN s(xpos,7)=12
2400 IF ypos=1 AND xpos<7 AND xpos>2 THEN s(xpos,2)=12
2410 END DEFine
2420 :
2430 :
2440 DEFine FuNction no_move
2450   LOCal lx,ly,px,py,sc,val
```

P.T.O.

Listing 16.1 continued

```
2460 px=0:py=0:sc=99999
2470 PRINT "Checking that you cannot move."
2480 FOR lx=8 TO 1 STEP -1
2490   PRINT lx;
2500   FOR ly=1 TO 8
2510     val=score(lx,ly,0)
2520     IF val>0 AND val<sc THEN px=lx:py=ly:sc=val
2530   NEXT ly
2540 NEXT lx
2550 PRINT"0"
2560 IF px>0 THEN PRINT "You can move at ";px;",";py
2570 IF px=0 THEN RETurn 0
2580 RETurn 1
2590 END DEFine
2600 :
2610 :
2620 DEFine PROCedure game_over
2630   PRINT\"Game over"
2640   com=0:user=0
2650   FOR xloop=1 TO 8
2660     FOR yloop=1 TO 8
2670       IF b(xloop,yloop)=1 THEN com=com+1
2680       IF b(xloop,yloop)=-1 THEN user=user+1
2690     NEXT yloop
2700   NEXT xloop
2710   PRINT"White:";user
2720   PRINT"Black:";com
2730   IF user>com THEN
       PRINT#0,"Congratulations - you win!"
2740   IF user=com THEN PRINT#0,"Draw!"
2750   IF user<com THEN
       PRINT#0,"Computer wins - you lose!"
2760 END DEFine
```

Appendix

Glossary of BASIC terms

This is an overview of BASIC terms for the QL. For a fuller description, see the User Guide.

ABS   absolute value
ABS(p) turns a negative value of p into a positive one of the same magnitude. It leaves a positive value of p unchanged.

ACOT
ACOT(p) returns the arc-cotangent of the angle p in radians.

ACOS
ACOS(p) returns the arc-cosine of the angle p in radians.

ADATE   adjust clock
ADATE p advances the clock p seconds. If p is negative, the clock is moved back.

AND
AND is a Boolean operator which can be used in an IF ... THEN statement, for example: IF A=B AND C=D THEN ... . There is also the operator && which is a true bitwise AND.

ARC   ARC_R
ARC [channel,]x1,y, to x2,y2,A draws the arc of a circle between x1,y1 and x2,y2. A is the angle, in radians, through which the arc turns.

ASC   American Standard Code (ASCII)   See CODE

ASIN
ASIN(p) gives the angle in radians whose sine is p.

ATAN   arc-tangent
ATAN(p) gives the angle in radians whose tangent is p.

AT
AT line,column sets the position at which printing will next occur. It must be used outside the PRINT statement.

AUTO   automatic
AUTO supplies line numbers for an entered program. It starts numbering at line 100 and continues in increments of 10. AUTO p,q starts numbering at line p and continues in increments of q. Other forms are: AUTO ,q AUTO p, and AUTO.

BAUD
BAUD p sets the baud rate to p for both serial channels. For example BAUD 9600 sets to 9600 baud.

BEEP
BEEP duration,pitch causes a sound to be emitted. Duration is in units of 72 microseconds. A pitch of 1 is highest and 255 lowest.

BEEPING
BEEPING is a function which is true if the QL is currently emitting a sound. (True here means non-zero.)

BLOCK
BLOCK [channel,]width,height,x,y,colour fills a block of the specified width and height at position x,y. All quantities must be specified in pixel co-ordinates.

BORDER
BORDER [channel,]width,colour draws a border of the given colour with a width which must be given in pixels.

CALL   transfer control to a machine code subroutine
CALL p calls a section of machine code at address p. Up to 13 parameters can be given in the call. They will be placed in the 68008 data and address registers in sequence.

CHR$ character string
CHR$(p) gives the single character string whose code is p. If p is too large, the least significant byte is taken.

CIRCLE CIRCLE_R
CIRCLE [channel,]x,y,r[,eccentricity,angle] draws a circle with centre x,y and radius r. Eccentricity is optional and specifies the ratio between the major and minor axis. Angle is the angle of the major axis relative to the vertical in radians.

CLEAR
CLEAR causes all variables - including string variables and arrays - to be cleared.

CLOSE
CLOSE #p informs the system that the file with channel number p is no longer required. Any channel associated with the channel will be de-activated

CLS clear the window
CLS [channel,][part] clears the window associated with the default or specified channel. Part=0 - whole window; part=1 - above the cursor line; part=2 - below the cursor line; part=3 - cursor line; part=4 - to the right of the cursor + cursor position.

CODE
CODE("s") gives the internal code for the first character of the string. Other examples are CODE(A$), and CODE("hello") which is same as CODE("h").

COLOUR   See PAPER and INK

CONTINUE   See also RETRY
CONTINUE causes a program, stopped by an error or with CTRL+SPACE, to be restarted at the following line. It does not work after editing.

COPY and COPY_N
COPY device to device. Copies a file from any input device to any output device until an end-of-file marker is found. COPY_N removes the header associated with a microdrive device to allow microdrive files to be copied to any other device.

COS cosine
COS(p) gives the cosine of p where p is in radians.

COT cotangent
COT(p) returns the cotangent of the angle p where p is in radians.

CSIZE
CSIZE [channel,]width,height sets the character size for the default or specified channel. Width =0 to 3, height =0 or 1.

CURSOR
CURSOR [channel,][xg,yg,]xp,yp sets the screen cursor at the position xp,yp in pixel co-ordinates, and at xg,yg in graphics co-ordinates. If both sets of co-ordinates are given, the pixel co-ordinates are measured relative to the point set by the graphics co-ordinates.

DATA
DATA p,q,r,... stores numerical and string values in a program, strings must be surrounded by quotes.

DATE
DATE is a function which returns the date as a floating point number.

DATE$
DATE$ is a function which returns the date and time contained in the QL's clock. The format of the string is "yyyy mm dd hh:mm:ss". See SDATE for setting the value.

DAY$
DAY$ is a function which returns the day of the week as a string.

DEF define
DEF is part of the statement which declares a user-defined function or a user-defined procedure. Examples are DEFine FuNction mean(A,B,C), DEFine PROCedure calc_areas(X,Y).

DEG degrees
DEG(p) gives the degree equivalent of p radians.

DELETE
DELETE filespec deletes the file specified. For example DELETE mdv1_filename.

DLINE
DLINE range deletes the lines included in the range. For example DLINE 10 to 50 or DLINE 30,40,80 or DLINE 10 to 40,50,100 to 200.

DIM dimension of an array
DIM is part of a statement which declares an array. The dimensions of the array are given in brackets, as for example: DIM Num(22), Names$(3,4). For string arrays the last number is the maximum length of each string.

DIMM
DIMM(arrayname,dimension) is a function which returns the maximum size of the specified dimension in the array. If no dimension is given, the first is the default.

DIV   integer division of whole numbers
Supplied numbers are converted to integers. Then division takes place. The result is given as an integer value, e.g. 7 DIV 2 is 3.

DIR
DIR devicespec is a command which causes the device specified to be searched and a directory of the files on it to be presented. e.g. dir mdv1_.

EDIT
EDIT p causes line p to be listed ready for editing. The cursor left and right keys become operational and characters can be inserted and deleted as required. Pressing ENTER signals the completion of the editing.

ELSE
ELSE is part of an IF ... THEN ... ELSE statement.

END
END FOR, END DEFine, END IF define the end of the respective block.

EOR   exclusive or   See XOR

EXEC and EXEC_N
EXEC and EXEC_N loads a sequence of programs and executes them in parallel. EXEC causes a return to the command processor after all processes have started execution, whereas EXEC_N waits until all the processes have terminated before returning.

EXIT
EXIT loop_identifier causes an exit from the current loop structure. For example IF n>5 THEN EXIT loop_identifier.

EXP   exponent
EXP(p) gives the exponential e raised to the power p.

FILL
FILL switch turns the fill routine on for switch=1 and off for switch=0. This fills the horizontal area between any graphics drawn on the screen. It also fills circles, if it is turned on for just the circle drawing.

FILL$
FILL$(string$,n) is a function which returns a string made from n repetitions of the string$, which must be only 1 or 2 characters long.

FLASH
FLASH [channel,]switch turns the flash state on for switch=1 or off for switch=0. Flashing only works in mode 8.

FOR
FOR is used at the start of a FOR ... NEXT and FOR ... END FOR loop.

FORMAT
FORMAT drive_cartridgename formats the cartridge in the microdrive specified and gives the name to that cartridge. The operation destroys all information previously stored on that cartridge.

GOSUB go to a subroutine
GOSUB p calls a subroutine starting at line p. The subroutine finishes with RETurn which causes execution to continue at the statement following GOSUB p.

GOTO go to a line number
GOTO p causes the execution of the program to jump to line number p, which may be given as a number or a variable.

IF
IF precedes a condition in an IF ... THEN [ELSE] statement. For example: IF ans$ = "YES" THEN 100 or IF G=1 THEN PRINT "hello".

INK
INK [channel,]colour sets the colour for further printing and graphics on the default or specified channel.

INKEY$
INKEY$(p) is a function which returns the string value of the next key pressed. If p is positive, it waits for p television frames and returns the null string if no key is pressed in that time. If p is -1, it waits till a key is pressed. #p represents a channel number and reads the next character from that channel.

INPUT
INPUT [channel,]p,p$ reads in values entered from the current, or specified channel. Examples include INPUT A,B,C,"Name",N$,D,d.

INSTR
INSTR an operator which gives the character position of the left-hand string in the right-hand string. If the string is not found, zero is returned. For example "a" INSTR "mat" returns 2.

INT integer part
INT(p) gives the integer part of the number p. For example: INT(4.95) is 4 and INT(-5.1) is -6.

**LEFT$** Use A$(1 to p) to return the left most p characters of A$.

LEN
LEN(A$) gives the length of the string A$.

LET
LET is an optional part of the assignment statement, i.e. LET X=45 is usually abbreviated to X=45.

LINE and LINE_R
LINE x1,y1 to x2,y2 draws a line between the pairs of points given. More than one set of points may be given, for example LINE 5,5 to 8,90 to 105,200 to ... etc.

LIST
LIST p to q causes the current program to be listed from lines p to q inclusive. If p and q are omitted, the whole program is listed.

LN   natural logarithm
LN(p) gives the natural logarithm of p.

LOAD
LOAD file_spec loads a new program in place of any previous one. For example LOAD mdv1_Rates.

LOCal
LOCal p,a$ declares p, q$ and any other listed variables as local to that function or procedure. The original values are restored at the end of the function or procedure.

LOG10
LOG10(p) gives the logarithm of p to the base 10.

LRUN
LRUN file_spec loads and runs the program specified.

MERGE
MERGE file_spec merges the program specified with that which is already in memory.

MID$
Use A$(p to q) to return part of the string A$ starting at character position p and carrying on to position q.

MOD (modulus)
MOD is a binary operation giving the remainder of an integer division, e.g. A MOD B. 7 MOD 2 is 1.

MODE
MODE p sets the graphics mode to p. MODE 4 or MODE 512 selects the

high resolution graphics mode. MODE 8 or MODE 256 selects the low resolution graphics mode.

MOVE
MOVE p causes the graphics turtle position to move on by p graphics units in the currently set direction.

MRUN
MRUN file_spec merges the file specified with that currently in memory and then runs the new version.

NET
NET p sets the QL to be network station p.

NEW
NEW initializes BASIC for a new program to be typed in. It clears any previous program in readiness.

NEXT
NEXT is part of the FOR ... NEXT construction. With the QL it is more usual to use END FOR to complete a FOR loop.

NOT
NOT is a Boolean operator.

ON
ON facilitates multiway switching. Examples include: ON X GOTO 10,100,350,35, ON X GOSUB 1000,2000. See also SELect.

OPEN
OPEN #p,device associates channel p with the specified device. e.g. OPEN #3,SER1 opens the serial device as a channel and assigns 3 as the channel number. Also OPEN #4,mdv1_file_name to open channel 4 as a file.

OPEN_IN
OPEN_IN #p,file_spec opens the file specified as channel p. For example OPEN_IN #4,mdv1_accounts.

OPEN_NEW
OPEN_NEW #p,file_spec opens a new file as channel p. For example OPEN_NEW #4,mdv1_accounts.

OR
OR is a Boolean operator which can be used in an IF ... THEN statement, for example: IF A=B OR C=D THEN ... . There is also the operator || which is a true bitwise OR.

OVER
OVER p selects the method of printing. p=-1 selects print in ink over the previous contents of the screen. p=0 selects print in INK on strip. p=1 selects print in INK on a transparent strip.

PAN
PAN p pans the entire screen p pixels right (or left if negative). PAN p,3 pans the cursor line only and PAN p,4 pans the line to the right of and including the cursor.

PAPER
PAPER colour selects the background colour of the screen for future actions such as writing, CLS, PAN etc.

PAUSE
PAUSE p causes the program to pause in its execution for 20*p milliseconds. The program starts executing again at the end of the time or immediately if a key is pressed.

PEEK, PEEK_W, PEEK_L
PEEK(address) is a function which returns the contents of the memory address specified as an 8 bit number (0 to 255). PEEK_W returns a 16 bit number (0 to 65535). PEEK_L returns a 32 bit number (0 to 4.29 E9)

PENUP PENDOWN
PENUP and PENDOWN are turtle graphics commands which turn the turtle's drawing ability off and on respectively.

PI
PI is a constant (the ratio of the circumference of a circle to its diameter). It is 3.141593 in the QL.

POINT, POINT_R
POINT x,y plots a point at the position x,y. POINT_R interprets the co-ordinates as being relative to previous ones.

POKE, POKE_W, POKE_L
POKE address,p pokes the number p into the address given. POKE p must be used for an 8 bit number (0 to 255). POKE_W p must be used for a 16 bit number (0 to 65535). POKE_L p must be used for a 32 bit number (0 to 4.29 E9).

PRINT
PRINT [channel,]p prints p. PRINT #p,q causes q to be printed to channel p. The separator ! represents an intelligent space; a comma causes printing in columns;\ causes a new line, a semicolon causes the next item to be printed at the current position without formatting.

RAD radian
RAD(p) gives the radian equivalent of p degrees.

RANDOMISE
RANDOMISE p 'reseeds' the random number generator using p which may be a decimal value.

READ
READ instructs the QL to read in one or more variable values. Values are assigned to the variables by reading from DATA statements.

RECOL
RECOL a,b,c,d,e,f,g,h causes the colours to be reset. Each parameter in the list should be a number between 0 and 7, representing one of the eight colours. The first parameter sets the colour which 0 should now represent; the second the colour which 1 should represent; etc. The effect of this command is retrospective.

REMark
REMark causes the rest of the program line to be ignored. It is useful for writing comments into a program to explain its operation and to divide the program up visually into parts.

RENUM
RENUM p,q causes the lines of a program to be renumbered starting at line number p with increments of q. If p is omitted, its default is 100. If q is omitted, its default is 10. A section of program can be renumbered provided the new numbers do not overlap any surrounding ones. This version of renumber is: RENUM a TO b;p,q where p and q are as before, and a and b are the first and last lines of the old program to be renumbered.

REPeat
REPeat is the first word of the REPeat ... END REPeat loop.

RESTORE
RESTORE p sets the line number p of the DATA statement from which values will be taken using the next READ statement. p may be a number or a variable.

RETRY
RETRY allows a program statement which has reported an error to be re-executed.

RETurn
RETurn ends a function or a subroutine. For a function it returns the required value and for a subroutine it causes execution of the program to

return to the statement following the most recent GOSUB.

**RIGHT$**   Use a$(LEN(a$)-p+1 TO LEN(a$)) to return the right-most p characters of the string a$.

RND
RND(p to q) gives a random number between p and q. RND(p) gives a random number between 1 and p.

RUN
RUN causes a program to start executing from the beginning. All the variables are set to zero.

SAVE
SAVE file_spec causes the current program to be saved. Parts of programs can be saved by, for example, SAVE mdv1_accounts,10 to 100

SBYTES
SBYTES file_spec addr1,addr2 saves the area of memory specified to the file specified.

SCALE
SCALE scale,x,y sets the scale (height of screen) to that specified, and the bottom left-hand corner of the screen to x,y as measured from the new origin.

SCROLL
SCROLL p scrolls the screen up p pixels (or down if -ve). SCROLL p,1 scrolls the screen above the cursor line. SCROLL p,2 scrolls the screen below the cursor line.

SDATE
SDATE year,month,day,hours,mins,secs sets the clock with the specified year, month, etc.

SELect
SELect ON p causes multiple actions to take place depending on the value of p. This line must be followed by lines such as ON p=1 to 50 PRINT "message". At the end of a whole series of lines selecting various actions depending on the value of p, a final line must be: END SELect.

SIN   sine
SIN(p) gives the sine of p where p is in radians.

SQRT   square root
SQRT(p) gives the square root of p.

STEP
STEP is the part of the FOR ... END FOR loop which specifies the size of the step to be added to the loop variable each time the loop is completed. If it is omitted, a step of 1 is the default. For example: FOR J=1 TO 7 STEP 0.2.

STOP
STOP causes the execution of the program to stop.

STRIP
STRIP p sets the colour of the current strip i.e. the background for any text written on the screen.

TAB See AT

TAN tangent
TAN(p) gives the tangent of p where p is in radians.

THEN
THEN is part of the IF ... THEN structure.

TURN
TURN p alters the heading of the turtle by p degrees.

TO
TO is part of the FOR ... END FOR loop structure.

UNDER
UNDER p turns underlining on for p=1 and off for p=0.

WINDOW
WINDOW [channel,]w,h,x,y alters the window to w pixels wide by h pixels high at position x,y, also in pixel co-ordinates.

XOR exclusive or
XOR is an 'exclusive OR' Boolean operation between the binary version of two integers. SuperBASIC also provides ^^ as the bitwise alternative.

Index

adding 54,104
ALGOL 4
AND 103,104
APL 4
ARC 143-144
arcs 143-144
array variables 164,165
arrays 163-177
  dimensioning 165
  one dimensional 165
  two dimensional 172-173
AT 20
AUTO 56,57

background colour 148-150
backslash 55,57
BASIC 4,9,25,53-66,106
  BBC 5
  characters 54
  expanding terms 26-28,31
  keywords 54
  letters 54
  shorthand equivalents 26-28,31
  Super 4-5
  symbols 54
  terms 249-260
BEEP 109
BEEPING 111
binary codes 4
BORDER 154
brackets 104,201
branching 221-223
business packages 4

capitals 16,18,21,26-28,31
CAPS LOCK key 9,11
cartridges 36-37
  file-storage 210
  formatting 36-37
  getting a directory 38-39
case, upper or lower 16,18,21, 26-28,31
channels 121-131,
  closing 130
  default 126-127
  number 125,211
  opening 127-128
character to code conversion 207
characters 54
CHR$ 207
CIRCLE 143,144
circles 143,144
CLOSE 211
CLS 20,127
COBOL 4
CODE 207
code to character conversion 207
coercion 66
colons 27
colour 134,147-162,
  available 148
  background 148-150
  filling 151-152
  foreground 148-150
  mixing 155-156
  number 148
  stippling 155-156

Index

commas 55,57,58
comparisons 96-97
CON 130
conditional statements 97-100
co-ordinates 128-130,
  graphics 135-138
  pixel 128-130
COPY 215-216
crashing 10
CSIZE 84,85,87
CTRL key 6,7,10
cursor 6,
  graphics 144-145
CURSOR 144-145
cursor keys 7,24
curves 140-142

DATA statements 72
database program 4
date 190-191
decisions 95-106
DEFine FuNction 193
DEFine PROCedure 26
delays 92
deleting 7
DIM 166,172
dimensioning arrays 166-167
directory of cartridge 38-39
DIV 104
dividing 54,104
DLINE 24,45
dollar 62
drawing,
  arcs 143-144
  circles 143
  curves 140-142
  ellipses 143,144
  lines 138-139
  points 138
duration 108-109

EDIT 23
editing 7,23-24
ellipses 143
END DEF 26
END FOR 78-79
END IF 97-100

END REP 83-85
ENTER key 7,24
entering 7
EOF 214
EOR 104
equals 97
error messages 8-9,10-11,17,
  18,42,52,72,73,74
EXIT 84

files 209-217
  copying 215-216
  creating 211
  reading from 212-214
  writing to 211,214-215
FILL 151-152
FILL$ 206
flowcharts 223-231
FOR loops 78-79
foreground colour 148-150
FORMAT 37
formatting cartridges 36-37
FORTRAN 4
frequency 108-109
functions 187-198
  built-in 188-191
  user-defined 193-194

games 4
games program 233-247
GOSUB 220-223
GOTO 221-223
graphics 133-146,
  turtle 17-18
graphics co-ordinates 135-138
graphics cursor 144-145
graphics package 4
greater than 97,103,104
greater than or equal to 97,103,
  104

hash 125

IF...THEN 97-100
IF...THEN...ELSE 97-100
immediate actions 14-15
index 54,104

INK 149-150
INKEY$ 200-201
INPUT 68-69,127
inputting data 67-75
INSTR 203
INT 61
integer variables 60-61
intelligent spaces 56
inverted commas 14-17,54-57

jumping 221-223

key,
   CAPS LOCK 9,11
   CTRL 6,7,10
   cursor 7,24
   ENTER 7,24
   RESET 10
   SHIFT 9,10-11
   SPACE 6,9,10-11
keyboard 3
keywords 54

languages 4
LEN$ 202
less than 96-97
less than or equal to 97
LET 68
letters 54
LINE 138-139
line numbers 18-20
lines 138-139
LIST 18-20,128
LOAD 39
loading programs 39,43-45
LOCAL 168,197
loops 77-93
   FOR 78-79
   nesting loops 88-89
   REPEAT 83-85
   variable 78-79
   within loops 88-89
loudness 108-109
LRUN 43

MDV 37,38,43,211
memory 38
menu-selection program 49-51
merging programs 43-45
microdrives 3,36-37,
   channels 124-125
   number 38
MOD 104
mode 134-135
MODE 134-135,148
monitor 6,8,126
MOVE 17-18
multiplying 54,104
musical intervals 111-114
musical scales 110,114-117

naming programs 38
nesting loops 88-89
NEW 23
NOT 103,104
not equal to 97

ON...SELECT 105
OPEN 127,129,214
OPEN_IN 212-214
OPEN_NEW 211
operations 102-105
OR 103,104
OVER 150

PAPER 149
Pascal 4
PAUSE 92
PENDOWN 17-18
PENUP 17-18
percentage 60
pitch 108-109,118-119
pitch number 109-114
pixel 134-135
pixel co-ordinates 128-130
PL/1 4
POINT 138
points 138
ports 125
PRINT 14,15,127
priorities of operations 102-105
procedures 25-27,220-221

Index

programming 13-33
programs 18-20,
  debugging 25
  editing 23-24
  line numbers 18-20
  loading 39,43-45
  menu-selection 49-51
  merging programs 43-45
  naming 38
  running 19
  saving 37-38,43
  structured 5,25,219-223
punctuation,
  backslash 55,57
  colons 25,26
  commas 55,57
  inverted commas 14-17,55,57
  semicolons 55,56,58,69

QL 1-4
quality 108-109
quotation marks 14-17,54-57
QWERTY 3

raising to a power 54,104
READ 72-73
recursion 194-195
REM 28
RENUM 19-20,46
REPEAT loops 83-85
repetition 77-93
RESET key 10
RESTORE 74
RETURN 193,220
right$ 202
RND 100
RPG 4
RUN 19

SAVE 38
saving programs 37-38,43
SCALE 135-137
scaling windows 135-137
SCR 129

SDATE 190-191
semicolons 55,56,69
SHIFT key 9,10-11
sorting 99,168-173
sound 107-119,
  duration 108-109
  frequency 108-109
  harmonics 108-109
  loudness 108-109
  pitch 108-109,118-119
  pitch number 109-114
  pure 108-109
  quality 108-109
SPACE bar 6,9-11
spaces 17,31,59
  intelligent 56
Spectrum 3
STEP 79-80
stippling 155-156
string variables 61-62
strings 54-57,199-208
  inputting 200-201
  joining 61-62
  length of 200
  manipulating 201-202
  searching within 202-203
  specifying a portion 201
STRIP 149
structured programming 5,25, 219-223
subroutines 220
subtracting 54,104
SuperBASIC 4-5 (See also BASIC)
symbols 54

tables 163-177
tabulating 20
television 6,124,126
training aids 4
TURN 17-18
TURNTO 17-18
turtle graphics 17-18

underline 59

variable names 59
variables 59,
  array 164-165
  inputting data 70-71
  integer 60-61
  loop 78-79
  string 61-62

WINDOW 128
windows 121-131,
  controlling 128-130
  default 131
  scaling 135-137
wordprocessing 4

ZX80 3
ZX81 3

The authors

Neil Cryer obtained his BSc and PhD in physics at the University of Exeter and is now a lecturer at Royal Holloway College, University of London, where he teaches physics and microprocessors. He acts as a consultant to industry on microprocessor control and is on the Computer Science Advisory Panel of the University of London.

Pat Cryer obtained her BSc in physics and mathematics at the University of Exeter and her PhD in educational studies at the University of Surrey, where she is now a lecturer. She has been a visiting lecturer at the University of Malaya; Makerere University, Uganda; Ramkhamhaeing University, Thailand; and Chiangmai University, Thailand. Her specialism is education and training through printed materials, in which connection she has undertaken various consultancies, including one to a major international computing company. She acts as co-ordinator and editor for the Society for Research into Higher Education working group to produce materials to support the training of university lecturers.